Struggle for the Spirit

To my parents
Alfred and Lilo Lehmann

Struggle for the Spirit

RELIGIOUS TRANSFORMATION AND POPULAR
CULTURE IN BRAZIL AND LATIN AMERICA

David Lehmann

Polity Press

First published in 1996 by Polity Press
in association with Blackwell Publishers Ltd.

2 4 6 8 10 9 7 5 3 1

Editorial office:
Polity Press
65 Bridge Street
Cambridge CB2 1UR, UK

Marketing and production:
Blackwell Publishers Ltd
108 Cowley Road
Oxford OX4 1JF, UK

Published in the USA by
Blackwell Publishers Inc.
238 Main Street
Cambridge, MA 02142, USA

ISBN 0–7456–1784–0

A CIP catalogue record for this book is available from the British Library and the Library of Congress.

Typeset in 11/13pt Garamond
by Photoprint, Torquay, Devon
Printed in Great Britain by Hartnolls Ltd, Bodmin, Cornwall

This book is printed on acid-free paper.

Contents

Abbreviations		viii
Glossary		ix
Preface		xiii

INTRODUCTION   1

Invocation, competition and comparison   1
Problems of method: religion in the context of popular culture   9
Field work   19

PART ONE: *BASISTAS*   23

1 *Basista* Catholicism: its Context and Character   25

2 Movements of Conservation and Renewal in Modern
Catholicism   37

3 Vatican II, Medellín and Liberation Theology   48

The Council and its aftermath   48
CEBs – base Christian communities   52
The legacy of Catholic Action   58
Liberation theology's diverging paths   65
The Church under pressure   75

4 Concepts and Usages in the Texts and Speech of the
Basista Church   78

O povo/el pueblo   78
The pamphlet literature   82
Organizations and institutions of *basista* Catholicism   90

5 Discourse   97

   The conflict between individual and collectivity, and the
      conciliation of faith with real-life commitment   97
   A popular structuralism   101
   The critical consciousness   103
   A post-conciliar religious practice   106
   Form and content in religious life   108

6 Conclusion   112

PART TWO: PENTECOSTALS   115

7 The Organizational Dimension of Pentecostalism and
      Neo-Pentecostalism   117

   Managing growth and marketing   117
   Education and training   129
   Women and men in the organization   131
   Conclusion   134

8 The Religious Dimension   135

   Ritual and liturgy   135
   Libertação – the collective expulsion of devils   139
   Pentecostalism and 'Afro-Brazilian' beliefs and practices   143
   Pentecostalism and race   155
   Religious culture and taste, high and low: changing the rules
      of engagement   163

9 The Experience of Pentecostals: Exaltation, Loyalty
      and Liminality   189

   The relation between officiant and congregation   189
   The personal service Church   191
   Restructuring the calendar   192
   Conversion: sex, empowerment and the family   194
   Identity and liminality   200
   Money: symbolic and material delimitations of the elect   203
   Conclusion   208

Appendix: Pentecostalism's Social Base   210

CONCLUSION

Fundamentalism, Globalism and Politics   215

   Politics   215
   The role of intellectuals   220
   Modernity: cosmopolitanism and globalism   222
   The projected image of the people   226

Bibliography   229

Index   240

Abbreviations

ACO *Ação Católica Operaria* – Catholic Workers' Action
CEB *Comunidad Eclesial de Base/Comunidade Eclesial de Base* – Base Christian Community
CELAM *Conferencia Episcopal Latinoamericana* – Latin American Bishops' Conference
CIMI *Conselho Indigenista Missionario* – Indian Missionary Council
CL *Comunione e Liberazione* – Communion and Liberation
CNBB *Conferencia Nacional de Bispos Brasileiros* – National Conference of Brazilian Bishops
CPT *Comissão Pastoral Da Terra* – Pastoral Land Commission
GSO Grassroots support organization
ISPAC *Instituto de Serviço para una Ação Comunitaria* – Institute for the Support of Community Action
ITEBA *Instituto Teológic da Bahia* – Bahia Theological Institute
JOC *Juventude Operaria Católica* – Catholic Workers' Youth
NGO Non-governmental organization
PNAD *Pesquisa Nacional de Amostragem por Domicilio* – National Residential Sample Survey.
PT *Partido dos Trabalhadores* – Workers' Party
TL Theology of Liberation

Glossary

(All words listed are Portuguese except for those designated by 'Sp.', which are Spanish.)

agente/agente pastoral activist or official in Catholic Church-sponsored work involving consciousness-raising or promotion of popular organization.

animador person who leads discussions, meetings.

auxiliar auxiliary.

bairro (Sp. *barrio*) neighbourhood.

basismo/basista a *basista* is a believer in *basismo*; *basismo* is an outlook on social, religious and political issues which starts from the viewpoint that the people are possessed with special, albeit often hidden, insights and untainted beliefs.

boia fria literally 'cold lunch'; a reference to agricultural workers who, being hired only by the day, do not receive a hot lunch from the farm owners.

caboclo protective spirit, a person's 'double' in possession cults, communication with which can be established through a medium; also, in Amazonia, a person of mixed *indio* and African descent. In Salvador, *Candomblé de caboclo* is a form of *candomblé* (q.v.) which is learnt more rapidly and practised by less elaborately trained people than the more prestigious 'pure' *candomblé*.

caminhada a long march, or wandering through the wilderness (from *caminho*, a road).

campamento camp/illegal settlement.

candomblé the form of possession cult prevalent in and identified with the culture of Salvador da Bahia, and claiming a West African, especially Yoruba, origin.

capóeira a stylized, dance-like version of unarmed combat whose roots are said to lie in slave culture and in Africa; Lewis (1992: xxiii) says that it is 'a martial art involving a complete system of self-defence, but it also has a dance-like, acrobatic movement style'.

cargos (Sp.) an Andean and Mesoamerican term: obligations which rotate among community members, to hold office and sponsor annual festivals.

cassação the act of depriving a person of their political – or other – rights.

centro(s) centre(s), but here usually establishment where a *mãe-de-santo* receives adepts, or clients, and practises her skills of divination and mediumship.

chutar to kick (cf. the English football term 'shoot for goal').

compadre/compadrazgo (Sp.) close friend, literally a man who is godfather to one's child, or to whose child one is oneself godparent. *Compadrazgo* is the institution of co-godparenthood, particularly in the Andes, Central America and Mexico.

Comunidade de Base (Sp: *Comunidad de Base*) Base Christian Community. Strictly speaking a *Comunidade Eclesial de Base*, with the institutional connotation of 'ecclesial'. Hence the abbreviation CEB.

congregação congregation; in the Assemblies of God, a small chapter operating under the authority of a *matriz* (q.v.).

cordel literally a string, but used to refer to popular poetic literature (*literatura de cordel*) in Northeast Brazil, because the booklets containing the poems are, or were once, sold at market stalls attached to a piece of string.

corrente literally a piece of thread, but also a necklace and thus a circle of worshippers. The Universal Church borrowed this term from possession cults and applied it to theme-services taking place regularly on particular days of the week.

crente 'believer', but the word now refers exclusively to Pentecostals and Evangelicals.

criolo/criolinho dark-skinned person/dark-skinned little man (cf. 'creole').

cura divina divine healing.

diacono literally 'deacon' – an office in church.

direitos de posse ownership/usufructuary rights.

dízimo/dizimista the tithe/person who contributes one-tenth of his or her income to a church. A practice associated nowadays exclusively with Evangelical and Pentecostal Churches.

doutrina literally 'doctrine'. Among Pentecostals, observance of codes of austere behaviour, as in prohibitions on provocative or even frivolous dress, smoking, drinking and illicit sex.

evangélicos literally 'Evangelicals' – broad term very frequently used in Spanish and Portuguese to refer to followers of Pentecostal and other charismatic Protestant Churches. Its meaning is nevertheless stronger – i.e. more charismatic – than in English.

evangelista 'evangelist' – an office/rank in some Pentecostal Churches.

exu a Yoruba deity, also a strong presence in Brazilian possession cults, analogous to a God of fortune who can bring about good as much as evil.

favela usually translated as a shanty town, but better thought of as an urban settlement permanently under construction by its inhabitants.

festa a feast.

focolare a Catholic devotional movement which developed out of Majorca in the post-war period.

folheto a pamphlet, but also a generic term for *cordel* literature (q.v.).

futebol football.

guía a personage in the relating of gods to humans in possession cults.

invasão a piece of urban land seized, marked out and built on by illegal or semi-legal occupants. Gradually it will become a *favela* (q.v.).

lavadeira/s washerwoman/women.

libertação liberation, personal and political – but also the liberation of a person from possession by the devil, or the liberation of a demon from the prison of a person's body.

macumba set of practices used in possession cults particularly associated with the casting and, conversely, dispelling of evil spirits.

mãe-de-santo a priestess in possession cults; owner of a place of worship or *terreiro* (q.v.).

maligno/malo the evil one/the devil.

matriz the seat of the Assemblies of God in an area – for example one *matriz* is in charge of the whole of Recife or Salvador and administers all matters concerning personnel, finance, membership, etc.

militancia active membership in a movement or political party.

Mina form of possession cult practised in Belem.

missionario/a a missionary; a rank or office in some Pentecostal Churches.

nagô term used to designate people originating in Dahomey and Yoruba-land, but also used to describe cults deemed to be 'pure' in contrast to others 'tainted' with Amerindian and other 'extraneous' elements.

obreiro/a literally a worker, but by extension a person who does the work of God, and thus a warden or low-level office-holder in Pentecostal Churches.

ofertorio the Offertory in the Catholic Mass.

olhar eye/look/approach.

orixá a god in the Yoruba pantheon, object of worship in the possession cults.

pãe-de-santo (male) priest in possession cults; owner of a place of worship or *terreiro* (q.v.).

pastor pastor.

Pastoral Pastoral Commission in the Catholic church. This term, which has largely replaced 'mission', is used generically to refer to specialized activities in the social field, at the parish, diocesan, or national level.

pedidos de oração written petitions for solutions to personal problems deposited in churches by Pentecostal worshippers.

pelegos compliant union leaders named thus by analogy with the sheepskin (*pelego*) protecting a horse-rider from bruising by the harsh saddle.

periferia periphery of large cities, inhabited by low-income groups.

población (Sp.) Chilean term to describe low-income neighbourhoods.

pomba-gira deceitful woman in possession cults' Pantheon. Adaptation of a Yoruba figure.

povão from '*povo*' (q.v.) – 'lumpen'.

povo people.

presbítero 'presbiter' – office in Evangelical and Pentecostal churches.

pueblo (Sp.): people.

sambódromo 'sambadrome' – official monumental parade area purpose-built in Rio de Janeiro in the 1980s for the Carnival parade and competition.

Santa Ceia lit. Holy Banquet – ritual in Evangelical and Pentecostal Churches resembling Holy Communion.

saudade a feeling of languorous nostalgia, sadness and longing, above all expressed in music.

seita (Sp. *secta*) sect – term used pejoratively by the Catholic Church and others to refer to both possession cults and to Pentecostal Churches.

sertão the drought-prone hinterland of the Northeast of Brazil.

spirita practitioner of or believer in spiritism.

suburbio suburb (in Salvador), with low-income inhabitants.

terreiro place for the enactment of the rituals of possession cults, under the control and ownership of a *pãe/mãe de santo* (q.v.).

trevas darkness (an archaic formulation).

umbanda version of possession cult developed from the early twentieth century in Rio de Janeiro, initially intending to distinguish itself clearly from cults of African origin such as *candomblé* (q.v.).

vedettismo (c.f. French *vedette* – film star – also used in Brazilian Portuguese) the propensity to make a prominent person into a celebrity.

Preface

This book owes it existence to three cities — Salvador da Bahia, Paris and Cambridge. Like all my other work, it could not have been produced without a network of people of limitless generosity who, knowingly and often unknowingly, have joined in it during the past five years. Although in the end it was I who wrote it down, the result would have been inconceivable without them.

In Salvador I benefited from the warmth, friendship, hospitality and stimulating conversation of Sylvia Maia, Mary Castro, Ione Gonzalez, and Sister Joanete. William Tavares provided me with the educational materials he himself had written, and gave indispensable help in carrying out field work, as did Alaide Costa. The research and conversation of Claudio Pereira and Wilson Gomes provided important points of departure. The late Fr Paolo Tonucci welcomed me in Camaçari, as did Fr Clovis in the parish of São Jorge. In Recife I was lucky to receive assistance from María-José Dias Monteiro.

In São Paulo and in Cambridge José and Heloisa de Souza Martins have, once again, been a source of strength as well as information and ideas which I can never adequately repay.

Thanks to the initiative of Christian Gros I was invited to spend three months as a Visiting Professor at the Institut des Hautes Etudes de l'Amérique Latine in Paris in 1995. I am enormously indebted to him and to the Institut's Director, Georges Couffignal, for it was during that period that my ideas were clarified and the writing process got under way. Michel Adam, Catherine Bidou, Antoinette Molinié, Hélène Rivière d'Arc, Katia Mattoso, Elisabeth Roudinesco, Patricia Birman, Véronique Boyer-Araujo, and Graciela Schneier all contributed sometimes crucial intellectual pointers and encouragement.

In Cambridge I have benefited from the security of a loving family and from membership in a unique academic community. Hence my enduring love for Ilona Roth and our children Benji, Jessica and Raphael. And hence also my debt to my colleagues Geoffrey Hawthorn, Graham Howes, David Brading and Jack Goody, and to Peter Fry on his occasional visits.

No one could ask for a better place to work than the Centre of Latin American Studies, and this is thanks to Ana Gray, the Centre's librarian, and to Clare Hariri the Centre's administrator. It is impossible to express adequately my appreciation for Clare Hariri's steadfastness and generosity of spirit towards all of us, staff and students, who work in the Centre.

At Polity Press, John Thompson has again been unstinting in his support of this venture and in suggesting improvements in the text and in presentation.

Drafts were read at various stages by Marie Howes, Sylvia Maia, Katia Mattoso, Charles Elliott, David Martin and Peter Fry. All of them responded generously to my encroachment on their time and made extremely helpful comments. If there are not more errors in my biblical references, that is thanks to the expertise of Jenny Roberts.

No research is without expense, and I wish to record my gratitude to the Leverhulme Foundation for the award of a Research Fellowship in 1991; to the Nuffield Foundation for Travel Grants in 1991 and 1993; to the Cambridge University Travelling Expenses Fund, and to the British Council and Brazil's CNPq which supported a Cambridge-Bahia 'link' in 1992–1995.

Salvador da Bahia de Todos os Santos
January 1996

Introduction

Invocation, competition and comparison

On Good Friday 1983 I attended service in the Catholic Church of Santa María de los Angeles in Managua. Its priest was noted for his strong commitment to the Sandinista government, to the cause of the poor, and to what the followers of liberation theology describe as the People's Church. His church was a new construction, built with the help of Italian volunteers who had painted on its walls the history of Nicaragua through revolutionary eyes: the Spanish conquerors massacring the Indians; the American occupying troops of the early twentieth century; Sandino with tall hat and riding boots in the posture of defiance which had become the emblem of the Sandinista revolution; Carlos Fonseca, founder of the Sandinista Liberation Front and martyr to the cause, in his heavy-framed spectacles. During the service, as the priest read St John's account of the Passion of Christ with a powerful sense of drama, the image which came to my mind was that of Jesus as revolutionary leader, the Pharisees as profiteers prepared to sell their country if the price was right, and Pontius Pilate as a vacillating *gringo* ambassador. Parishioners succeeded each other at the altar offering special prayers for particular groups or individuals: let us pray for the Sandinista government, for although they may not believe in God, still they are doing the work of God; let us pray for the revolutionary forces of Guatemala and El Salvador; let us pray for the Holy Father, even though he may have been badly advised during his visit last month – but as for the Archbishop, Lord forgive him for he knows not what he is doing; and so on. On the altar was a photograph of Archbishop Romero of El Salvador, assassinated in 1980 and already elevated *de facto* to the status of saint and martyr.

Not far away the reviled Archbishop was holding his own, much larger, service in the open air. It was a more orthodox occasion. Afterwards a lady walking away was heard to express her surprise, in the most matter-of-fact fashion, that this year the statue of Christ had not bled as it usually did. The Pope's celebration of an open-air mass in Managua a few weeks previously had been the scene of a shameless struggle for religious legitimation by both revolutionary and counter-revolutionary forces, and Archbishop Ovando y Bravo himself was the psychological and symbolic leader of the opposition to the Sandinistas. So for many people attendance at the Archbishop's service on Good Friday must have been more than a routine religious gesture.

The experience of this Good Friday posed a question which led eventually to the writing of this book: what did the progressive, or 'People's', Church have to say to the mass of the people? What did they think when the figure of the Pope, whom they had been brought up to treat with reverence and respect, was derided by their own priests? How could they make sense of the bitter conflicts over political issues which opposed their Archbishop to many members of the hierarchy and of holy orders? I could not suppress within myself a feeling which from then on slowly shifted my perception of liberation theology and the movement to which it had given rise. It was a sense of factitiousness, a suspicion that in their overconfidence the proponents of the People's Church were hiding even their own awareness that the people were not as they were proclaiming them to be, that their hope of yoking together their version of Christianity with the people's faith ('popular religion') was an illusion and a fantasy.

Once these questions had been raised, to ask what the 'people' thought, believed, or imagined inevitably entailed asking the same about the intelligentsia. The interdependence and interweaving of popular culture with the culture of the educated classes became increasingly evident and increasingly fascinating as I explored both the evidence collected in the field and certain contemporary cultural theories. Although the usefulness of the two terms remained unquestionable, so also the notion that they denoted distinct watertight compartments became unsustainable. Rather the relationship between them seemed one of reflexive interplay. And so that mirror play between the popular and the erudite became a central theme of this book.

My interest in the Catholic Church, and my realization that its presence and importance had gone unrecognized in all my work in Latin America since the late 1960s, led me first to study liberation theology and base Christian communities (CEBs) (Lehmann, 1990), but by the time I came to conduct more detailed work in Brazil from 1991, I realized that a relationship which I had hitherto thought of in terms internal to Catholicism had been vastly complicated by the presence of Protestantism, and of a particularly explosive version thereof, namely Pentecostalism — whose followers are variously known in Latin American as the *sectas* (*seitas* in Portuguese), as the *evangélicos*, and as the *creyentes* (believers — *crentes* in Portuguese).[1] By 1991, the work of David Martin and David Stoll had brought the phenomenon of Pentecostalism vividly to the attention of the English-speaking public, as had the cruel deeds of Guatemala's dictator Ríos Montt,[2] and above all the unavoidable spectacle of small chapels sprouting all over impoverished neighbourhoods throughout the cities of the region as well as among indigenous peoples in Central America and in the Andes.

Evidence of the massive scale of conversion, especially among the poor, led to a recasting of the questions which had arisen in my mind that Good Friday in Managua, framing them now in terms of the meaning attached to both 'progressive Catholicism' and Pentecostalism. This meant analysing the discourse and the mind-set of the people involved at the grassroots in relation to the specificity of the cultural context, based on fieldwork and a multiplicity of other sources. If this was to be grasped in all the richness of what J.-F. Bayart (1989) would call its historicity, then a contextualization of the two phenomena was required, complete with organizational background and the national and global framework in which this struggle is taking place.

For my research showed that the comparison undertaken was inseparable from a real confrontation, and that the religious field in Latin America is now an arena in which contending forces 'struggle for the spirit': it is a struggle not just for numbers, or for 'market share', but for the ability to legitimately invoke the people and speak in the name of the people. Thus the book which has emerged is forced to take the macro as well as the micro view, to provide an account of the forces in contention as well as their impact on individuals at the grass roots. The big questions are very big: do the people feel more faithfully represented by, or identified with, the revolutionary priests and nuns in their jeans and sandals, promising a long period in the wilderness travelling towards an uncertain Promised

---

[1] The mere fact that I had omitted even once to mention the word 'Protestantism' in the earlier book, despite its sub-title 'Economics, politics and *religion*', and that no reviewer had drawn attention to this, shows how discussion of these topics among the intelligentsia was an inward-looking — in a sense provincial — affair.

[2] Ríos Montt governed Guatemala for a brief period in 1982–3, and refused to cede to the Pope's insistent demands that he halt the execution of a group of peasant leaders which took place during the Pope's presence in the country. Ríos Montt was a born-again Christian and a member of the small but influential California-based Church of the Word.

Land, and offering a diet of agonized self-questioning, of seminars and consciousness-raising combined with mini-projects, to sustain the People of God on their journey? Or will they be drawn towards the pastors, uniformly respectable in their suits, white shirts and black ties, as they proclaim the tangible happiness that will follow from a fulminating conversion experience, a herculean effort to get their lives and their families under control, and the financial discipline of a weekly contribution to church funds? The research questions are an operational and partial version of these big questions: what do the priests, the Catholic activists, and the pastors and preachers actually say? How does their language relate to that of the people? How do their metaphors, symbols and rituals relate to the traditions of the people's culture? How do they themselves 'think the people'? And how are these radically opposed projects of salvation, each in their different ways both this-worldly and other-worldly, interpreted in the language of the people?

While the Catholic Church has made a 'preferential option for the poor', with all that has implied in the way of collective — but not collectivist — solutions to the problems of poverty, many of the poor themselves seem to have opted for Pentecostalism, and while Catholics express reverential devotion to the people and their culture, the Pentecostals use modern methods of marketing to 'target' the poor, ignoring social themes and describing salvation in terms of personal prosperity.[3] Could it be, in the words of Nathan Wachtel, that we are witnessing, 'finally, after 500 years, the extirpation of idolatries'?

That is too apocalyptic. Doubtless for decades and probably centuries to come the Catholic Church will remain a weighty presence in Latin America, but it will not be the same institution, either internally or in relation to the wider culture and society. Weakened paradoxically by the tardy and embarrassing implementation of its sixteenth-century policies by these Protestant upstarts, it will have become 'a church like any other' and be less of a hegemonic institution. It will have responded of necessity to demographic realities and recruitment difficulties. But it will also have been changed from within, and it is that process which forms the subject matter of the first part of this book.

Since the Second Vatican Council in the early 1960s, followers of liberation theology and similar progressive Christian ideas have set out to reinvigorate the church by 'going to the people' and bringing to them a

---

[3] An additional irony arises from the Portuguese word for 'liberation' — *libertação* — which for Catholics means a prophetic liberation from oppression and structural sin, but for Pentecostals means the expulsion of devils.

message of empowerment – an empowerment inspired by revolutionary reinterpretations of the Bible and the life of Christ, but whose implications have been more ecclesial[4] and political than spiritual. In that message, the Christian base communities (CEBs) have become the repository of many people's hopes for church renewal in the post-conciliar period, and also a symbol of the provenance of that renewal – from the poor, specifically from the poor of Latin America. This book concentrates, in its first part, on the *basista* faction of Catholicism but the reader should keep in mind that, despite serious differences over certain matters of theology and politics, *basistas* and the official Church share the same concept of the 'people', speak the same language of erudite culture, and rely for their survival on the same hierarchy of bishops and priests.

I speak of *basismo* rather than Christian base communities because, far from being the hard and fast and 'actually existing' category depicted in the literature and in political discourse, base communities are one part of a broader phenomenon in Brazilian and Latin American political culture, which can be described as a sensitivity to, and even veneration for, the beliefs and interests and practices of 'the people'. Furthermore, although the idea of a base community and the ideas of *basismo* are highly influential among the intelligentsia, this influence is out of proportion to the number of base communities and of participants in them, and, more importantly, even to their real weight within the institutions of Catholicism. Thus it is necessary to broaden the category to make it analytically defensible. I could not assimilate it to populism, partly because of the pejorative connotations of that word, especially in English, partly because in Latin America populism denotes a complex of institutional features of the state, of party organization and loyalty, and of economic policies, characteristic of many countries (most famously Argentina and Brazil) during the 1930–80 period. In contemporary parlance, the term *base* in both Spanish and Portuguese has come to mean the grass roots, occasionally even replacing the usage *pueblo/povo* (people), and just as *populismo* has a pejorative connotation, so sometimes can *basismo*, though in this text the latter (abstract) noun denotes a sensibility and not a political judgement.

Basismo in connection with Catholicism emphasizes the cultural and analytical delineation of the movement, avoiding even the appearance of political labelling, as would be the case with the words 'progressive' or 'radical' for example, whose use would impoverish and distort the interpretation rather than enrich it. To speak of 'progressive' Catholicism, as people often do, is to give the impression of a political faction, of a

---

[4] That is, related to the structures of the Church.

Catholicism modified only in response to extra-religious, principally political pressures and concerns, which is not what its protagonists intend, while 'liberation theology', though obviously relevant and influential among *basistas*, would, if used on its own, give the equally misleading impression of a purely doctrinal movement. The usage '*basista* Catholicism', in contrast, couples two cultural categories, leaving open rather than closing off their political consequences and the political intentions of their bearers, and thus making it possible to compare the political effects of different types of *basista* and *basismo*, or to compare their functioning in different contexts.

Once the model of *basismo* has been set out, the second part of the book is pervaded by an implicit comparative agenda. If in the first part the emphasis in the interpretation of *basista* discourse was on institutional and doctrinal history and context, in the second part Pentecostalism is treated in the manner of an open-ended exploration of the multi-levelled character of culture change, in which religion plays the role of a kaleidoscopic lens, combining and recombining diverse elements of a society and its culture. The contrast with *basismo* is a constant counterpoint: the one is concerned very seriously with theology, the other cares little for theology; the one is little concerned to draw boundaries around its membership, the other does so with great care, as if drawing the frontiers of an ethnic group; the one insists that the path to belief lies through rational analysis, the other rejects such an idea and accepts only the fulminating descent of the Holy Spirit; the one minimizes ritual in favour of belief, form in favour of content, the other continually recreates ritual and equates belief with an emotional state and an array of practical prescriptions for everyday life; the one insists on the indissoluble connection between religious belief and political commitment, the other rejects such a connection totally.

So the list goes on. It is hard to believe that both are appealing or responding to the same needs, desires, frustrations and alienations of the mass of poor people whose adherence they seek, and this emotional and imaginary asymmetry calls into question even the notion that both forces are adequately described by the term 'religious'. As a result a straightforward comparison between the two in structural, sociological terms, though by no means impossible, would miss out the dynamic of their interaction with history, culture and institutions. *Basismo* projects itself as heir to a historically rooted Catholic and Brazilian culture, and to the erudite–popular interaction which is so central to those cultures; for all the radicalism, even the iconoclasm, of its message, its symbols, images, and language are redolent of that heritage. The other force, Pentecostalism, is conducting an onslaught against the feasts, celebrations, rituals and rhythms – musical and chronological – which together make up the people's culture, and no doubt in the process is creating another variant of that culture. Although it even adapts the rituals of Catholicism and of the possession cults which pervade the Brazilian cultural system, it advertises itself as something completely new and completely foreign, and is in no way ashamed of its Anglo-Saxon ideological inspiration, however modified and adapted. Pentecostalism finds strength in its lack of historical depth and in its lack of local roots, while Catholics, mainstream and *basista*, believe the opposite approach is the right one.

If this is an account of the struggle for the 'people', that is for control of the meaning or the invocation of 'the people', it is because the element of 'projection' in the invocation of the people – be it in art, literature, culture, politics or religion – is extremely important, especially in Brazil. Some of the themes taken up here had already appeared in the 1930s: Mario de Andrade (1893–1945), a leader of Brazil's modernist movement, was calling for a revolt against the formalistic and rhetorical archaisms of elite cultural expression in favour of the use by the literary elite of the language of the people. The 'Brazilianization of Brazil' was to be achieved, among other ways, through the development of 'national' artists who would penetrate the 'deep structures' of the country. In this way, he said in the late 1920s, 'we could be more ourselves'. The themes of authenticity and faithfulness to the people's traditions already appear in Andrade's fear that the search for the 'real' Brazil, the Brazil which did not 'ape' Europe,[5] could be hampered by folkloristic concerns or by exoticism, and thus could succeed only through the thorough assimilation by the artist of the people's culture, researching his own subconscious. Yet Andrade was a vanguard representative of aesthetic modernism, who captured the indigenous by using the device of an almost surreal allegory – *Macunaima* (1928) (Schelling, 1991: 121–43).[6] Reflexivity, as William Rowe and Vivian Schelling (1991) have shown, though they do not use the word itself, has been a constant underlying theme of the region's culture at least in the twentieth century, as versions of the 'mind', 'spirit' or 'soul' of the masses were successively fertilized, tended, recycled and imbibed by generations of intellectuals of all political colours. For it is the intelligentsia, especially in Latin America, who invent the people and would themselves be invented by the people – and the revolutionary

---

[5] In a presumably intentional wordplay, Andrade uses the word *macaquear* from *macaco*, a monkey.

[6] In this alliance Brazilian modernism was far from unique: the Spanish poet and dramatist Federico García Lorca also used the style of modernism and surrealism to capture the 'deep structures' of Andalucía.

character of Pentecostalism comes from its will to turn away from this complex, dialectical relationship and thus destroy it.

This reflexivity is also a feature of Catholicism more generally, and translates itself into a cosmopolitan Catholic culture. The Church is cosmopolitan in that it has a long history of attempting to assimilate 'other', or 'local' cultures, to draw them in to itself or, as current jargon would have it, to 'inculturate'.[7] Apparent differences in practice from one country to another may therefore mask common meanings. Pentecostalism is better described as global rather than cosmopolitan, and moves in the opposite direction: Pentecostal churches all over the world, in the most diverse cultures and societies, exhibit astonishingly similar patterns of growth, use similar techniques of oratory and proselytization, and similar forms of organization and leadership, and also resemble each other strongly in their ritual practices (see Martin, 1990; Marshall, 1991; Gifford, 1993).

In these circumstances of cosmopolitanism and globalism, the comparative method and its accompanying structural explanations couched synchronically in terms only of particular societies or cultures can hardly be convincing. The contribution of this book is to counteract two contrasting biases in the existing literature: whereas committed *basistas* emphasize the way in which *basismo* is rooted in local popular cultures, I have emphasized its relationship with other tendencies and movements in the Church worldwide. And where other writers have tended to emphasize how Pentecostalism differs from local cultures, I have tempered a recognition of this undoubted truth with a detailed account of how it finds points of entry into local cultures, returning in the Conclusion to the global theme, which is evidently very important indeed. The hallmark of the comparative/ structural approach is the search for propensities: the overarching research question would in that context ask what factors lead different social groups to adopt this or that religious persuasion. But the globalism of a phenomenon makes it extremely difficult to pursue such an interpretative strategy, because of the disproportion between the highly differentiated character of the explanatory variable (the circumstances and character of the social groups) and the highly unified character of the process to be explained. The interpretation offered here focuses instead on the creative role of the religious movements themselves, and on their capacity to open

---

[7] Defined as follows by the late Superior-General of the Society of Jesus, Fr Arrupe: 'The incarnation of Christian life and the Christian message in a particular cultural context in such a way that this experience not only finds expression in elements proper to the culture in question . . . but becomes a principle that animates, directs and unifies the culture, transforming it and remaking it so as to bring about a "new creation" ' (quoted in Shorter, 1988: 11).

up spaces and carve out niches for themselves in a variety of cultural settings.

Problems of method: religion in the context of popular culture

Researching Pentecostalism in Brazil (and probably in many other places too) is at first a unique and frequently shocking experience. The wailing, shouting and above all the electronic amplification which accompany religious celebrations often assail the ears with almost unbearable force, and the response to the researcher's request for information or opinion can be a ferocious assault on his soul. Not always, but often enough to place this type of research in a category all of its own. In one respect it is salutary: whether in their own or in a foreign country, social scientists are accustomed to docile subjects, all the more so when they themselves are light-skinned and comfortably off, and are conducting their inquiries among poor people of much darker colour. This is different.

The world of Pentecostalism has no place for neutrality or detached observation of religious life: working on the subject introduces a further, more subtle, discomfiture — more subtle at least in the writing, if not in the crossfire of field research. In the field the researcher is being alternately hounded and hectored, seduced and befriended. Whereas in conducting research on, say, politics, one can feign acquiescence, by sagely nodding in conversations with politicians or activists, charismatic Christians often reject or evade the connivance necessary for an untroubled interview relationship. On the researcher's part, it is difficult, indeed impossible, to affect politely an appearance of agreement with evangelicals, especially where this requires a cathartic conversion: who will be prepared to kneel in a gesture of submission, 'accepting Jesus' in the name of science? And who, having done so, could keep up the pretence and cope with its ramifications?

With this experience behind him, the social scientist, in reporting and analysing the field data, will have extreme difficulty in suppressing an attitude of contempt, disdain, amusement, even shock, or, alternatively, of admiration and wonderment. If a person describes a miraculous cure, or even a cure which has no medical explanation, how can I describe the account without inviting the reader to share those attitudes of mine in some sort of complicity? How can I reproduce a testimony of conversion, complete with fits, healing and claims of moral regeneration, without either betraying patronising disbelief or, conversely, implicitly inviting the reader to believe all these claims?

The answer, of course, is that I cannot. On the other hand, to evaluate these situations, which are so central to the Pentecostals' experience as they see it, surely falls outside a social scientist's competence. It would require a psychiatrist or a certain kind of psychologist, and also a research/ interview setting of a very different kind from that on which we rely in fieldwork. In my research I have had conversations in churches and in people's homes, and some of the most revealing, emblematic comments have been picked up in almost casual encounters – precisely occasions when people are off their guard and have not either put up their defences or prepared themselves to project a certain image. These are useful settings for my own research purposes – that is for analysing conceptions and definitions of words and situations – but hardly appropriate for any sort of assessment or evaluation of accounts of healing or psychological transformation. Such assessment would involve placing them in a detailed way in the context of the individual's life history, and also asking some prying questions – questions which most social scientists would regard as unethical, extraneous or plain risky, and which would require the interviewee to be a client or a patient, and to enter into a relationship in which the interlocutor is allowed, even encouraged, to 'pry'. Sometimes, of course, it 'all comes pouring out' and, like others, John Burdick for example, my conversations were once or twice punctuated by weeping or an unstoppable cascade of words. But these moments of personal revelation merely compound the social scientist's embarrassment because we are not trained to deal with them, we do not know, professionally, how to react or how we are expected to react, and above all we have not created an appropriate setting for their analysis as 'cases'.

This account of 'real fieldwork' should cast some doubt on the steady flow of self-doubting texts which have come from anthropology in particular and have gained currency under the post-modernist influence of Clifford and Marcus (1986), trying to confront the heritage of British imperial domination which marked the first two generations of social anthropology, and of post-war United States imperialism. The main arguments were neatly, albeit patronizingly, reviewed by Clifford Geertz (1988) who concluded simply that although the doubters are right to remind us that times and places have changed, and that the consensual superiority engendered by imperialist domination is no more, they need not implode or self-destruct, for there will be a place in the future for 'conversations across societal lines', 'to enlarge the possibility of intelligible discourse between people quite different from one another

. . . yet contained in a world where . . . it is increasingly difficult to get out of each other's way' (p. 147). The eirenic image of 'conversations', or the images of passive subordinate tribes and peoples in other more polemical accounts, fits uneasily with some of my own encounters with Brazilian Pentecostals: far from being the representatives of an uncontaminated indigenous or popular culture, they were involved in a frontal attack on central tenets and practices of their 'own' culture, in the name of values which they themselves glorified even though, or perhaps precisely because, those values came from another, foreign, culture which they usually referred to not even as Western but simply as the United States – a term which in their usage meant not so much a political or geographical unit, but rather a land of wealth and Protestantism, 'land' here being used, as in 'land of milk and honey', in a slightly fabulous way.

To compound the ambiguities of the encounter, much as they might see themselves as sharing in the culture of this imaginary white Anglo-Saxon world, they did not identify me with that culture, or apparently with any collective cultural identity. Rather they placed me as an individual, without social, racial or cultural referent, but exclusively in reference to their movement, and thus usually as a 'soul' – to be saved, or perhaps beyond salvation, but a soul nonetheless. When it is added that most of these Pentecostals were black – though this is a complicated category in Brazil which will later receive more extended discussion – and female, then doubt must be cast on the appositeness, in this situation, of the dominator/dominated model which underpins much anthropological soul-searching and self-questioning. Indeed, one reason why a person like myself finds the Pentecostals, at least occasionally, so shocking, is that they are not submissive, and thus they do not allow us to take shelter in a guilty (but also cosy) sense of privilege or superiority. The habitual roles were, in some encounters, reversed: the white male from a rich country was put on the defensive by groups of people who were poor, black and female.

The ironies are not insignificant and raise serious questions about our conceptualization of popular culture and religion: the Pentecostal onslaught against a local culture is conducted by local people who are clearly members of the popular classes, yet the campaign is ideologically derived from an advanced industrial society and specifically invokes the glorious economic achievements of the United States. The inspiration, admittedly, does not come from the core of the establishment of world capitalism, but rather from a quite specific cultural, racial and social niche of the USA, from the margins, and from a brew of belief and practice which was for long despised in North American evangelical churches (because of its insistence on gifts of tongues and healing and receipt of the Holy Spirit). Whereas in North America evangelical Protestantism is predominantly found among whites, in Latin America it has achieved a surprising degree of penetration among indigenous and black sectors of the population, though it could not be said to be predominantly identified with them. Our world view has great difficulty in accommodating these Pentecostals whose ideas, born and developed on the margins of 'our' societies, seem − numerically at least − to be flourishing at the heart of Latin America's popular sectors.

Although there was at first a reaction of hostility among social scientists to this wave of Protestantism, especially among those sympathetic to *basista* Catholicism or the theology of liberation, the evident success of the Pentecostals in particular has now produced the opposite effect. For example, David Stoll (1990) began by insisting on the role of US-based missions in the rise of Central American Protestantism, but has become increasingly distanced from that view. In his introduction to a recent book edited by him with Virginia Garrard-Burnett (1993), Stoll inclines more to blame the Catholic Church for its own troubles, and indeed his co-editor concludes the book in triumphalist tones by restating the view that Latin America is undergoing a Reformation of equivalent dimensions and implications to that which occurred in Europe in the sixteenth century. Stoll and others are writing from a perspective of 'reflux': they have undergone a conversion from an earlier position and assume that their readers are still lagging in this trajectory. John Burdick (1993) describes his disillusionment with a radical Catholicism to which his early political formation had drawn him, and then confronts and compares it with both *umbanda* (a congeries of possession cults) and Pentecostalism. His book is structured by the disappointment revealed in its Introduction: it is an account not just of why *crente* (i.e. evangelical or, literally, 'believer')[8] church attendance and membership are growing so fast, but also of all the 'good things', the emotional benefits, which their members find: solace for their suffering, control over (some of) their vices; anonymity; receptivity (on account of the predominance of blacks) and so on. His book, which has very many merits indeed, does then exhibit a certain complicity with the 'numbers game' which is currently demanding of students of this field an account in terms of a competition, or a race for market share.

The question of growth and numbers is particularly delicate because

---

[8] *Crente* is a term used in particular by the members of the Assemblies of God. Some other Pentecostal groups avoid it.

the churches themselves are so obsessed by it. The numbers game is their game: proselytism is one of their salient objectives, some would say their *raison d'être*. The triumphalism of announcing, even with some reservations, a Latin American Reformation, is a further extension of complicity in the numbers game, and in the Churches' own triumphalism. To transpose Europe's Reformation in this context is an abuse of the term: the political changes and the wars which accompanied, indeed were part of, the Reformation, are absent or radically different in content. Where is the counterpart to the Thirty Years' War, to Calvin's or Luther's political theory (Skinner, 1978, vol. 2)? And what then do we make of the rival view (Levine, 1992: 3) that a Reformation is surging from the Catholic base communities?

The example of Burdick shows an author's discovery that the images he once held dear of popular culture and religion, and which were shared by *basista* Catholics, were mistaken and idealistic, as were the *basistas'* own images of themselves. Other authors, like Le Bot (1993), follow a similar trajectory: a double disillusion sets in and is then transmitted to the reader.

For in *basismo*, idealization is not only a problem in the interpretation; it forms a constituent part of the phenomenon itself. *Basismo* is the belief that the people, the 'grassroots', have a distinctive culture and outlook on life and society, and that political and religious salvation necessarily involve listening to the people and gaining empathy, even a mystical communion, with their culture. It exists in the form of certain philosophies of development – 'appropriate' technology, 'putting the last first', the NGO emphasis on participation, are examples – and it also exists in Catholicism, indeed more broadly in Christianity. In writing about Catholicism in Latin America I use the term to avoid formulas such as 'progressive Church' – which inappropriately allies a political to a religious term – or 'People's Church' which gives a false impression of this movement's power and institutionalization. *Basista* Catholicism, or Catholic *basismo*, find their expression, obviously, in *comunidades de base*, in *Ação Católica Operaria* (Workers' Catholic Action), in the theology of liberation, and in innumerable parish-level initiatives in the fields of health, education, *capoeira*[9] and so on.

In studying *basismo* the sociologist faces a very different situation from that described in the case of Pentecostalism. *Basismo* is not a mass movement, but a movement which gradually creates a popular intelligentsia, so

---

[9] A stylized, dance-like enactment of their slave ancestors' form of unarmed combat, *capoeira* is a classic case of the (re)invention of tradition. See Lewis, 1992.

its activists are highly educated, often to university level, and they welcome an outside observer with open arms. Are these activists not themselves, in some way, also social scientists? They are accustomed to dealing with outsiders and foreigners, being reliant for many of their activities on links with NGOs and the Church, and their ideology is consonant with that of the international network of defenders of human rights and participatory development. It is therefore not surprising that the 1970s and 1980s saw an upsurge of enthusiastic writings by Latin American, North American and European authors, on 'social movements', the 'People's Church' and so on, in which the activities and discourse of this popular intelligentsia were taken to be representative of popular culture in general.

Once again, then, we find that there is a problem in the conceptualization of popular culture arising from the relationship between the observer and what he or she conceives of as popular culture, and it is here that the central methodological issue arises. I shall deal with it by starting from the much-cited but, in my view, little read, book *Os Deuses do Povo* by Carlos Rodriguez Brandão (1980). Brandão's book is little read because it is difficult, yet it is difficult precisely because of its proximity to the culture it describes and analyses, and because of its distance from the conventional language of social science: his style is littered with popular idioms and turns of phrase, and the richness of his Portuguese, worthy of a work of literature, stands in contrast to the poverty of much social science writing. The book is distinguished by a focus not on any particular religion in itself, but on popular culture as a whole, defined repeatedly – almost *ad nauseam* – in opposition to elite, or rather erudite, culture. For Brandão, this is the overriding and sole relevant categorical distinction in the study of religion, cutting across, dominating and even erasing the divisions between established, institutionalized, theologically delineated Churches, since all 'Churches', even the so-called Afro-Brazilian, spiritist or *mediúnico* (medium-based) possession cults, contain the 'erudite–popular' division within them. His focus would be best translated as falling on the 'little people' and on daily life, all condensed in the context of a small town in the interior of São Paulo, Itapira. For Brandão religious belonging is a dimension of everyday life and is often characterized by fluidity: people shift between Churches, small-time leaders constantly pop up and create new ones while others disappear or are absorbed. Where others describe religious life in terms of crises and ruptures Brandão's style emphasizes its routine character: the descriptions regularly dissolve into lists, in which an activity is shown to be distributed among a range of social groups, or in which a group is shown to engage in a wide variety of practices. Repeatedly he returns to the one single polarity which opposes the popular to the erudite, for even while the popular is shown to contain an extraordinary number of groups and institutions, they exhibit common features: Catholic fraternities and commemorative groups escape from the control of the hierarchy; proliferating Pentecostal churches and 'biblical groups' escape from the control of budding pastors, illustrating an endless dialectic of formation, institutionalization, flight and reassertion of the autonomy of the popular.

Brandão positions himself in relation to what French writers call '*le petit peuple*', and what he calls variously *as pessoas de baixo* (the people from below), or *a gente pobre* (the poor people), using frequently the adjective *subalterno*, in a manner reminiscent of the Indian journal *Subaltern Studies*. Often he refers also to what might be called 'social types' – peasants, landless workers, the people on one side or another of the river, from this or that type of neighbourhood. Religious identities are infinitely subdivided: some are *firme na fé* (solid in their faith'), others are *filhos da fé* (born into the faith, literally 'children of the faith'), most evangelicals are *crentes* (literally 'believers'), but very frequently that label is further qualified, as *crente fiel* (faithful believer) (pp. 136–7). Religious life is knitted into the texture of subaltern, or subordinate, culture, and that for him overrides many differences between belief systems, if only because of the predominance of practice, routine, the rhythms of the day, the week, the year and the life cycle, over belief and doctrine which, at least on the face of it, are so important to erudite culture and religion.

Brandão's book is littered with references to *trocas* (exchanges): between people, between religious levels, between religious intermediaries of all sorts and their followers, between the living and the dead, between 'the subject and the divine entity' (p. 131). All is routine: even the Pentecostals' 'miracles' – the cures, the descent of the Holy Spirit – are routine.

From the perspective of the mid-1990s, this use of the erudite and popular categories raises two questions. One is whether the Pentecostals can still be presented as a part of a continuous thread of popular culture, and the other is whether popular culture is itself as autonomous as Brandão assumes. Brandão's study focuses on a small town in the interior of São Paulo in the 1970s, going through profound social change, on account of the expulsion of the farm resident work force to the town's periphery (the *boia fria* phenomenon),[10] in a period of rapid economic

[10] Literally 'cold lunch': the period of rapid mechanization, and land concentration, from the early 1960s onwards, linked in Southern Brazil to a switch out of coffee and into other crops, or into new

growth. It is nevertheless presented as quintessentially provincial, a town of the interior, whose cultural life is defined, both by the author and by the people, in opposition not only to the seething metropolis of São Paulo, but even to the smaller, but very prosperous, industrial centre of Campinas.

The poverty which Brandão describes is one of stability, which fits into an established cultural order of domination. But 25 years later, and perhaps already at that time, this image of continuity in popular culture is ever more difficult to fit with observed reality, and the exchanges (*trocas*) on which Brandão insisted have become more numerous, reflexive, intense and above all more multifarious and inter-cultural, in keeping with the fraying of the frontiers of once national cultures and the omnipresence of television. During the intervening years, large-scale evangelical organizations have inaugurated a neo-Pentecostalism which is impossible to contain conceptually within the boundaries of pre-existing popular culture, overshadowing Brandão's small, independent Churches and Bible groups. These organizations, let us remember, have as their aim the conquest and total reshaping of popular culture and they bring to that task previously unimaginable organizational methods and financial resources. Brandão had pointed in passing to the ways in which Pentecostalism departs from the established patterns of popular culture: in its rejection, especially among the most 'popular' and irredentist churches, of the 'intermediary' figures which, in the form of saints, mediums and *mães de santo* are central to popular (and erudite) Catholicism and to possession cults; in their far greater intolerance of human weakness than Catholics or cult leaders; and in their concern to draw lines on the basis of individuals' moral performance. But these remarks were mere asides in his text; now, with hindsight, they can be seen as manifestations of features which have since become dominant in Brazilian and Latin American Pentecostalism.

Brandão insists that these evangelical or Pentecostal revolutions are perfectly normal phenomena rooted in popular culture, because for him resistance is a defining feature of that culture. Thus he also makes the participants active, creative bearers of meaning, rather than passive, reactive beings tossed about on the waves of social dislocation. This may be idealistic, but it does at least open the way to an actor-oriented understanding, grasping participants' involvement as they see it and

varieties suitable for more mechanized production, saw a drastic reduction in fixed, resident labour, and increasing reliance on contract and daily hired labour drawn from the former farm labourers, now living on the edge of small towns. These workers, no longer receiving lunch from the landlords, would have to take theirs with them and eat it cold.

above all as they express it. My own approach sees evangelical Christianity as an enterprise of cultural conquest in which the leaders, at all levels, of these large-scale religious organizations are attempting to change the entire face of popular culture. It draws its inspiration from an interpretation of Cortés's conquest of Mexico by Paul Hirst (1994), according to which the Aztecs simply could not understand Cortés's concepts of war and empire; their consequent ideological defenselessness, more than their technological disadvantage, spelt their total defeat. Accustomed to their own highly ritualized form of war and to its resolution by human sacrifice and treaty, the Aztecs could not imagine that the purpose of armed conflict could be total domination by the victor over the vanquished (Clendinnen, 1991). Likewise, these modern evangelical religious organizations are not an unwilled product of social strains, but an attempt to transform and conquer an entire culture – ranging from the calendar to domestic life, from liturgical music to patterns of cultural and other consumption. In this respect, maybe because of the spatial and temporal location of his research, Brandão's account appears too eirenic, too firmly imprinted with the assumption of continuity in the popular–erudite dialectic. By approaching the subject of Pentecostalism as a cultural onslaught one should be able to avoid (a) the adoption, however subconscious or unintentional, of the Pentecostals' own point of view; (b) the adoption of points of view deriving from a dialogue with one's own and/or the reader's past; and (c) the idealization of the category 'popular culture'.

What, then, of the notion that popular culture is somehow a culture of resistance? Brandão is ambiguously poised between a view of it as an autonomous force of resistance and the recognition that, especially in the religious field, it is involved in a dialectical relationship with erudite culture, in which the one seeks constantly to control the other, by co-opting some practices and trying to suppress others, while the other evades the control of erudite or official authorities, at the same time also adopting official practices and then turning them to its own ends. As early as 1974 Natalie Davis explained that the idea of popular religion had to be removed from the conventional opposition between superstition, or magic, and rationality, and recognized for the role it played in its social context. In 1981 Peter Brown explained the drawbacks of a 'two-tiered' concept opposing popular and erudite culture. Subsequently, ideas of reflexivity have come to the fore, and now it would appear that it is only by recognizing that the terms popular and erudite, or terms very much like them, themselves have a meaning for the culture(s) in question that one can salvage them. One extreme of this approach is that of Pierre

Bourdieu, for whom the very notion of 'popular culture' is an idealized fabrication by those who succumb to the illusion of the autonomy of the culture of the dominated. In fact, although Bourdieu does use terms such as 'the culture of the dominated' he means by this a culture which is a pale imitation of literate or erudite culture, consisting of 'dispersed fragments of a more or less age-old erudite culture' (1979: 459).

The conclusion is that Brandão is right to emphasize exchanges (*trocas*) and wrong to insist on resistance, while Bourdieu is right to emphasize the interaction between the two levels but wrong to depict it as a one-way street, especially if that approach is to be applied in the field of religion. Catholicism in particular is a religion in which the erudite and the popular have for ever been involved in the dialectic I have mentioned, and in which a certain image of the poor – a changing image, to be sure – has been a permanent presence and a projection. *Basista* Catholicism depicts an idealized image of popular culture in the face of which its activists and theorists prostrate themselves in an almost reverential manner: the result is that they try very hard to take up the habits and idioms of this popular culture in order to bring the Catholic religion, as they see it, nearer to the people and also in order to reform Catholicism itself in the direction of the 'point of view of the poor'. They are taking the sociologist's viewpoint into the Church itself, and they do so in circumstances where they themselves are not of the popular classes, though many could be considered members of a popular intelligentsia formed in the culture of *basismo*, and in a country where the projection of the other – the black,[11] the African, the *spirita*[12] – is a central element. The Pentecostals, for their part, transcend this dialectic: they are utterly oblivious to high culture and good taste, yet instead of adopting a servile attitude to the culture of the popular classes, they also attack many of its central elements, especially its rituals.

Unless we sort out our thinking on this subject and become much more self-aware in our treatment of it, we are liable to distort our writing in the way others have, by allowing our enthusiasms to run away with us, or by courting our readers with distracting complicities. In contemporary societies it is particularly risky to venture strong views about authenticity: cross-cultural borrowings combine with fantasies of imitation and projection on the part of the observer and the observed, thus imposing severe demands of self-awareness on the observer; and the claim that 'a

---

[11] See the apposite remarks by Maria Isaura Pereira de Queiroz (1986), in addition to an already abundant bibliography on the subject. The issue of race in Brazil is explored further in Part Two.

[12] Practitioner of one or other of the innumerable possession cults available in Brazil – not to speak of astrology, numerology, tarot card reading – or just plain hope.

people', let alone 'the people', require or desire some sort of authenticity or faithfulness to their 'own' culture, is meaningless because the very notion of boundaries delineating defined individualized 'cultures' is open to question.

Field work

The field data used here were gathered during two periods, one in May–September 1991, the other in December 1993, in the vast city of Salvador da Bahia, now the third biggest in Brazil, with more than three million inhabitants. Salvador – known simply as Bahia in daily speech – has grown beyond recognition in the past two generations. Apart from a fivefold growth in its population between 1950 and 1991, it has undergone a socio-spatial 'gutting'. During the nineteenth century and until the 1960s ornate stately mansions built by coffee planters overlooked All Saints' Bay (Bahia de Todos os Santos) and the port which for centuries received its distressing human cargo from Africa, and sent coffee and cacao to Europe. These constructions have almost all been torn down and replaced by tower blocks which cast a permanent shadow over the clifftop avenue. The lower classes, who once lived in the fetid valleys behind the cliffs, have been uprooted to make way for a network of highways facilitating communication between middle- and upper-class neighbour-hoods. As their numbers multiplied by waves of migrants from the hinterland (the *interior* as Brazilians love to call it), they were removed to the *periferia*, to *favelas*, self-built neighbourhoods often the size of small towns, built up gradually by the inhabitants' own efforts, and located in outlying areas tens of kilometres, and hours of travelling time, from their places of work. One of these, Nova Sussuarana, was the scene of some of my early field work in 1991. Another mechanism of urban expansion on the fringes has been the *invasão*, which simply means land invasion. In a by now established routine, a group of people organize themselves to seize a piece of unoccupied land, sub-divide it, and establish themselves as quickly as possible so as to secure squatters' rights (*direitos de posse* – literally possession, as distinct from ownership, rights) and thus fend off attempts by the authorities to dislodge them. In 1993 I conducted fieldwork in just such a neighbourhood – Nova Constituinte – on the edges of the well-established suburban working-class municipality of Periperi. This *invasão* was the poorest area in which I worked. Periperi is part of the extensive and extended necklace of urban developments stretching along the seashore to the south of the city and known as the *suburbio.*[13] In addition, I worked in the parish of São Jorge in Jardim Cruzeiro, an area already established as working class in the nineteenth century, and closer to the city centre, located not far from the Penha peninsula,[14] with its popular strip of beach leading at the tip to a colonial church adjoining a small cloister. I did a limited amount of work in a more recently established working-class area, Liberdade, home to many workers in the vast petro-chemical industry established outside Salvador in Camaçari during the 1970s. Liberdade has a more vibrant commercial activity than the other areas mentioned, and is also the location of the headquarters of the Assemblies of God for the entire state.

As the reader will discover, the most fruitful interviews were conducted in Periperi and in the parish of São Jorge, in Pentecostal churches dotted around the city, and with numerous activists and believers with whom I made contact through mutual acquaintances or casually in churches and chapels. My choice of location was dictated to no small degree by ease of access: in Nova Sussuarana the Catholic chapel was usually closed and I made no headway in the branch of the Universal Church; in Periperi I was guided by a local resident and former Franciscan who was well connected among both activists and Pentecostal believers; in São Jorge Padre Clovis, the parish priest, enabled me to conduct my research for a few days in the community school. Quite a lot of time was spent just hanging around in Pentecostal churches, observing and watching out for conversational opportunities.

Thus described the procedure sounds haphazard, but it should be remembered what was being attempted, namely an understanding of the functioning of these churches and groups as institutions and an under-standing of their core discourse across the city and beyond. This is neither a community study nor an attempt to gauge the characteristics of the average participant or activist – quite justifiable ventures but not a priority for the type of understanding I was seeking, and certainly not feasible in the time available. It was therefore important to spread my time and energy, to obtain a sense of the variety of practices and organizations, to draw a picture of the operation of the organizations and institutions at the level of the city and of the country, and above all to

[13] A term peculiar to Salvador and not to be confused with the *periferia* which is less urbanized and poorer in infrastructure and in its inhabitants' income, let alone with the Anglo-Saxon notion of a 'suburb'.

[14] The Penha neighbourhood developed around a flourishing textile industry in the nineteenth century, and was already described in that period as a *bairro popular* – a term best translated, given the context, as a working-class, not simply a 'popular', or 'people's' or even 'low-income' neighbourhood (Mattoso, 1992: 440). The São Jorge parish is also located not far from the church of Bonfim, centre of popular rituals in Salvador.

gain a grasp of the language and discourse of the movements and organizations of which individuals and their churches formed a part.

Why Salvador? It has often been said to me that, with its reputation of being the centre of African culture in Brazil, Salvador would produce quite special religious forms and more than usually charismatic and possession-based Pentecostalism. It has also been said to me that this is the Northeast which is 'like another country' compared with the industrial centres in São Paulo and with southern Brazil generally – Rio de Janeiro, capital of samba and carnival, being somehow half-way between the two. It is also plain to any visitor that Salvador is a city where, at least until the mid-twentieth century, the institutions of the Church have made an indelible imprint on architecture and topography, on the annual rhythms of life, and even on the very religious practices which the Catholic Church itself has in the past condemned as 'pagan' or the work of the devil – namely the possession cults.

The relationship between Pentecostalism and the possession cults is dealt with in detail in the text, but the analysis of the cults is undertaken to some extent at arm's length, on the basis of secondary sources, because I did not do any field research in the *terreiros* where varieties of *candomblé* (as the cults are usually known in Salvador) were conducted. The decision not to do so was taken early on because the study of the cults requires lengthy, detailed and concentrated involvement. Each one is different, each individual *māe* or *pai de santo* is in rivalry with the others, and guards his or her secrets jealously, just as his or her relationships are guarded. To study the cults would mean studying nothing else, and because each *terreiro* is so individual and because they all set so much store by mysteriousness and esotericism, it would mean studying only one or two *terreiros*. In the light of these considerations, I decided to avoid them in the field, though they could not be excluded from the analysis.

The Northeast is different – but that difference itself has by now been assimilated into the self-image of Brazil and of the Brazilian intelligentsia, and then recreated just as the category of the 'people' is recreated. The migration from the Northeast to the South, and the migration of all sorts of cultural traits, of music and art and festivities, has by now been accepted, adopted and reinvented as part of the country's imaginative life. And, in reverse, the habits of projection and display of difference have been adopted in a Northeast where once upon a time, when the sugar planters reigned supreme and the slaves and later the peasantry were compliant, maybe difference was not a matter for reflexivity or self-doubt. The Northeast may still be a byword for poverty and underdevelopment in Brazil, it may be the region where inequality is most pronounced and poverty most acute, but its boundaries are not those that might mark the fault-lines of a dualized national culture. No sooner had Gilberto Freyre and later the structuralist economists[15] defined the Northeast as a distinctive region of the country – for better or for worse – than it instantly became part of the nation's cultural complex. Although Salvador and the Northeast are different, it is not therefore to be thought that Brazilian culture cannot be usefully studied there, or that studies conducted there offer any more partial a vision of Brazilian culture than would studies conducted elsewhere.

The historical areas of Salvador are littered with baroque churches and monasteries built in the distinctive style of the Portuguese empire. Many older neighbourhoods (Graça, Piedade, Sé) are named after convents or churches. For centuries its '365' churches were the scenes of celebrations by the privileged, but also by brotherhoods of people of different races and classes. The central areas of the city give the impression of being built for Catholic solemnities, celebrations and processions. But this does not mean to say it is a very Catholic city in the sense of a believing, or even a very observant, sort of place – rather it is the home of a population enamoured of the celebrations and processions which mark the rhythms of the year and the life cycle, and many of these activities were in the past managed not by the clergy but by all manner of brotherhoods, that is by lay organizations only loosely supervised by the hierarchy – as was the case in much of the Spanish American empire as well. For a long period in Bahia ceremonials – civic, religious and domestic – regulated the lives of inhabitants of all colours and social standing. But today the areas dominated by these old churches form only a small part of a vast metropolis, and I do not think that one can assume that the religiosity of this population – less well endowed with priests than more prosperous cities in the south – is peculiarly influenced by its very Catholic architecture and the imaginary it might once have reflected. It is as secular, or as religious, in its culture, as Rio, São Paulo, Belo Horizonte, or any other large conurbation of the Americas, and as good a starting point as any other for a study of contemporary cultural change.

---

[15] Classically, Celso Furtado's highly influential *Formação econômica do Brasil* (1959) defined the economic problems of underdevelopment in the country as the exploitation of the North-East by the industrialized South – since when the Northeast has enjoyed permanent status, like Italy's *mezzogiorno*, as the country's 'number one problem' with no solution, and an insatiable appetite for public money.

PART ONE

Basistas

Je suis né peuple, j'avais le peuple dans le coeur . . .
Mais sa langue, sa langue, elle m'était inaccessible.
Je n'ai pu le faire parler.

                    Michelet, quoted in Roland Barthes: *Michelet par lui-même.*

1

Basista Catholicism: its Context and Character

The Introduction defended the usage *basista* Catholicism – or Catholic *basismo* – and provided a definition of *basista* Catholicism in terms of a mind-set; it is now necessary to situate it more precisely as a movement, or perhaps more accurately as a quasi-movement, combining features of a movement, of a faction, even of a theory and a theological doctrine, in a whole whose consistency is, at least intuitively, confirmed by the ease with which its followers, their meetings and their writings are recognized.

The ideas of Catholic basismo have been shaped by the 'social doctrine' of the Church and of the more mainstream modernizing and liberal ideas which, in Catholicism, inspired the Second Vatican Council, and above all by the theology of liberation (TL) (Lehmann, 1990). TL is distinguished by the central tenet that praxis, the apprehension of and intervention in the lives of human beings and in the conditions which shape those lives, is part both of theology as an activity and of its subject matter. Thus the 'father' of liberation theology, Gustavo Gutierrez, writes of theology as a 'critical reflexion on society and the Church' (1972: 36) which would ultimately become sterile if it were devoted only to establishing eternal 'truths' (p. 37 – quotation marks in the original). Yet it is not merely social denunciation in theological language. Jon Sobrino, one of its most prominent exponents, expresses this difficulty pointedly in the context of Christology: 'The social setting shapes christology and does so by action or omission that is, consciously or unconsciously, partisan. Liberation christology is at least conscious of this and has the honesty to recognize it: its thinking is done from the world of the poor and is done to liberate them. ' (Sobrino, 1993: 31) In liberation theology this issue of 'point of view' is extremely important – it hardly appears in Gutierrez' 1972 book, but dominates his work on Las Casas published 20 years later. In this TL fits in with other traditions: 'point of view' is central also to the tradition of activism which spread from France and Belgium to Latin America after the Second Word War and has been promulgated by organizations such as Catholic Workers' Action (*Ação Católica Operaria*). Here the theme is that of submitting oneself and one's environment to critical reflection, in a collective setting, and in solidarity with particular social categories – workers, students, for example – and committing oneself to a course of action. Furthermore, *basista* Catholics are concerned that this combination of systematic, organized reflection and socio-political activism is conducted *a partir de los pobres* – a phrase which means literally 'from the poor' (cf. the quotation from Sobrino above) but implies both 'from the point of view of the poor' and 'with the participation of the poor'. We will in due course have occasion to investigate the implications of such a position.

I have used the term 'quasi-movement' in relation to *basista* Catholicism because although it is not in itself a social movement, it does form a prominent part of a multi-layered, multi-faceted and indeed multi-national social movement. Catholic *basismo* is part of *basismo* in general: unlike the Pentecostals, who are highly self-sufficient and exclusive, it is heavily influenced by extra-ecclesial ideas and movements, and in its turn reaches out into secular ideas and movements, so that it is difficult to draw frontiers around it. Indeed, the absence of rites of passage in the one compared with the numerous staged rites in the other, as well as the absence in *basista* Catholicism of symbolic markers setting them off from others, such as proliferate among Pentecostals – distinctive rules of dress, abstention from alcohol and fiestas – make this difference very clear indeed.

Basismo, taken most generally, is a social movement. But it is a social movement which differs from 'classic' examples of the genre in ways that themselves reflect contemporary social changes, in technology and in ideology. The most exhaustive attempt to define social movements in both Europe and Latin America has been that elaborated in many places since the early 1970s by Alain Touraine. Touraine takes an Olympian view: he uses the term only to refer to a grand historical change, a 'movement of cultural reorientation', and specifically denies that particular organizations can count as social movements at all – they count merely as part of a grand project, of which his (implicit, hidden) ideal type seems to be European social democracy. Social democracy, for him, like any social movement worthy of the name, encompasses a 'historical actor' or subject (the working class), embodying the principle of identity, a historical adversary to that subject (the capitalist class) embodying the principle of opposition, and a historical project to lead society in a particular direction (a reorganization of the production system – social democracy) embodying the principle of totality. Social movements are not precisely interest groups or organizations, they are more than that; they engage in issues and conflicts which put at risk the entire social system: the stakes (the *enjeux*) are extremely high. This is why in a capitalist society they are class movements, but this is not to say that their agents – their bearers – are necessarily class organizations. Thus, writing in 1973, Touraine says that student movements reveal the social conflicts proper to a post-industrial society, but that does not mean to say that students are a social class (Touraine, 1973:363).

Touraine has from early on – at least since his *Sociologie de l'Action* (1965) – tried to construct a sociology which combined the idea that society is created with the idea that societies operate if not under a regime of laws of social change, then under a regime of 'principles', but of principles which are in tension. Touraine is not accustomed to dialoguing with the great traditions of social thought or with the great social thinkers, so that any interpretation of his aims and motives suffers from a greater element of speculation than usual, but it would seem that he is trying to construct a social theory which preserves a Marxian concept of systemic contradiction (without using the word itself very often), while insisting on human agency and avoiding the functionalist idea of 'society' in search of equilibrium.[1] He resolved the problem with the idea of historicity and of systems and fields of historical action. Society is not subject to the exigencies of an idea, nor does it merely evolve in response to material change: the idea of historicity is that of society acting upon itself, both materially and culturally: *{elle} se retourne sur elle-même.* To avoid the empiricism of identifying concrete collectivities as agencies of social change, and the functionalism of interpreting social change as responses to changes in the environment, he places social movements at a level not of society but of a field of historical action, defined as the locus of confrontation of principles whose outcome sets the direction of social change.

If this approach is to make practical sense it must mean that social movements are multi-levelled phenomena operating in the spheres of ideas, institutions, power struggles, the state, civil society and more.

---

[1] At the time of its publication *Sociologie de l'Action* could not but fail to evoke the Parsonian emphasis on 'action', yet Touraine took great pains to distance himself from Parsons while describing his own approach as *actionnaliste* – a term he has not used at all in his writings of the 1980s and 1990s: *'Je ne reproche pas á la sociologie fonctionnaliste d'avoir représenté la société comme un système: c'est son apport positif. Son tort est d'avoir conçu ce système selon des images mécanicistes ou organicistes si insuffisantes qu'elles obligent á recourir simultanément à une vision évolutionniste, heritée de l'optimisme libéral et positiviste du XIX siècle et qui est chargée de l'idealisme et de l'ethnocentrisme les moins acceptables.* (1973: 27).

Although, as Touraine repeatedly states, it is absurd to use their theories — and the many theories which vie for influence within each movement — as an explanation of the evolution of social movements, the activity of theorizing and theoretical dispute — and thus the role of intellectuals — must also be recognized as one of their essential features. If the notion that they are 'movements of cultural reorientation' has any weight, then social movements worthy of the name must in addition encompass a vast range of institutions and social groups. In the case of the labour movement or social democracy in Europe, for example, this includes education, health, industry, modernism in art and literature, and so on. The army of academics in universities and of policy-makers in the state apparatus, feeding the machinery and ideology of welfare; the welfare state itself legitimating the hegemony of social democracy; the parties and trade unions, the numerous local level institutions built to protect the rights enshrined in social democracy — all go together to make up social democracy as a movement. This list may seem dated, even antediluvian, evoking as it does a world which, as far as Europe and the Western Hemisphere are concerned, foundered some time in the 1980s, but underlying it there is a concept of social movements as multi-layered, multi-faceted and therefore uncoordinated phenomena which find their way into the interstices of society and thus, gradually, without recourse to revolutions or *coups d'état*, bring about historical change. A social movement, then, contains innumerable organizations and institutions within its purview, but it is more than a network, for although it cannot be thought of as a centralized organization, it does rely on institutionalization in the organizations which form part of its web.

How then can *basismo*, with its emphasis on grassroot participation and the resistance to institutionalization, merit the description of 'social movement'? Is not the anti-institutional bias in *basista* culture so important to its activists and protagonists that the means encapsulated by these emphases replace and undermine their ultimate ends, and thus somehow cancel out their vocation as a social movement?

In lacking an identifiable ultimate goal *basismo* would not be different from social democracy in its heyday, for however precise its original goals in the late nineteenth century — or in the English case in the early days of trade unions — social democracy grew into a multifarious set of organizations and institutions each with goals of their own. Indeed any large-scale social movement contains within itself habits, rituals and institutions which become ends in themselves to the point where it becomes necessary to admit that a social movement of the kind envisaged by Touraine is as much a sub-culture as a movement. The vagueness of ultimate goals is not therefore a disqualification in itself, but the question does arise as to whether the perennial resistance to institutionalization and even to institutions *tout court* has the effect of restricting *basismo* to little more than endless cascading expressions of localistic frustration, anger and immediate demands whose potential for achieving structural change in the long term is grossly exaggerated by overenthusiastic intellectuals in search of a new revolutionary paradigm – or perhaps merely of new rhetorical devices in which to dress an old paradigm.

In the Latin American context – and possibly in a much broader context as well – the question is further confused by the use of the term social – or 'popular' – movement to refer to quite concrete phenomena 'on the ground', invariably involving small-scale groups. It is in reaction to this 'empiricist' conception that observers like Touraine can belittle the potential of these local mobilizations as a force for social change. In Touraine's view the State enjoys overwhelming dominance in Latin American society and politics: its magnetic force weakens political parties and co-opts these 'movements' just as it co-opts the intellectuals who under other circumstances might provide the ideological inspiration of a 'movement of socio-cultural re-orientation'. It is a view supported and possibly inspired by Ruth Cardoso's widely quoted account of urban social movements under Brazilian military governments, in which she argued that the transformative potential of urban social movements was severely constrained by their vulnerability to co-optation even under authoritarian regimes (Cardoso, 1983). Lacking autonomy of ideas, leadership and means, the 'social movements' are from this viewpoint incapable of inaugurating the new forms of citizenship advertised widely by post-Marxist intellectuals (Lehmann, 1990).

As the following five characteristics show, the local-level social movements diverge significantly both from Touraine's ideal and from that of the apostles of the grassroots philosophy who are their most vocal supporters. On the other hand, they also depart from the standard model of interest groups. The distinctive features of *basista* movements in Latin American cities are: (a) their grassroots type of organization, which means they have flat hierarchies, in which followers participate in the management of organizations to a high degree; (b) the high proportion of women among leadership and rank-and-file participants, especially when compared with trade unions and political parties of the left; (c) their involvement in some sort of partnership with local government, often benefiting from the existence of sympathetic technical personnel in the bureaucracy; (d) their involvement in institution-building, however fitful this process may be; and (e) their reliance on international ideological and funding networks. Their existence is inter-dependent with that of the international NGOs which fund their activities and the centres and institutes (or GSOs – grassroots support organizations – Carroll, 1992) which help local organizations apply for funding and help the funding agencies in their search for projects and organizations.

Taken together, combined with the NGOs and GSOs which advise and support them, with their nationwide and international network of contacts, with the methods of organization which they have in common, with the growing body of ideas broadly identifiable as 'global populism', these initiatives can be said to constitute a social movement, even a sub-culture, but one which is distinguished from others, and to some extent defined, by its cosmopolitanism – its ability to straddle national, ethnic and cultural boundaries. This international sub-culture is characterized by a very broadly definable ideology, a network-based style of interaction among its followers, an intelligentsia which produces its ideology, and innumerable small organizations as defined in the previous paragraph. The ideology places great value on authenticity, on faithfulness to 'roots', to the culture especially of indigenous or non-Western peoples, or simply of the poor, the people, while expressing fierce hostility to the threats to that culture, by Western culture, transmitted by international media and corporations, or indeed by local elites.[2] The combination of authenticity – the defence of difference – and economic betterment may seem strange, especially when the advocates of the former so frequently denounce economic development, but the two are compatible when it is remembered that the denunciations concentrate their fire on a particular model of capitalist and authoritarian development, and are made in the name of 'another', or an 'alternative' development attuned to the cultures and interests of 'the people'.

These ambiguities fit in with the broader irony of a posture whose hostility to 'Western' habits, culture and especially capitalism, is founded on concepts of authenticity, tradition and respect for the other which would be unthinkable outside that selfsame Western tradition.[3] Likewise its idealization of the harmonious communities existing in 'traditional' societies and, by extension, among the poor, echoes the sociological tradition born of Marx and Durkheim and the biblical elevation of the

[2] This orientation evidently has an affinity with the identity-based mobilization in which Melucci (1989), for example, sees a new type of politics, as to some extent does Castells (1983), but whereas identity-based movements, from the Corsicans and the Bretons to the gay community of San Francisco, are almost exclusively focused on difference, *basismo* combines a 'Third-Worldist', universalistic ideology of economic betterment with the right to difference.

[3] Two of the most prominent exponents of a *basista* approach to development are John Clark (1991) and John Friedmann (1992).

poor as inheritors of the kingdom of God (see Luke 6.20), while the idea that harmony can be restored by the intervention of disinterested parties and by the taming of 'savage' capitalism is drawn from European social democracy.

The network-based style of interaction and coordination is also central to *basismo*, because it is uncodified, and because it forms something like the sub-conscious of the movement, reproducing itself without needing to be set out in an explicit form. The movement has taken up with alacrity the opportunities afforded by a period of revolutionary changes in information technology.[4] Ease of communication, the difficulty of controlling information from centres of power, and even the small scale of operation available to activists and leaders, make for networking rather than the construction of bureaucratic hierarchies. An anti-authoritarian, even anti-hierarchical ethos, coupled with the difficulty of accumulating either political or economic power in this environment, accompanies an amoeba-like institutional pattern, in which new leaders, once they emerge in an organization, strike out on their own, creating new organizations.

Financial dependence on international agencies notorious for their shifting priorities and short time horizons accentuates this pattern, which is detectable at all levels of the movement: (a) that of the grassroots organizations proper, where hierarchies are flat, administrative roles widely distributed, and objectives quite specific and concrete; (b) that of the domestic NGOs which operate in the manner of institutionalized interest groups or charities, providing documentation to local groups, defending particular causes, in the manner of the innumerable cause-oriented charities in the UK and the USA; (c) that of the GSOs (Grassroot Support Organizations) (Carroll, 1992) which could be described as research and consultancy cooperatives providing support services both to the grassroot organizations (in their search for financial support) and to the international charities (in their search for worthwhile projects and groups). GSOs are usually small and their income flow is unsteady and unpredictable. The international charities vary enormously along innumerable dimensions, but they are usually larger and more bureaucratic, enjoying a steady income from a broad donor base and sometimes from governments. GSO leaders depend heavily on personal contacts to keep their organizations going, and there are opportunities for individual entrepreneurship for anyone who can develop his or her own contacts. At the international level the networking pattern is no less in evidence: the international charitable aid organizations encourage a fellow feeling of mutual ideological

---

[4] The use of the Internet made by the Zapatista leaders of the 1994 Chiapas uprising in Mexico is a striking example of this point.

supportiveness among their staff, and the balance between the need for a common ideological perspective and professional expertise is thought of in different terms from those one might encounter in, say, the World Bank.

The members, activists and personnel involved at all these levels of organization are in constant circulation, attending meetings and conferences, and putting together a very dense international network and sub-culture, in which participation is extended beyond the circle of the privileged few to the less privileged and even to grassroots leaders. Occasionally a figure from among 'the people themselves' like Rigoberta Menchu or the late Chico Mendes achieves prominence and circulates extensively at this level. The enormous importance of this network for those who participate in it is illustrated, perhaps more faithfully than the writer intended, by the following passage from a book about women and development: 'One of the greatest benefits of the UN Women's Decade and its three conferences has been that women from almost every country in the world have been able to meet, share experiences, debate needs, priorities and strategies' (Young, 1993: 42). It is a paradox of the grassroots movement that the high value placed on cultural authenticity facilitates the development of a multi-cultural community of activists, scholars, organizers and donor officials who share a sub-culture of dissent from dominant models of development, of going against the tide, of informality and brother/sisterhood. This in turn generates strategies to enable the movement to reproduce itself: people 'at the bottom' know they must appeal to the proclivities of distant funding agencies, and develop a sensitivity to changes in fashion among them; the small scale of organizations and agencies, and their independence from national and international officialdom, enables them to find new audiences, new needs, new 'markets', new strategies and slogans; they even appeal increasingly to official multilateral agencies because they have the ability to make projects reach the poor for whom they are designed, and they can also produce new ideas by drawing on the goodwill they enjoy among academics, experts and advisors.

These academics and experts are the intelligentsia of the movement, operating at the crossroads between academic research, advocacy and consultancy, in far-flung centres of research and in universities. They are in some ways the counterpart to that intelligentsia of international development whose ideas support the neo-liberal orthodoxy known as the 'Washington consensus' on development policy. However, they differ from their counterparts in the belief that they have a mission, that they are not technicians or managers, but exponents of ideas which dissent from the mainstream and which, they hope, will eventually bring about change. If they are researchers or writers they talk of the subjects of their research, the people they study and write about, as if they were real-life partners in a common endeavour, with names and addresses, not anonymous subjects of research projects. In short, members of this intelligentsia write and speak as if they are part of a movement of what Touraine would, indeed, call 'socio-cultural reorientation'. They are found at the international level, and also at the national level, where they often combine participation in GSO-type institutions with academic or technocratic employment.

Cultural authenticity, a stress on listening to the poor, the down-trodden, the salt of the earth; networking, dissent from the international establishment, cosmopolitanism — all these dispositions form the core of *basismo*. If a social movement, to merit the name, needed a coherent set of beliefs or an elaborate ideology, as Touraine's definition seems to imply, then neither this nor any other comparable movement would qualify. On the other hand, if his formulation could be slightly modified so that by social movement he meant a sub-culture of dissidence and transformation, then *basismo* does qualify. The diversity of instances knit together by common participation, the institutional niches it has created or colonized, the style of interaction between people of the most diverse cultural backgrounds, national origins, and social status, a remarkably global reach — all these elements contribute to the gradual invention of an environment in which otherness becomes sameness, and taken together they form a social movement sprawling across contemporary international civil society.

There remains the nagging question of *basismo*'s disappointing 'results'. After a decade or more during which these ideas have gained increasing acceptance in the international development community, both govern-mental and non-governmental, the pattern of development in Latin America and Africa remains stubbornly inegalitarian: the broad pattern of income distribution continues to deteriorate, in contrast with the much less polarized picture observed since the 1960s in the fast-growing but politically authoritarian Asian economies. It is even more disappointing to observe these trends when one considers that during the 1980s many Latin American countries shifted back to electoral rule. Possibly, the results of *basista* mobilization and of the activism of its networks have produced more results than appear on the surface, which will emerge over the long run, but for the moment many supporters find it unfortunate that so much of what *basismo* advocates has been co-opted by the major international development institutions and even by the rhetoric of national governments, sensing the watering down of their theses and the reduction of their autonomy *vis-à-vis* the State apparatus. Yet is this co-optation not a measure of success? The social revolution has not come, but the fact is that nowadays no development project, especially if it is a rural project, is complete without provision for 'participation', and the same is also true for projects in deprived urban areas of North America and Western Europe.

These doubts are reflected by Bebbington et al. (1993), who describe the rapprochement between NGOs and the state in the period of transition from authoritarian rule in various Latin American countries in the late 1980s, and also their involvement in the 'emergency' social funds supported by the World Bank to alleviate or palliate some of the sufferings inflicted by the harsh medicine of structural adjustment (1993: 50). The authors are doubtful about the depth of the participation, and are quick to point out (cf. p. 79) that where there is participation it is of a contractual or consultative kind, and does not place the 'base' in a position to influence the institutions of the state – thus raising the issue of co-optation once again. The discourse and themes of *basismo* – participation, respect for local communities – are omnipresent but not many authors would venture to claim that this in itself has brought about a sea-change in either the official approach to development or in the pattern of development itself.

If *basismo* is a social movement, where is its 'mass base'? If this is understood as an organized mass, with membership in formal organizations, as in a trade union movement for example, then clearly it does not exist: like much modern pressure group politics, *basismo* receives different degrees of support and involvement from different groups, depending on the issues at stake and the benefits available. The notion of membership is in any case not strictly relevant because on the ground few of its activities are conducted in a formalized context. Yet as in the case of the Catholic *basistas*, *basismo* more generally has a qualitative influence on the major institutions of society out of proportion to its numerical weight at any given moment: because it has a well-connected intelligentsia, because it is 'plugged in' to a wide variety of institutional niches, both national and international, governmental and non-governmental, in education, in research, in the media. In Brazil, it played a central role in moulding the ideology of the Workers' Party (Keck, 1992) – though that Party has since developed a powerful trade unionist element which resembles traditional social democracy more closely than *basismo*.

The penetration of many established institutions of society by the networks of *basismo* stands in contrast to its slow and halting penetration of precisely those popular sectors where, on a purely ideological reading, it might have hoped to find a ready welcome. If we look once again to Brazil, we find that the leaders of the NGO movement, at least in Rio de Janeiro, have recently become national figures: Hebert de Souza (universally known as Betinho), founder of a National Campaign against Hunger, and Rubem César Fernandes, the Director of the Institute for the Study of Religion (ISER), are high-profile individuals who, after many years in the shadows leading their NGOs, broke into the limelight in the early 1990s and were able to gain media attention, governmental support, and large-scale donations from business and from the general public. Their campaigns *Natal sem fome* (Christmas without Hunger) and *Viva Rio* had a major public impact, but cannot be said to have brought about mobilization among the poor: they were closer to charity than to mobilization, but they did at least mobilize a middle-class public in a collective symbolic gesture, as thousands gathered to hold hands in a vast circle around the Candelaria Church in Rio in December 1993, in a gesture of protest against the city's endemic violence.

In diluted form, *basismo* has even penetrated the State, for example in the case of Mexico's Solidarity Programme, which was the centrepiece of the Salinas government's efforts to alleviate the social costs of structural adjustment between 1988 and 1994, and in a similar programme adopted by the Cardoso government in Brazil. The programmes rely on projects presented by community groups and include a substantial contribution by the community, usually in the form of labour. To be sure this is only the official version, and makes no mention of the undoubted political management of Solidarity in Mexico, but it illustrates the influence of *basista* thinking even in extremely important policy initiatives.

These examples show that the idea of *basismo* presents precisely the inverse movement to that presented by Pentecostalism: penetrating the elite, the intelligentsia and the technocracy with greater ease than the popular sectors – for we see how the idea has to be converted by intermediaries (charities, bureaucratic apparatuses) into projects and packages, before being 'transplanted' into the social milieux to which it is primarily addressed. In contrast, the Pentecostals, as shall be seen in greater detail in separate chapters, have had enormous success in penetrating the interstices of the popular sectors, to the embarrassment of those in the Catholic Church who have applied the 'preferential option for the poor', but have achieved little impact at the level of educated culture. Certainly, they are gaining attention and are even finding negotiating partners in the political arena because they mobilize votes, but that is not the same as achieving ideological influence. Indeed, despite their efforts to increase their influence in Congress through the election of prominent

Church members and through electoral deals with different parties, there is no sign of an intention on the part of Pentecostal leaders to translate this presence into the advocacy of a particular ideological or political cause.

Translated into the structures and culture of Catholicism the *basista* disposition acquires distinctive and multi-faceted features, and a specific identity: it becomes what I have called Catholic *basismo*. Some of its impact is at the level of formal institutions, of which obviously the Church itself is our concern, or written texts and ideas, of which the documents and theories of Catholic Action, Vatican II and liberation theology are most relevant to the present exposition. Some of the impact is at the level of local-level organization and mobilization connected in a variety of ways with the parish or diocese, and carried along by networks of committed activists, priests and religious. Taken together, all their initiatives and the influence of their ideas make up an identifiable world, a sub-culture, probably more important for its projection beyond the institutions of the Church, which has had an impact throughout the 'development community' internationally and on the language of national development initiatives and policy. In the struggle for control of 'the people' — that is of the legitimate utterance, not of the people themselves — it figures as the depository of the hopes of the progressive intelligentsia: if the Catholic identity of the people, so deeply rooted in popular culture, can be reinterpreted in such a way as to become of itself the identity of a people aware of being 'chosen' — in the sense of having special access to the liberating message of the gospel precisely on account of their poverty and innocence — then the gates to liberation, political, social and therefore also religious, will finally be open.

2

Movements of Conservation and Renewal in Modern Catholicism

During the second half of the twentieth century, in a Church shaken by change, there has been intense competition to influence the future direction of the Church, of the hierarchy, of national Churches, and of numerous institutions and movements which fall within its purview. Whereas once kings and princes vied for political control of the papacy, now a vast range of pressure groups and movements of different types battle for ideological influence. They are striking not only for the variety of their aims and projects, but also for the variety of types of organization they represent: some are religious orders – or factions within the orders – some are mass movements, some are lay evangelical movements, some, like *basismo*, do not fall easily into any organizational classification at all.

In order, therefore, to place Catholic *basismo* in the context of the culture and structures of Catholicism, this chapter begins by describing other successful tendencies and organizations which in some way have had success in areas where *basistas* would also like to succeed, namely Opus Dei, the Italian *Comunione e Liberazione*, and the Charismatic Renewal movement. Opus Dei is chosen as an example of a strategy to hold back the advance of modernism in the church and also to penetrate the elites of society so as to influence ideologically highest levels of secular power. The Opus is also as diametrically opposed to the spirit of *basismo* as is possible, so that although its growing influence is not necessarily a reflection of the opinion of the mass of Catholics, it obviously raises questions about the difficulties faced by *basismo* in influencing the direction in which the Church is moving, despite the latter's evidently closer conformity to the official doctrine of the modern Church – namely Vatican II. *Comunione e Liberazione* is chosen because in mobilizing a very large number of people in Italy in a lay evangelical but highly politicized movement, it has succeeded politically and at a quantitative level to which *basistas* themselves aspire. And the Charismatic Renewal is chosen because it has succeeded, again at a quantitative level, but in the propagation of a distinctive form of religious practice and doctrine among Catholics.

Opus Dei is the sort of organization which St Ignatius of Loyola would have created had he lived in the twentieth century. While the older religious orders are losing people, despite concessions to liberalism and modernity, the Opus seems to have no difficulty in attracting adherents. Opus Dei is said (by Walsh, 1989:15, and Olmi, 1987) to have 70,000 members worldwide – far more than the Jesuits, though the comparison is distorted by the dissimilarity between the organizations: only 2 per cent of Opus members are priests and only 30 per cent are what the Opus calls 'numeraries', or full members who have taken vows of chastity and live in communities. Opus Dei, which is organized along the lines of a religious order, has found a way, through the legally obscure formal status of a prelature *nullius*, to become something very similar to an established order, with an elaborate system of authority and training, and distinguished from others by what would appear to be militant commitment to an extremely puritanical, male-dominated, almost flagellatory version of Catholicism, in which officially approved modern ritual and liturgical changes are avoided so far as is possible without violating the letter of Vatican II. It stands in contrast to the Jesuits, for example, not only on account of its different system of organization and different type of members, but also in its ability still to follow a distinctive religious and personal doctrine – in effect an ideology which is laid down in the writings of its founder José María Escrivá y Balaguer.[1] The sense of combat is accentuated by details evocative of clandestinity such as the Papal dispensation whereby its members need not answer to the bishops in the diocese where they are working except in matters concerning their priestly office, if they are functioning as priests. The Society of Jesus can no longer be thought of as an army committed to a single cause in the way Loyola imagined it:[2] it is a diversified, complex, set of communities with highly educated members, many of whom are accustomed to thinking independently. Obedience may be the vow, but meetings and discussions are the reality of Jesuit life.

The fact that so few Opus members are priests reflects the organization's clear commitment to penetration of the institutions of the modern world,

[1] The book by Walsh is a useful source of information but readers should be warned that allowance needs to be made for its muckraking character. Indeed, the literature available on Opus Dei at present is divided between the apologetic and the denunciatory, and the reader simply needs to have an intuition for the point at which it starts to exaggerate.

[2] Loyola named it the *Compañía de Jesús*, the word *compañía* coming from military usage. Later the Pope decided that the official name would be *Societas Jesui*.

especially the professions. Although many Jesuits exercise their profession, they do so at the same time as exercising the priesthood and as a 'second string' to it, whereas Opus goes out into the professions, and concentrates its recruitment heavily among people with a very high level of education. Thus whereas the Jesuits regard their worldly involvements as a way of complementing their work on behalf of the Church, Opus seems to regard them as a strategy of penetration of the institutions of society.[3]

Another organization which, in a very different way, has achieved considerable success in accumulating influence in the Catholic world is the Italian *Comunione e Liberazione*. CL, as it is generally known, has concentrated on mobilizing young people, especially students, and in renewing Catholic culture, if not on a mass scale, then certainly on a scale of hundreds of thousands,[4] and it has carved for itself an ideological 'niche' which, though hostile to the values of modernity, looks outward to participation in the modern economy and polity, proclaiming a revival of the traditions of the Church, especially the Italian Church, and remaining hostile to the socialist and Marxist currents which attracted so many Catholic militants in the 1960s, including many of its own top cadres, most of whom left CL's predecessor movement, *Guiventú Studentesca* (Student Youth) for the revolutionary left. Subsequently, CL was formed with its new name, and eventually it established an arm's length alliance with the Christian Democrats – a party it criticized severely for selling out on fundamental Catholic moral issues in pursuit of secular power.

Founded by the charismatic Milan prelate Don Giussani, who remains the movement's leader, CL has established numerous student residences in Italian university towns, and undertakes business ventures in the form of cooperatives designed to create employment, with a strong emphasis on self-sufficency rather than 'hand-outs', even while fomenting 'solidarity' among its members and followers. According to Abbruzzese, CL's main objective is to 'transform an experience of faith into an instrument of cohesion and a concrete social bond' (1989:23), and to build a new society from below, which would undermine what Giussani sees as the over-

---

[3] It is for example well known that the Opus played a crucial role in reorienting the Franco regime towards an opening to the world economy and to international capital during the 1950s.

[4] Abbruzzese (1989) writes of a core of *militants* numbering between 120,000 and 150,000, but which, when added to the vast number of associates in cooperatives and at the annual Rimini gathering of CL, can reach 300,0000 or even 500,000. Since CL does not operate on a formal membership basis, all these figures are pure guesswork. Abbruzzese's work suffers from a pious tone and from a confusion of theological and sociological categories – despite a laudatory Preface written by one of France's most prominent sociologists of religion. Zadra's (1994) paper, though shorter, is much more informative.

secularized character of a society in which young people are morally disoriented, especially through its 'works', namely the cooperatives and student residences alluded to above.

The example of CL is instructive in the context of a comparison with *basismo*, on account of its elaborate organizational apparatus, which penetrates business, politics, the professions, the media (through numerous weekly and monthly publications and a prestigious wide-ranging publishing house – Jaca Book), and also in the contrast between its mostly middle-class base and *basismo*'s intended focus on the poor (Zadra, 1994). It does not have a formal membership, but rather a range of institutional forms each of which creates different ties of affiliation and is 'organizationally and financially independent', though 'ideology and organizational policy are highly centralized' around Don Giussani (Zadra, 1994:134). Thus it includes special organizations for professional people, and also one for people who have committed themselves 'for life by vows of poverty, celibacy and obedience' – though in contrast to Opus Dei, they are not the core leadership of the movement, but rather one of its many branches. Its political arm – the *Movimento Popolare* – established itself as a powerful faction in the Christian Democractic Party and after the disintegration of the party in the 1990s its leaders made common cause with businessman-politician Silvio Berlusconi.

CL does not lack ambition: 'it is the place where individuals become Church and the Church comes into being within society', enjoying at the same time the official approval of the Pope as an 'association . . . having an autonomous international status' (Zadra, 1994:134) – and indeed it has established itself in 30 countries, though nowhere with anything like the impact it has had in Italy. *Basismo* may have political influence on account of the coherence of its ideas, but it has nowhere been able to combine missionary Christian activity with business and politics and the penetration of social groups to the same effect, and if a single reason were to be sought for this it would be found, as José Comblin (1990) argues, in its dependence on the parish as its organizational base, and its concomitant inability to establish institutional apparatuses of its own beyond a network of small-scale institutions and ginger-groups. Although CL also uses a similar network method to the *basistas*, it takes care to ensure that the networks are linked together by an articulated apparatus which sets doctrine and policy, and of course by the commanding figure of a charismatic leader – a style of leadership which would be utterly out of place among *basistas*.

The other phenomenon – apart from Opus Dei – which provokes among *basistas* both irritation and puzzled admiration, is the Charismatic

Renewal movement, regarded by them as little more than an elaborate hoax, an entrapment in bourgeois ideology. The charismatics count hundreds of thousands of followers and sympathizers worldwide, though once again this is a mere order of magnitude, given their lack of a membership system. Their growth has never been a subject of debate or excitement as have the Base Christian Communities (CEBs) among the Catholic intelligentsia, who in Brazil regard the charismatics, not without some reason, as a purely middle-class affair and uninterested in social causes. Yet there is evidence that they are not entirely middle-class and that their growth may quite early on have outstripped in pure numbers that of the CEBs.[5]

Charismatic Renewal is respectful of hierarchy, creates a clear differentiation between leadership and other roles, has a system of training for leadership roles which seems to be a central focus of the organization, and is careful to place itself under the patronage or sponsorship of the hierarchy. It is an organized movement with cadres, structure, and a centralized production of, for example, training materials and methods. In Salvador in 1991 it ran courses for preachers, for people aspiring to practise 'ministries' (which does not mean to be ordained but rather to take on leadership roles in the movement and in prayer meetings), in music, and also a *Seminario dos Dons* (Seminar of Gifts) in which people could learn to make an appropriate use of their gifts, especially the gift of speaking in tongues, of healing, and the like. There was even mention of a national conference of *Renovação* (i.e. Renewal) music, for the purpose of developing and diffusing the movement's own style of worship.

The Charismatic Renewal movement is a disconcerting phenomenon because although it remains firmly and faithfully within the Catholic Church and its members are eager to point out that it has received a nod of approval from the Pope, it propounds a message almost word for word the same as that of the Pentecostal churches: its members speak in tongues during meetings, practise healing, believe in the gift of the Holy Spirit as a spontaneous experience rather than a ritual sacrament administered by authority of the Church, and emphasize the opportunity afforded to individuals to change their lives by 'accepting the Holy Spirit'. Although

[5] A national enquiry by the Brazilian church in 1975–6 indicated that the Renewal movement was of largely middle-class composition and exhibited little commitment to 'social' causes (Marin, 1995: 330), while a local inquiry in the northeastern city of Recife – Archbishopric of Dom Helder Câmara – as early as the 1970s discovered 40 prayer groups belonging to the Renewal movement with some 2,000 adherents (ibid.). These indications are not without weight when compared with 4,000 members of *Encontros de Irmãos* (literally Meetings of Brothers – equivalent of CEBs) for the whole of the state of Pernambuco, of which Recife is the capital, around the same period, especially in the light of the subsequent growth of the one as compared with the other.

some doctrinal issues cause concern at the hierarchical and theological level, I do not think that the people involved are especially concerned by it so long as they can meet in a Catholic church and thus continue to remain within the fold.[6]

The Auxiliary Bishop of Salvador, Dom Thomas Murphy, who is the movement's head, or at least its patron, in the Archdiocese, told me that the Charismatic Renewal movement started at Duquesne University in the United States in about 1964. The movement's size is unknown, but one indication is the attendance of 10,000 people at a conference in Rome in 1975, which was addressed by Pope Paul VI. The movement has enjoyed the support of the influential Belgian Cardinal Suenens from its inception, and the Cardinal has tried hard to keep it within the spirit of Vatican II, to demarcate it from the Pentecostal Churches and especially to deal with sensitive issues such as the proper status of baptism by the Holy Spirit. The sensitivity is highlighted, for example, by Pope Paul's careful avoidance of the word 'charismatic' in his written address to the 1975 conference (McDonnell, 1980, vol. III). At the same time, the evident popularity of the movement among Catholics in Europe and the Americas, and its indifference to issues of politics and power either within the Church or in society, is a reason for the hierarchy to look upon it with benevolence, even if only very few bishops welcome it with open arms and even if the idea of charismatic gifts received directly from the Holy Spirit may implicitly threaten the clerical monopoly of spiritual power. They are caught between the danger that the movement will violate certain basic tenets and the risk that if it is not welcomed its members will begin to meet outside church, and drift away from the Church. This was clearly expressed to me by Dona Celeste, a lay leader in Salvador who insisted that they must only meet in church. On the other hand a parish priest whose sympathies for the 'People's Church' are well known from his writings, the late Paolo Tonucci, said to me in 1991 that he told the charismatics they could not meet in his church because 'you believe in the private property of the Holy Spirit whereas I do not believe in private property'! As early as 1977, the Brazilian hierarchy was openly critical. Cardinal Arns of São Paulo, a strong defender of liberation theology and of the option for the poor, had already in 1976 criticized the movement's

---

[6] There is one crucial doctrinal difference: whereas Pentecostals insist on baptism being a unique personal experience of the Holy Spirit, and one which can only occur after the age of reason, and as a result of a personal conversion, the Catholic Church views it as a sacrament and a ritual which can and should be administered to infants and is independent of the individual's experience or level of understanding. The form of words found to bridge the gap between official Catholic doctrine and the Charismatic Renewal involves recognition that the gift of the Holy Spirit grows as a person's life unfolds.

middle-class composition, its neglect of the poor, its ignorance of his diocese's pastoral priorities, and its 'dangerous' character. Then in 1977 the National Conference of Brazilian Bishops issued a statement in the form of a report on a survey and some comments, criticizing 'the infiltration by elements of spiritism, an excessive emphasis on baptism by the Holy Spirit to the detriment of the other sacraments, religious emotionalism, and preference for the extraordinary gifts to the detriment of ordinary daily Christian life.' (McDonnell, 1980, vol.II: 350). Although the bishops made some sympathetic remarks, these were outweighed by their doubts and criticism. The Secretary-General of CELAM, the Latin American Episcopal Conference, Cardinal Alfonso López Trujillo, was slightly more sympathetic, seeing in the movement a possible reaction to the strong 'social' and 'political' emphases in the post-conciliar Latin American church with which he is widely thought to be unsympathetic. But he still drew attention to the danger the movement could represent to hierarchical authority and also to the issue of baptism in the Holy Spirit (ibid.: 358).

During 1991 I attended meetings and celebrations of the movement in Salvador and interviewed several activists. The resulting observations could be used to support some of the views expressed by Cardinal Arns, which I have heard repeated by *basista* Catholics, but they also give grounds for asking whether further investigation might not produce a rather more nuanced picture. On the movement's social composition, the participants in a Course for Preachers certainly showed an overwhelmingly middle-class predominance: there were 20 people, all but one women, of whom 17 had completed their secondary schooling, and 9 had completed their university education. I also attended prayer meetings of a group in the middle-class neighbourhood of Barra, where the social pattern seemed the same and again there was an overwhelming female presence. But Dona Celeste told me that the movement counted 70 prayer groups in Salvador, and that 70 per cent of the movement's followers – estimated by another participant at 2.5 million in Brazil as a whole – are of 'low income', and when I went to the meeting of the movement's 'Youth Group' I found a large church packed out with hundreds of young people who – to judge by the mulatto complexion of the gathering – were clearly much more disadvantaged than the participants in the preachers' course. Even the leader of this very large youth group earned her living as a shop assistant, while the leader of a 'men's group' was a solderer whose wife had a clothes shop and who owned a minibus. Dona Celeste, a retired, university-trained pharmacist, was of the sort of social group who would have a fairly exalted image of the level at which incomes would be counted as 'low', but nevertheless Cardinal Arns may also have been erring in the opposed direction – having perhaps a fairly diminished image of where people begin to be 'middle class'.

Dona Celeste spoke of the movement's charitable activities, and another woman activist spoke of a food distribution organized by members of the movement, but Dona Celeste's opinion of liberation theology could have been plucked straight from a speech by a conservative political hack:

> Its followers go to the people and preach no spiritual message, and they go to the rich and preach only hatred and aggression. In the countryside one finds nuns teaching the people to seize land and then when they get it it turns to desert, or they sell it, and someone else starts the accumulation process over again. If someone is landless that can only be because they do not want to work the land. In short what are the fruits of liberation theology? And is there not a saying 'by their fruits you shall know the tree'?

Her view was that if people are poor it is because they are lazy and that only a personal transformation, and the right way of praying, can produce fruits. Another activist (an electrical engineer) said the people do not necessarily want liberation, but rather spiritual renewal. Yet Dona Celeste also spoke of the Charismatic Renewal as enabling her to live her religion to the full, and that meant rendering a service to her 'brother'. This person did not fit the caricature of a conservative Catholic: rather she criticized the church itself for being too 'conservative' and not opening itself as it should to the Charismatic Renewal; she was critical of the way the Archbishop takes lay activists like her for granted, of the lack of time for prayer in church meetings, in contrast to charismatic meetings where sometimes they might first pray for one and a half hours and then get through the business without friction.

Basistas have little time for what they see as the charismatics' endless *louvor* – chanting of praises, and giving thanks for small miracles which Jesus has brought about in their lives – or for their emphasis on the individual's personal relationship with God. There is no doubt that this last is a prominent feature, as the following phrases and paraphrases (in English) from a prayer session of a 'men's group' illustrates:

'*Deus te ama não porque voce é bom, mas porque ele é bom*' (God loves you not because you are good, but because he is good)

'Say your name! Say "Carlos, God loves you!"' . . . I am happy because God took away my sins.'

'*Jesús fez uma cura em mim* (Jesus healed me): I discovered I had a feeling of rejection towards my father so I forgave my father, and I thank Jesus for that cure.'

'Many are called but few are chosen.'

'We often think that the best witness is that of others . . . but it isn't . . . the best witness is *my* witness.'

'*Diante do poder da oração eu fico tocado por essa força*' (In the face of the power of prayer I fell touched by that power)

These are all phrases which could just as well be heard in a Pentecostal service, as the reader will see in subsequent chapters; the same could be said of the leader's admonitions to resist the temptation to do wrong at the coming festivities to mark the feast of São João. Maybe more significant than the content was the style of the leader himself: his use of the microphone, his hectoring delivery, were barely distinguishable from those of a Pentecostal preacher, and there were hints of tension between the movement and 'mainstream' Catholicism: the mere fact that the service leader reminded people to take the sacraments — especially the Eucharist — and to go to confession beforehand, could be seen either as a sign that charismatics have a propensity to rely on their prayer meetings and the personal gifts they feel they possess, to the detriment of the obligations of institutionalized religion, or as a sign that, faithful as they are in the mainstream context, they should align themselves with the more conservative practices.

The small prayer group meetings I attended in the Barra neighbour-hood were more than anything reminiscent of group therapy sessions. Leadership was benign, a guitar would strum in the background while participants, sitting in a circle, revealed and confessed their thoughts, told of the small miracles Jesus had brought about in their lives, and called for the Holy Spirit to wash over them (*derramar*), or for the 'water of Jesus to wash our hearts' (*Que a agua de Jesús nos lave a coraçao*). Here the contrast with Pentecostalism is very clear, with regard to style and atmosphere and the externalizing of emotion, and of course income and educational levels.

Clearly the Charismatic Renewal is out of tune with the preferential option for the poor which has become the watchword of even mainstream Latin American Catholicism. But its growth is widely recognized to be enormous. What is not clear is whether it is changing the culture or institutions of the Church to the extent that might be expected from such a large and apparently elaborately structured movement, and why it has such a minimal socio-cultural impact as compared with the Pentecostals, even though 'on paper' it is saying and in many respects also doing the same things. Differences over adult baptism are insignificant when set against the similarities of stated belief and of central practices such as healing and speaking in tongues. The sociological differences are, in contrast, much more patent, for the Charismatic Renewal is a primarily middle-class phenomenon which has succeeded to some extent in filtering down among the poor, while the Pentecostals, in precisely the opposite movement, direct their proselytism emphatically at the poor, gradually filtering up through the social structure. In addition, obviously, there is the simple difference that the charismatics regard themselves as Catholics whereas the Pentecostals do not, with all that this implies for their positioning *vis-à-vis* the identification of Catholicism in the popular imaginary as the hegemonic culture of the country. To be a charismatic would not imply the dissidence implied by commitment to a Pentecostal Church, even if the beliefs were religiously identical, and indeed, even though both in their different ways offer a support to the upwardly mobile.

The examples of Opus Dei, CL and the Charismatic Renewal show that if the papacy of John Paul II has been a period of consolidation, even reversal, of the legacy of Vatican II, that must be due to the support his agenda has found in many quarters. Indeed, it may even indicate that these movements reflect trends to which his opponents shut their eyes but which he is content to follow. Richard Marin's masterly study of the Helder Câmara years in Recife, and their national and historical background (1995), shows that the 'Church of the Poor' was a minority phenomenon, on the defensive within the hierarchy, among the laity at large and in the political arena. While, to the international media, the saintly Archbishop who alone stood up against dictatorship and was the driving force behind the Church of the Poor, seemed to incarnate the entire Catholic community and hierarchy of the Northeast of Brazil, among the laity in his own diocese the highly apolitical *cursilhos de cristiandade* (catechistic 'mini-courses') and the *focolare* – both international devotional movements of southern European origin – had a burst of popularity which presaged the wildfire spread of Charismatic Renewal among whose members many former *cursilhistas* would find a new home (Marin, 1995: 295, 330).

The Opus strategy is to penetrate the modern professions and the institutions of modern capitalism and the State – especially in Spain; CL's insistence on creating institutional forms which can stand on their own feet in a modern capitalist economy is all too evident. Their influence, and that of the Charismatic Renewal, on Catholicism worldwide has been far greater than that of *basista* Catholicism – even though *basismo* may have been far more influential in social and political spheres beyond the frontiers of Catholicism – despite the impression given in a proliferating literature about 'the Catholic Church' or 'religion' in Latin America especially (including Lehmann, 1990). The contribution of *basismo*, for its part, can be seen in innovations such as the well-known but little understood base communities and the *pastorais* (pastoral commissions) specializing at the operational level in different social problems – which have changed both the way in which the Church relates to social and political problems and also the character of boundaries between institutions of the Church and civil society. This is the legacy of Vatican II, and it is to the Council and its intellectual consequences that we now turn.

3

Vatican II, Medellín and Liberation Theology

The Council and its aftermath

For most Catholics, Vatican II (1962–5) probably meant a change in the style and language in which services are conducted, and in the way in which priests and members of religious orders dress. But among a vast number of religious professionals – from theologians to priests and religious to activists in lay organizations, though in unknown numbers – it has by now brought about profound changes in their lives, and in the way they relate to each other, to authority and to all kinds of social, political and moral issues. The Council inaugurated a change of the climate in the Church with respect to discussion and debate, but it evidently destabilized the entire apparatus, as shown by the mass of clerical resignations which took place in the years following it. Indeed, it must be a source of disappointment to the protagonists of the Council that the very measures taken to change the 'stifling' atmosphere in the Church, and to reform 'outdated' practices, brought about – or at least presaged – a continuing decline in church attendance over a 20-year period in Europe and the Americas, waves of resignations (1,000 for example in Brazil alone between 1965 and 1970, amounting to 8 per cent of the total number of priests in the country – Smith, 1991: 127), and a collapse in the number of candidates for the priesthood, in a trend which, in Brazil, again, only began to reverse itself in the 1970s.[1]

---

[1] On the basis of internal documentation of the Archbishopric of Olinda and Recife and numerous other institutions in its area, Marin states that between 1965 and 1985 there were 33 resignations and only 17 ordinations of secular clergy in the Archdiocese. In the North and Northeast of Brazil 191 secular and religious (i.e. parish priests on the one hand and members of religious congregations on the other) were allowed to renounce the priesthood between 1964 and 1973 (Marin, 1995: 242). The proportion of secular clergy under 40 was 33 per cent in 1965 and declined to 10 per cent in 1985 (p. 346).

Those protagonists were the European theologians who under the previous papacy had been marginalized or even silenced – names such as Congar, Küng, Schillebeeckx – and for whom the Council represented one of the most important moments in the entire history of the Church. They were able to see the highest instance of the Church adopting a series of texts in which community seemed to receive preference over hierarchy, in which the idea of the People of God became standard usage, and they thought that these would put an end to the climate of distrust of other Christian Churches, of Enlightenment philosophy, and of the ways of life of modernity. Latin Americans were also influential, indeed the Council's frequently cited document on the laity – *Gaudium et Spes* – seems to owe its very existence to active and highly effective lobbying by the Chilean Bishop of Talca, Manuel Larraín – a powerful advocate of land reform and strong influence on Chilean Christian Democracy, tragically killed in a road accident shortly afterwards – and the Brazilian Dom Helder Câmara – at that time still Secretary of the CNBB and Auxiliary Bishop of Rio de Janeiro. Together with John XXIII's encyclical *Mater et Magistra* (1961) and Paul VI's *Populorum Progressio* (1967), *Gaudium et Spes* was a central legitimizing text for 'third-worldist' activism in the Church during the papacy of Pope Paul VI (1963–78).

The disappointment of the Council's protagonists – combined in some cases with disciplinary measures taken against them by Pope John Paul – should be tempered by an awareness that many of these difficulties might have come about even in the absence of the Council, as a result of the pressures of a changing world, even if the Council, by providing an authoritative text legitimating change, contributed to the intensification of certain conflicts, especially those concerning the option for the poor and the scope of authority within the Church apparatus. These last two themes, joined in the body of thought known as the theology of liberation, came to dominate theological and political debate in the Latin American Church during the period from 1968, with repercussions for the Church worldwide: in the Vatican, where it caused a great deal of concern about both doctrine and episcopal authority, and elsewhere in the developing world where many – but by no means all – priests and nuns, male religious and activists, saw in TL (as I shall call it) a set of ideas which spoke directly to their situation, their predicament and their concerns, and of course to those of the people among whom they were working. These tended to be the most vocal, articulate and cosmopolitan clergy, and for that reason Catholic opinion in Europe and North America also came to believe that they were, if not a majority, at least representative of a sensibility which commanded substantial support, especially among the poor.

If some of the consequences attributed to Vatican II could be seen as arising from the broader structural and social circumstances of the time, the same may be less true of the Latin American Bishops' Conference (CELAM) which took place in the wake of Vatican II at Medellín in Colombia in 1968. As has been described elsewhere (by Lehmann, 1990; Levine, 1980, and many others), this conference produced a surprisingly[2] radical and political document which opened the way to even more radical subsequent interpretations, and provided a raft of legitimizing quotations for much more radical theories and initiatives than the bishops had probably intended. The bishops probably also did not imagine how important the meeting would be. At the subsequent meetings in Puebla (1979) and Santo Domingo (1992) more elaborate procedures were adopted to ensure there were no more 'surprises' (Berryman 1980).[3]

The Medellín 'Conclusions' contained an analysis of the social problems of the region very close to that being developed at the time by the 'dependency' school of economists, and to the chapter on the subject later to be published in Gustavo Gutierrez' *A Theology of Liberation*; indeed Gutierrez, who had already attended Vatican II, had a prominent advisory role in drafting the document, together with José Comblin, a Belgian priest, long based in Brazil. The continent was in a state of 'structural sin' and 'institutionalized violence', and the task of the Church was to make an 'option for the poor' and fight against these 'unjust structures'. In other circumstances these statements might have passed unnoticed, or been dismissed as left-wing eccentricities, but perhaps there were particular circumstances which made of them, in some quarters, watchwords of Church renewal and episcopal pronouncements, and in others bones of contention during the following 10 years. The resulting polemics only served to raise the stakes in internal ideological and power struggles, now conducted in full public view. It was not just the stakes – in terms of power and influence over the direction of the Church and its institutions – which were raised: it was also the public profile as younger, sometimes European, often European-trained, priests, chose to 'stand up and be counted', to 'bear witness' to their beliefs, as a guarantee of their purity and authenticity, in contrast to the preference for discretion and

[2] In his concluding remarks Marin (1995) wonders whether the official adoption of this radicalism was not the reflection of the post-Conciliar disarray of authority in the Vatican and the fast-footed action of a small group who saw their opportunity – in other words that it did not reflect the true feeling even of the institution's members as a whole, let alone of the laity.

[3] So much so that few have ever heard of previous CELAM meetings. It was formally founded as a body at the Rio meeting as early as 1955.

gradualism which usually marks internal Church politics. Although at first this pressure seems to have placed the hierarchy and the Vatican on the defensive, the counter-offensive did not fail to come.

Apart from the internal struggles and challenges, the watchwords of Medellín also distanced the Church hierarchy, in the public image disseminated by the media in many places, from the friendships and sodalities which it had come to take for granted. Dom Helder Câmara, for example, never took public positions against any hierarchical instance, or placed in public view his disagreements with other members or groups in the hierarchy. However, his absolute, undiluted frankness in highly embarrassing public pronouncements whose scandalous effects he could perfectly well foresee – for example before the Legislative Assembly of Pernambuco state, or at the inauguration of a seminary, always in the presence of civic and military dignitaries (Marin, 1995:170–84) – obviously provoked tensions in the hierarchy. In Dom Helder's case his unique position, venerated almost as a saint in certain *favelas* of Recife and surrounded by an aura of adulatory international publicity, always led to declarations of solidarity from his colleagues, even from those who disagreed with him. But each time a personality of rank, or even a lower-level priest or religious, created a scandal, the reserves of solidarity were drained just a little, and the grounds for future reappraisals were prepared. Thus we see how, for a time, the watchwords of Medellín could hold sway, but that the quite special circumstances which enabled them to do so also foreshadowed their subsequent gradual domestication.

In Latin America, political differences were pitting the hierarchy against lay Catholics in evangelizing movements such as Catholic Action and its 'specialized' offshoots, in several countries. Conflicts arose within Christian Democracy in Chile over the interpretation of the social doctrine of the Church, of Vatican II and Medellín, and between the hierarchy and lay organizations in Brazil (of which more below). In Argentina a coalition of 'Third World Priests' and former Christian Democrats and *cursillistas* were drawn into an alliance with radicalized versions of Peronism; the Argentine hierarchy, unmoved by either the post-conciliar spirit or that of Medellín, responded with repressive measures. Even Colombia, reputedly one of the most conservative religious establishments in the region, had suffered the shock and scandal of the death in 1965 of Camilo Torres – a priest of impeccable oligarchic extraction who had publicly abandoned the ministry to join an armed revolutionary organization. In Bolivia the guerrilla of Teoponte (not to be confused with the earlier expedition led by 'Che' Guevara) was started by a breakaway Christian Democratic group.

The spread of the Medellín message surely owed much to the high levels of social mobilization then prevalent and the wave of political repression which was about to hit the continent in the form of the bureaucratic authoritarian regimes which, in the months and years following Medellín, came to power, or significantly increased their repression, in Brazil, Argentina, Chile, and Bolivia.[4] In the face of this unprecedented institutionalized violation of human rights, sometimes directly affecting even its own religious personnel, the Church was able to react, and to do so without endangering its internal unity. The time was therefore ripe for a radicalization which, in tune with the Medellín text, extended denunciations from the institutional conjuncture and misbehaviour of individuals, to a structural analysis of political institutions and of the capitalist model of development itself. The degree of radicalization varied, obviously, but even where bishops did not share these positions fully, those who did hold them within the Church were free to speak and write and propound them in the most varied contexts.

CEBs – base Christian communities

One of these contexts was that of the base Christian communities (CEBs – *Comunidades Eclesiasticas de Base*, in Portuguese *Comunidades Eclesiais de Base*). The term CEB received an impulse from a chapter in the Medellín 'Conclusions' which dealt with the Church's need to remedy its personnel deficit, by training lay people to perform religious and catechistic functions. But it was adopted by *basismo* and extended in meaning and purpose to the point where the international Christian community believed that the CEBs were in the vanguard of a revolutionary process of Church renewal in the entire continent (Levine, 1992). Many – but by no means all – bishops and priests encouraged the creation of CEBs, or similar local groups under different names, which devoted themselves to a wide range of activities. Sometimes their members took leading roles in organizing the urban and rural poor, especially around land conflicts and invasions (Banck, 1990) and peasant organization, sometimes they formed Bible study groups; sometimes, as in the Brazilian coastal city of Vitória, they were integrated into parish and diocesan decision-making (Oliveira, 1986; Banck, 1990); sometimes their members and leaders took them to be a nucleus of a 'People's Church' which would ultimately displace

---

[4] There is, of course, a vast literature on this subject which it would be inappropriate and tedious to review here. I have already reviewed it in Lehmann (1990).

the hierarchy's authority itself (as argued in numerous publications by the Brazilian theologian Leonardo Boff, e.g. Boff, 1977, 1985).

In the words of a priest in Guadalajara, Mexico, which could equally have been heard in Brazil and other places (Napolitano, 1995: chap. 5), the 'true CEB' is a seed sown in the community, embodied not in the institutional life of the Church at all, but in prayer, sacraments, missionary spirit and social service in the community. That is, whereas these practices or rituals are regarded officially and traditionally as linked to and regulated by institutional religion, the emphasis and priority here is on their identity with the life and spirit of the community – with the implication that it is for us, for outsiders, to go and find them, as it is for the 'insiders' who are not aware that these ways of worship and signs heralding the Kingdom are there in their midst.

It was in Central America that the close identification of CEBs and similar organizations with revolutionary causes reached its height and eventually also provoked the most severe reaction, both from the State and from the Church hierarchy. The close identification of the 'People's Church' faction of priests and religious in Nicaragua with the Sandinista government – expressed most scandalously in the slogan 'In the name of God and the Revolution' (Lancaster, 1989) – led to the suspension of the clergy involved from saying mass in the Managua diocese and to repeated papal reprimands. In El Salvador grassroots consciousness-raising from the 1970s, initially of a non-revolutionary character, laid the way for recruitment by the FMLN revolutionary army. In Guatemala in the same period priests joined with, or at least lent their spiritual support and religious services to, the revolutionary *Ejército Guerrillero de los Pobres* (Poor People's Guerrilla Army) in the bloodiest conflict of the entire isthmus (Le Bot, 1993). There were moments in the mid-1980s when it seemed that a large number of committed priests and religious throughout the region saw in the Nicaraguan revolution the beginnings of God's Kingdom on Earth, speaking of themselves as re-enacting the persecution suffered by the early Christians at the hands of the Roman Empire. Yet it gradually became clear that this was a minority phenomenon sustained by the enthusiasm not only of those directly involved, but also of an international network of support provided by NGOs and sympathizers in Europe and the United States whose enthusiasm lulled the protagonists into a triumphalist illusion of power.

Recent studies have begun to subject some of this triumphalism to the cold eye of research, and their findings are too strikingly consistent to be ignored. The studies by Swope (1992), Hewitt (1987), Burdick (1990, 1993), Mariz (1989), Marin (1995) and Napolitano (1995), all carried out in the 1980s, show that whatever the content of discussions inside CEBs or similar lay groups at the local level, much of their impact depends on the degree of support they receive from their bishop – or, in the case of Guadalajara the Jesuits, operating independently of, if not in opposition to, the local bishop. In Santiago de Chile, São Paulo, and the vast Rio de Janeiro suburb of Duque de Caxias the diocese provided strong moral support, guidelines, and in some cases study materials. In each case the socio-economic status of the participants was above that of the 'poorest of the poor' imagined by the programmatic writings of the 'People's Church', and in the case of Santiago (Swope) and Rio de Janeiro (Burdick) survey data showed that participants were above the average educational and employment status for their neighbourhoods, while Hewitt (1987) in his São Paulo study speaks directly of 'middle-class CEBS' as a sub-category. Mariz (1989: chap. III) writes that the educational level of the CEB participants in her Recife sample was above that of the Pentecostals.

   The studies also shed light on what goes on in CEB meetings. Swope showed that most of the discussion in them concerned questions of personal morality rather than political questions, a finding mirrored by Hewitt (1991), who describes CEB activities as mostly concerned with charitable works, Bible study and religious festivals. In São Paulo it required the presence of politically active priests and religious for CEB meetings to engage in 'consciousness-raising'. Burdick describes how poorer, less literate, and even darker-skinned participants felt marginalized by more educated and high status fellow members, and also by the atmosphere of gossip which pervaded these rather tightly-knit, inward-looking associations – tensions only heightened by the replacement of the (private) practice of confession by public face-to-face discussions and consciousness-raising (1990: chap. 5). Mariz refers to the need to have a talent for speaking out if a person is to participate fully in CEBs (1989: chap. IV), while Hewitt observes conflicts in which some oppose or simply stay away from the 'more innovative forms of political involvement' while others, in contrast, avoid 'devotional activities deemed to be somewhat irrelevant' (1991: 48–9). Burdick insists on the difference between CEBs and both possession cult leaders and Pentecostals in their response to personal emotional problems and conflicts: the former would say that such things were 'not for here' whereas both the latter would offer some form of what in another context would be called counselling (1990: chap. 5). Indeed Burdick constructs much of his analysis around the opposition between 'cults of affliction' (namely Pentecostalism and the possession cults), which create 'socially safe spaces' and relieve guilt by shifting the blame for domestic conflict away from the individual, and post-conciliar Catholicism which places all the burden of guilt on the individual and avoids treating personal/social problems – especially those of marriage – as anything other than manifestations of structural features of society (1990: chap. 5).[5] Likewise, Napolitano (1995: chap. 5) quotes a Church activist not involved in the 'new' (i.e. *basista*) wing of grassroots activism, asking what 'they' can do about everyday problems like drug addiction: 'why, since they cannot remove the ills of society, cannot "they" at least rid me of my personal ills?'. The same person attacked priests for whom the 'Christian Family Movement' was an artifice of 'the right' and who refused to talk about themes such as the family, which was what people in the parishes want to hear them talk about. For the *basista* wing of the Church in Guadalajara as in many other places, propagates the view that 'becoming a person' means being 'able to stand for one's social and human rights' and full personhood is achieved through group activity.

Even where the 'line' promoted by activists is a strong version of the option for the poor there is no question of following Leonardo Boff's model of rebuilding episcopal authority from below, beginning with the CEBs. On the contrary, there is much evidence that the CEBs, especially those where the link between political and religious commitment is made with most emphasis, rely heavily on hierarchical support and authority. Hewitt quotes both authoritative statements of policy and survey evidence which insists on the need for CEBs to be 'always united with their priests and bishops' and to resist political manipulation from right and left,[6] while Napolitano's description of the 'construction of knowledge' by the Jesuits of the 'new' Church carries strong undertones of imposition. These indications, like my own fieldwork reported below, show that although CEBs in certain dioceses have become deeply involved in the politics of community self-management, it would be wrong to think of them as a strong political force, or even a highly politicized one in society as a whole. On the other hand, they also show that CEBs, or CEB-like groups and communities, have a role to play in the institutional survival of the Church.

If this is the case, then the Church would do well to pay closer attention to their institutional dimension and less to their supposed political activities. In the diocese of São Paulo – which may well be the only place

[5] An extreme case which he mentions is that of a priest who in response to a woman's account of her marital difficulties, especially domestic violence, told her that these were very common and the best she could do was to join the women's movement.

[6] On the other hand, he also points out – in another connection – that in 1986 Cardinal Arns, Archbishop of São Paulo, and another bishop, published a list of approved candidates for elected office (1991: 99).

where the whole CEB operation is accompanied by an active administrative apparatus – the number of CEBs grew from 470 in 1980 to 765 in 1983 and 938 in 1988 (Hewitt, 1991: 37). Yet the 'inter-ecclesial CEB meetings' periodically organized at the national level (1981, 1983 and 1989) do not enjoy formal national hierarchical support, and thus appear as partial, and even partisan, occasions.[7] For a bishop attendance or non-attendance on those occasions was a political gesture, and so long as they are tinged with this suspicion of partisanship or factional politics, the CEBs are unlikely to fulfil their institutional promise. Yet it cannot be denied that the impetus to their development in the 1970s and 1980s came from political commitment among members of the Church hierarchy: later, the Church, divided, had difficulty in deciding whether to use their success as a basis for its own institutional purposes: in short, routinization.

The fact that in São Paulo and in Duque de Caxias – the sprawling Rio working-class suburb studied by Burdick – the Archbishop and Bishop respectively propounded a highly politicized and committed Christianity, seems incidental to the broader observation that possibly the CEBs were filling a time-honoured function of lay organizations – namely that of confirming individuals in their aspirations for social status and mobility by enabling them to identify with and in some ways partially replace the figure of the local priest and acquire recognized roles in local parish life. Indeed, by the end of his book Hewitt (1991) is describing an evolution of CEBs towards 'bona fide mini-parishes', and the expression CEB itself has almost disappeared from Church documents in Brazil on account of its conflictive connotations – especially after Pope Paul's bitter remark in *Evangelii Nuntiandi*.[8] At the level of ritual, the description by Burdick of the 'discourse of the progressive Church' as resembling, in its unintelligibility, 'the Latin of pre-conciliar prayer' (1990: 564) points even to the domestication/ritualization of that discourse itself. Insofar as the 'progressive' language becomes ritualized it loses content and is 'mouthed' for form's and ritual's sake. These signs of institutionalization

[7] Marin (1995) reminds us that 'only' 95 out of 370 bishops were present at the 1989 'inter-ecclesial' meeting of CEBs in Brazil. He regards this as a symptom of lack of sympathy for the movement, whereas I would be inclined, given the unofficial character of the entire CEB movement, to regard it as rather a positive figure! At every turn, the literature and discussion of this subject hinges on judgements of this kind, which are difficult to ground empirically because of the contrast between the heterogeneity of the CEBs themselves and the illusion of homogeneity or comparability purveyed by their apologists.

[8] This 1975 encyclical distinguished between those CEBs which remain 'firmly attached to the local Church' and 'do not allow themselves to be ensnared by political polarization or fashionable ideologies', and others which 'come together in a spirit of bitter criticism of the Church which they are quick to stigmatize as "institutional" . . .' (para. 58).

must in the long run lead to the taming of the politics of the CEBs. This point is reinforced by the further observation that as CEBs matured so they developed community centres and their role changed from one of transformation to a more institutional one, both in relation to the Church and in relation to their neighbourhoods, thus compensating for the shortage of priests.

Despite their undoubted *vraisemblance*, these writings may be tinged with the authors' disappointment at finding that CEBs were not hotbeds of revolutionary activism; indeed Burdick (1993), in his Preface describes his own disillusion in that respect with some feeling. Furthermore, the institutionalization and diocesan involvement which seem to be essential to the success of CEBs but also to their domestication in São Paulo and in Santiago de Chile, are themselves problematic in the far less developed Northeast of Brazil, where people are poorer, institutions weaker, and priests fewer in relation to the population.

Whatever the verdict on the nature of their impact, these examples show CEB networks which have achieved a degree of visibility, but the comparison with the Northeast of Brazil also shows that this is due to the institutional backup they receive from priests and especially nuns. In contrast, on arrival in Salvador in 1991, I discovered that the CEBs which I wanted to study were a non-existent category in the city. The Archbishop gave no support to CEBs or similar organizations of lay people, so that such initiatives gained little recognition outside the parishes of the few priests who were committed to the *basista* ideal. Likewise Marin's description of the *Encontros de Irmãos* (1995: 309–15), as CEBs were known in Recife, shows not a failure to reach the poor, but rather very weak institutional back-up. Despite the personal support of the Archbishop, the movement is described as having failed to spread beyond the immediate zone of influence of its priests and activists, and as being unable to sustain itself after Dom Helder's retirement (Marin, 1975). Mariz (1989:44) adds weight to this perception when she says that the *Encontros* were independent of local priests and 'managed' directly from the Archdiocese, implying that local priests were unenthusiastic about them. The movement in Recife was predominantly feminine and middle-aged, and does not seem to have mobilized more than 5,000 people in the entire state of Pernambuco, let alone in its capital Recife, though taken on its own this figure is open to many interpretations and does not take into account the substantial number of Catholic Action activists in Recife, who would also normally be counted in the *basista* movement.[9]

[9] If they were a highly motivated and intensely mobilized 'popular intelligentsia', those 5,000 could have achieved an enormous amount.

Marin's judgement, like that of some of the other authors mentioned, may be coloured by excessive expectations. Recife – as he himself points out – has a weak tradition of institutional Catholicism, so that initiatives from that source are unlikely to fall on fertile ground. On the other hand it has a robust tradition of popular political mobilization, was one of the few places in Brazil where the Communist Party had a capacity for mobilization in the 1950s and 1960s, and currently has numerous very active lay grassroots movements. It is therefore not surprising that many of the *Encontros de Irmãos*, in addition to Bible-reading, were heavily involved in what has been called 'collective consumption unionism' (cf. Castells, 1983) – local mobilization for water, flood protection and the like.

From all this it may be concluded that the name CEB covers a wide array of activities, quite a wide range of social groups, and numerous social situations and styles of mobilization and evangelization, and also that many activities associated with CEBs by some – especially perhaps theologians of liberation and their readers among the Latin American and European intelligentsia – are found elsewhere, while many devotional activities supposedly foreign to the philosophy of the CEB not infrequently constitute their central activity. In short, the CEB has been reified.

The legacy of Catholic Action

In Latin America, the irruption of Vatican II and of TL took place in a context already strongly influenced by the approach of Catholic Action. This is important to remember so as to correct the impression that the modern history of Catholic political involvement in the region dates only from the late 1960s, from Medellín and liberation theology, and also because it leads us to differentiate between a traditional concept of a working class and its culture – which would come from this Catholic Action background – and a more mystical *basista* orientation to the poor and to the grass roots, which emerged from it.

The publication of Pope Leo XIII's landmark encyclical *Rerum Novarum* in 1891 marked the beginnings of what became known as the 'social doctrine of the Church', and the first recognition by the Church of the legitimacy, even the merits, of trade unions, so long as they were not socialist. Leo XIII had already approved Italian Catholic Action, and it grew quite rapidly, but under his successors it suffered a similar fate to other evangelical (as distinct from ritual and celebratory) and quasi-political organizations of lay people: the hierarchy grew frightened of losing control and by 1940 Pius XII had 'practically eliminated the laity from its coordinating body' (Lehmann, 1990:91). Elsewhere in Europe a slightly different approach was adopted, centred more on the working class, as embodied in the *Jeunesse Ouvrière Catholique*, founded by the Belgian priest Fr Cardijn in 1923 (Heloisa de Souza Martins, 1994: 95), and after the Second World War in the French worker-priest movement which was suppressed by the Pope (Lehmann, 1990: 91). These movements were centrally concerned with the working class – not with the peasantry or with the *'déclassés'* – and particularly in Brazil this same emphasis was adopted. Unlike Argentina and Chile, where during the inter-war and post-war period the social doctrine of the Church was a powerful influence on political parties and movements (Peronism and Christian Democracy), in Brazil it was felt much more in the world of evangelical movements – Catholic Worker Youth (*Juventude Operaria Católica* – usually known as JOC – and later Catholic Workers' Action (*Açao Católica Operaria* – ACO), which were particularly active in São Paulo and in Recife. Their growth was remarkable: according to Mainwaring (1986: 121), by 1961 the movement had almost 26,000 members and was one of the biggest of its kind in the world, but already at that time incipient *basismo* could be observed in the tense relationship with the trade union movement. JOC's concern to be faithful to the true beliefs and interests of the workers led to conflict with the *pelegos* or compliant leaders who were all too ready to do deals with employers or governments, and it also had problems with the Communist Party for ideological reasons and because of the Party's overbearing methods of political penetration and control (Heloisa de Souza Martins, 1994). In 1967, in São Paulo, still in the aftermath of the coup of 1964, the tension reached a peak when the Communists struck deals with the authorities who 'intervened' – or took control of – certain unions (ibid.: 190).

In the work of Heloisa de Souza Martins we see described the beginnings of *basismo* in Brazil, in the form of *obreirismo* – faithfulness to the true beliefs and interest of the workers and only the workers. Her interviews with former activists, whose history of commitment to Catholic Action went back to the 1950s, are littered with the jargon of Christian 'workerism': less value was placed on 'class consciousness' than on pride in one's work and thus 'conscientiousness'– p. 114)[10] and the awareness of workers' rights as established – significantly – in Brazilian

---

[10] The words used in Portuguese are *conciencia de trabalhador* – a worker's conscience/ conscientiousness – and only secondarily 'class consciousness'. A second term is *valor do trabalho* referring to the value of work and thus to pride in one's work.

corporatist legislation. At the same time, they foreshadow later themes in their hostility to what they already call *assistencialismo*, the politics of temporary remedies as opposed to structural solutions to social problems.[11]

As the political situation grew more tense, polarized and even violent in the 1960s, JOC moved radically to the left and outsiders from more seasoned political organizations found a way to influence its top leadership (Heloisa de Souza Martins 1994: 185, 200). While some people felt the movement was being taken over, and were disconcerted by 'parachuted' ideas (p. 185), others swam enthusiastically with the tide, in a confluence of Maoism and religious commitment: 'we had to go to the shop-floor to . . . purge ourselves of the sins of capitalism'. When Martins describes going to the 'point of production' as a rite of passage marking the baptism into a new religion (p. 189), she is describing the early manifestations of the quasi-religious dimension of *basismo*.

Although Heloisa de Souza Martins' account is centred on the industrial ABC area of São Paulo,[12] the influence of that experience on the organizations and networks of Church-sponsored social activism in Brazil was enormous. After the decline of JOC (Mainwaring, 1986: 133) it was transmitted through the activists who went 'down' to live among the workers during the most repressive period (1968–74), through others who worked in building CEBs and other types of popular movement in the 1970s and 1980s, surfacing again in the newly created Workers' Party (*Partido dos Trabalhadores* – PT) which was founded in 1979 and continues to depend on trade unions for its core support. In Recife it is now clear that the activism encouraged by the advent of Helder Câmara in 1965 drew on the personnel and tradition of Catholic Action, and only much later, in the early 1970s, on the new theology of liberation. Indeed, it is striking to note, that in his speeches in the late 1960s, before his words and even his name were prohibited by the military government from being mentioned in the press, Dom Helder made frequent and even privileged reference to specifically workers' rights embodied in Brazilian labour legislation – the '13th month',[13] the right to free association, to a pension, to job security and so on (Marin, 1995). It is impossible to read

---

[11] Thus already in a 1967 manifesto, the JOC criticizes unions who do not operate 'in the framework of their specific mission which is the defence of workers' rights', but rather 'in an *assistencialista* line', 'committed to the employers and the government' (Martins, 1994: 181).

[12] So called after the first letters of the three municipalities which make up the area: Santo André, São Bernado and São Caetano do Sul.

[13] It is the practice in many Latin American countries, usually enshrined in law and thus transformed into a right for certain categories of workers, to pay a 13th month of wages at Christmas each year.

about Catholic workers' movements in the 1960s without seeing the continuity between that sensibility and the *basistas* of the 1980s and 1990s: first the desire that the organization should translate as authentically as possible the needs and interests and consciousness of the workers themselves, without intellectual mediation, and secondly, as if in dialectic with the first element, the intense efforts of intellectuals or educated activists to bridge the gap between themselves and the *base*, the workers or grass roots. Indeed, the word *base* became a talisman: had not the radicalization of the 1960s already revolved to a large extent around the interpretation of the 'basic' reforms and the struggle of different parties and ideological positions to gain possession of the term (Lehmann, 1990)?

In the intervening period Brazilian society – like that of other countries in the region – went through momentous changes, and the social base of *basismo* changed in accordance with those processes. The working class of the ABC in the 1960s was a classic proletariat and, in Brazilian terms, as even the photographs in Heloisa de Souza Martins' book reveal, its culture was one of respectability, masculinity, and security. At that time half of Brazil's population was still living in the countryside, manufacturing employment was growing very fast, and *favelas* were scenes of small-scale capital accumulation through self-built housing. In the mid-1980s, and certainly by the 1990s, the social base of *basismo* – no longer remotely *obreirismo* – was heavily female, concentrated at the place of residence rather than the place of work, and consisted of people with only precarious access to labour markets.[14] Years of savage capitalism followed by endemic economic crisis had brought about profound changes.

A similar evolution can be observed in Argentina and Chile where, during this same period, young Catholics were also trying to bridge the gap with the 'people', trying that is to pierce the veil of opacity separating them from an image of the people or the working class created by different historical projects – Peronism, Christian Democracy and Marxism. In Argentina *Peronistas de base*, influenced by similar currents of Catholic social or even devotional activism, such as the *cursillos de cristiandad*, went to live in working-class suburbs, distancing themselves from the trade union hierarchy and Peronist 'verticalism' they regarded as corrupt and authoritarian and also from the advocates of armed revolution. In the

---

[14] Paradoxically, the PT, the party of *basismo*, in whose foundation *basista* Catholicism took a significant role side by side with new trade union leaders such as Lula, found its voting base not among these 'marginalized' groups, but rather among employed people, especially in the demoralized public sector (Banck, 1990; Kinzo, 1993). Lula (Luis Ignacio da Silva) came to prominence, first as a trade union leader in São Paulo in the late 1980s and later as a founder and national leader of the PT (Worker's Party) and as its presidential candidate on two occasions, 1990 and 1994.

1960s and 1970s the *Sacerdotes del Tercer Mundo* (Third World Priests) unleashed fierce conflicts within the Argentine church and, in a dramatic gesture equivalent to the 'Marxist' conversions of some Brazilian Catholic groups (in particular *Açao Popular*), declared that only Peronism could solve the country's and the people's problems.

In Chile, the Catholic University students of the early 1960s who took part in *Acción Católica* would spend their vacations 'going to the people' in the countryside, and they formed the shock troops of the Christian Democrat Party's youth wing in the 1964 presidential campaign of Eduardo Frei announcing a 'Revolution in Freedom' to the tune of a song entitled *Brilla el sol de la Juventud* ('The sun of youth is shining'). But by 1968 some had already found their way into the ranks of Althusserian Marxism (such as that tendency's best known Latin American exponent, Marta Harnecker),[15] while many of those who remained in the ranks of Christian Democracy became disillusioned with Frei's caution and broke away to form a 'United Popular Action Movement' — MAPU — which joined with the Communist and Socialist Parties in the ill-fated *Unidad Popular* coalition.

In all three cases the Catholic element was present as an inspiration to intellectuals to go in search of the true, concrete (the word 'concrete' was pervasive) essence of the working class, and, despite different points of departure, in all three cases the enterprise of *basismo* sooner or later fell outside the mainstream organizations of the working class. When we perceive the common Catholic element in the three cases, and when we remember the common background in French, Belgian and Southern European[16] initiatives in evangelization of the working class, then a type of Catholic invocation of 'the popular', a sense of distance and wonderment in the face first of 'the working class' and later of 'the people', as the embodiment of an almost ungraspable virtue, comes to the fore. What starts out as a programme to recapture the working class for Catholicism, becomes in the end a programme in which the intelligentsia, though not necessarily the intelligentsia of high culture, go to learn from the working class.

The shift of the Brazilian church to support for grassroots activism was

[15] Author of the wild and unlikely best-seller: *El Capital: conceptos fundamentales*. Outsold only by Gabriel García Marquez, the book turned Althusserian Marxism into a canon and hammered out generations of students on the anvil of revolutionary structuralism (Castañeda, 1993: 57). Marta Harnecker, presumably benefiting from her status as the wife of one of the country's senior security officers, became for a time the only person exercising proper journalism in Cuba, publishing articles in *Bohemia* on sensitive issues such as rationing in the 1970s.

[16] In Argentina *basismo* owed a certain amount to the *cursillos*, a Spanish innovation, and less to Fr Cardijn, worker-priests or 'specialized' Catholic Action.

not only the consequence of the activities of a faction or of a group of intellectuals. In the post-war period bishops in Brazil (José de Souza Martins, 1994: 126–7), as in Chile, gradually adopted a reformist attitude to rural problems in the interests of preserving the social order against the ravages of proletarianization and urban migration, and of stimulating the development of modern industrial capitalism. Even bishops who later appeared as 'conservative' figures, especially in the Northeast, were encouraging innovative forms of literacy training, using the method of Paulo Freire, and the formation of trade unions in the countryside, in the name of the most elementary and reformist conception of rights. These rural workers' organizations, and the fact that the Church as an institution stood behind them, were among the most powerful motivations for the military coup of 1964, a coup which was to inaugurate the period of 'bureaucratic authoritarianism' in the region. According to Martins, the experience of the clash between this ethical commitment, which they initially saw as consistent with the established order, and the violence and oppressive forms of employment (slavery, debt bondage, servility) in the countryside, led many – but by no means all – bishops to adopt radical positions in the late 1960s.

The renewal and social commitments of the hierarchy in the period after 1960, and after the loss of control over Catholic Action, brought the creation of Pastoral Commissions, constituting yet another institutional mechanism in the social activity of the church. The *Conselho Indigenista Missionario* (CIMI – Indigenist Missionary Council) was created in 1972 and the *Pastoral da Terra* (CPT – 'Land Pastoral Mission') in 1975, to support the self-activism of indigenous peoples in Amazonia, small farmers and landless workers – and similar organizations in other sectors were to follow. Falling under the sponsorship of the Bishops' Conference (CNBB) through governing councils composed of bishops, rather than under a particular hierarchical instance, staffed by lay people and ex-priests, the *Pastorais* (plural of *Pastoral*) provide educational and promotional support services – courses, pamphlets, meetings – for unionization, organization, and non-violent, often judicial action through which these groups could defend their land, their rights, their livelihood, their interests, sometimes even their lives. They publish documents explaining the inequalities and oppression reigning in the countryside and the legal provisions and procedures available to the social groups who suffer thereby, the function and operation of trade unions, and so on. Although they do not follow hierarchical instructions, the Church is prepared to stand by their actions, and until 1994 – when there was a serious crisis in the CPT as a result of disputes among the landless and farmer organizations themselves[17] – they were consistently supported by the bishops.

Whether coming from below or from above, *basismo* required the full-time commitment of priests and nuns and also funding from international organizations such as *Misereor*, a charity operating under the sponsorship of the German bishops. But the support of priests, and not only of elderly priests, was not always forthcoming. In 1975 seminarians in Recife – supposedly the stronghold of commitment to the poor – reacted collectively against the programme of social commitment (Marin, 1995: 273ff.). These potential recruits – most of whom would never make it to ordination – came from a much more humble background than earlier generations of priests, let alone than their often European teachers, and this call to sacrifice in the cause of the poor fitted ill with their hopes of achieving social mobility for themselves and their families through their calling. It seems that this apparent exhaustion of approaches deriving from Catholic Action opened the way in the late 1970s to liberation theology proper, at least in the Northeast of Brazil (Marin, 1995: 284).

We may begin to see a crystallization of conflict within and between several traditions and tendencies in the late 1970s: the excitement of Vatican II and Medellín has given way to tension and anxiety in the light of vertiginous falls in vocations and in clerical personnel; the counter-revolution in the Vatican, tentatively initiated by Paul VI, is intensified by John Paul II; Central America is erupting in revolutionary violence, increasing the pressure on the Church to take sides; the movements inspired by the social doctrine and the Catholic Action tradition are making their mark in the conscience of the Church but not in political reality. At the same period, some theologians of liberation come to espouse more activist positions, publishing work in response to immediate political situations and organizational needs. This may explain the change in Leonardo Boff's output from erudite works of reflection such as *Jesus Christ Liberator* (1971) to programmatic works of ecclesiology advocating the restructuring of the entire apparatus such as *Church, Charisma and Power* (1985), and numerous other works on the relationship between religious and political commitment (*Ecclesiogênese*, 1977; *Da Libertação*, 1979; *Cristãos: como fazer política*, – 'Christians – how to be active in politics' – 1987). Likewise in the early 1980s,[18] the increasingly

[17] It seems that these disagreements concerned the role which the Pastoral staff should play in the organizations of the landless (*Movimento dos Sem Terra* – Landless People's Movement).

[18] This was during the heyday of the Central American revolution, when the Sandinistas had not yet been weakened by the counter-revolution, the FMLN of El Salvador had forced the government of that country onto the defensive, and in Brazil Catholic activists and groups were prominent in the mobilization in favour of direct Presidential elections (the '*Diretas Ja!*' campaign).

vociferous use of the term People's Church (*Igreja Popular* in Portuguese, *Iglesia Popular* in Spanish) cannot have been uncalculated by people who knew very well that it provoked fury in the hierarchy, containing as it did the hint of breakaway Churches or at least of a severe downgrading[19] of episcopal and papal authority. These writings, produced almost as primers for a non-specialist readership, and containing as much social as theological reasoning, may well reflect the perplexity of theologians and their difficulty in finding a language which could respond to the pressure on them 'from below'.

When therefore we consider this wave of activism from the point of view of Church politics, and indeed of theology, we can understand why Gutierrez speaks, as he has done so often, of the 'irruption of the poor' in the life and thought of the Latin American Church (Gutierrez, 1990: 21). Although TL spoke early on of poverty in radically new terms when compared with established discourse, that new register merely provoked debate, whereas high-profile social activism in land invasions, CEBs, proliferating social projects, and protests against human rights violations put the Church firmly on the political stage, inviting pressure from governments and civil society; it also placed lives at risk, sometimes even the lives of priests and nuns. These circumstances must have contributed significantly to the agonizing reappraisals which took place during the 1980s, both among theologians and in the hierarchy which, apart from challenges to its authority, bore the moral and political brunt of these political pressures, and not infrequently faced decisions implicating individual lives.

Liberation theology's diverging paths

Theology is a subject, a profession and a discipline, with theories and techniques and expertise of its own, which at least the most distinguished liberation theologians possess in abundance: the repetition of their most striking and occasionally (to the ecclesiastical authorities) scandalous conclusions by social scientists reduces a thick textured argument almost to a mouthing of slogans, because the elaborate arguments derived from biblical and patristic texts, from the philosophical and theological traditions themselves, from linguistic analysis of the Bible, from historical contextualization and much besides, are missing.

---

[19] The most scandalous moment was when the Pope, standing in front of a deeply divided and increasingly unruly crowd in Managua in 1983, denounced the 'absurd and dangerous character' of the '*Iglesia Popular* (People's Church'), defined as a 'parallel' ministry (speech of 4 March 1983).

The ahistorical treatment of the TL school as if it were revealed truth rather than as a school of thought with all the differences and arguments and contradictions which any school would have, and above all a school capable of change through time, has produced an excessively homogenous picture of TL and also a tone of preaching which is inappropriate to social science. In place of this apologetic, timeless, almost moralistic, discourse – which theology is not but which non-theologians sometimes take it to be – a grounded approach is needed in which it is treated as a school of thought and in which the multiple pressures and orientations required of its practitioners are taken into account. For theologians are not, and rarely have been, producers of dogma or doctrine. The production of dogma is the role of authoritative, in effect political, institutions, which may employ theologians, and even be led by persons trained in theology, but are not theological in their vocation. The Catholic Church is the religious institution which has taken the production of official doctrine most seriously, and indeed may be unique in this regard: many religious traditions – Judaism, Sunni Islam – are able to dispense entirely with such authoritative/dogmatic bodies – but this does not mean that they dispense with theology. Theologians are professionals of recognized erudition in specialized fields. Often they are historical or archaeological specialists – as those who might be concerned with the Dead Sea Scrolls, or with Gnostic texts – or legal artesans, such as Talmudic scholars – and sometimes they are moral philosophers, but they are not preachers.

However, the producers of TL have revised the role of theology and of the theologian and although their revisionism is mostly concerned with methodology, they have in so doing added an unusual prophetic voice. It is this voice which propelled TL out of the libraries and classrooms and into the headlines, yet if we read the path-breaking publications of the school, we find that they are taken up principally with detailed scholarly argument and analysis, leading up, to be sure, to prophetic conclusions. By separating those conclusions from the preceding analysis commentators have contributed to the impression of a theology guided by political idealism or strategy. If this were a political theology in that simple sense then it would have no claim to distinction as either theology or politics, but its protagonists would also probably have displayed more political skill and ruthlessness. If TL had been a truly political theology – not in Metz's sense but in the sense of a theology aiming to place its ideas at the centre of power within and outside the Church – then it would have lost prestige as a school of thought but would not have remained the prerogative of a marginal – albeit vocal and prophetic – network of research and documentation centres. The contrast with Opus Dei once again comes to mind.

For liberation theology the 1980s were the decade of respectability and differentiation: its status as an established school of thought was confirmed when, after much hesitation and argument, Rome produced a 'sanitized' version,[20] while at the non-official level, and at the more scholarly level, different tendencies and specializations began to emerge, likewise reflecting TL's coming of age. We have already noted the 'activist' tendency which developed in Brazil, but in contrast we find a significant shift of emphasis in Gutierrez's own work, and yet another strand among Central American theologians.

Although the term theology of liberation is more closely associated with the name of Gustavo Gutierrez than with any other, it is Gutierrez' own thought which has perhaps moved further away from the positions he took up in the early 1970s than those of any other of the movement's prominent exponents − so that today he appears to have evolved while others remain more faithful to the programme originally outlined in his *A Theology of Liberation* (1972). Gutierrez has shifted away from class analysis, from an account of society in terms of social classes which can be observed 'out there', towards a much more prominent, even dominant, concern with the poor as 'the other', as other cultures and races. Although this may be his way of accompanying the Church's own growing concern with culture, heralded first in *Evangelii Nuntiandi* and later developed at Puebla and in John Paul II's approach more generally, it takes up, but now with much more emphasis, his own early idea of doing theology through the eyes of the poor. His work has contained fewer and fewer political or activist allusions and has tended to concentrate much more on themes related to how theologians and ordinary believers think about their belief − through what eyes, and whose eyes, are they looking? Partly perhaps because of the turn of events in his country Peru, references to Marx have all but disappeared, Gutierrez being now prone to say that the issue of Marxism simply lies outside the field of theological discourse,[21] and clearly finding it an irritating distraction. The tone of his work is much less contestatory *vis-à-vis* the Church establishment, so that even though its implications may continue to be as revolutionary as ever, he seems unwilling to pursue them explicitly, preferring not to write 'socio-political' books with a theological bent such as those which Leonardo Boff and his brother Clodovis have been producing, and whose provocative statements jump from the page when read by anxious censors in the Vatican. In the end Gutierrez' vast scholarly apparatus may hide a more innovative theological contribution because, being less confident as social

[20] Congregation for the Doctrine of the Faith: *Instruction on Christian freedom and liberation, 1986.*
[21] As he repeatedly stated in lectures in Cambridge in 1989.

science, it leaves less room for the flight into activism. After all, has this flight not saddled TL with too many hostages to fortune?

This has involved a delineation of Gutierrez' position on Marxism. In his doctoral defence in Lyons in 1985, in a short section on theology and social science, Gutierrez stated firmly that theology calls upon the social sciences in order to gain a better understanding of the social reality of Latin America, but although 'in contemporary social science there are a certain number of elements which derive from Marxism', this 'in no way justifies an identification of social sciences with Marxism, above all not if one means thereby the Marxism which Father Arrupe (the late Superior-General of the Society of Jesus) called "its exclusive version" ' (Gutierrez, 1990: 25). The distance is polite, but nonetheless palpable. In a related passage, Gutierrez seems to be taking pains also to distance himself from overpoliticized or overconcretized versions of the Kingdom, when he says firmly that 'one must not identify the coming of the Kingdom with the historic achievements of human liberation'. Rather, 'the historical, political, liberating event is the growth of the Kingdom, is a salvific occurrence, but it is not the coming of the Kingdom, nor total salvation' (1990: 29). Gutierrez is here obviously placing a distance between himself and those who would identify 'the Kingdom' with 'socialism', but is trying to do so without giving comfort to the enemies of either socialism or TL.

Thus far one might interpret these words as a political distancing from uncomfortable interpretations of his own work and even from his own earlier views,[22] but other works of this time, and above all later work, shows that all along Gutierrez has been thinking very hard about what his contribution really was and could become.

The accent on the poor in Gutierrez' work has acquired an increasingly subjective emphasis, in which the call is neither to 'do something' about poverty nor to wallow in guilt about it, but rather to work out how the scandal of poverty, as it is repeatedly called in one of his favourite usages, affects thought, especially theology. The poor, who also are oppressed by political violence, 'are not fooled: they see the truth and speak out where others remain silent'. In particular, Gutierrez writes, they understand martyrdom (1984: 23). So theirs is a particular awareness of the operancy of the divine in daily life born of their suffering. The poor and oppressed appear in this context more as a distinct ethnic or cultural group than as a

---

[22] It is impossible not to recall at this point a similar sequence in the writings and actions of another icon of the high point of Latin American radicalism, namely Fernando Henrique Cardoso, who spent several years trying to correct apocalyptic interpretations of his work on dependency theory; the story is told in Lehmann, (1990).

social class, because they are distinguished by their way of thought, and when Gutierrez speaks of a theology developed from the perspective of those people, he thinks of a long, hard, maybe impossible struggle to penetrate their world, not of an instant perception, let alone an instant solution. There is a delicate, unresolved doubt here concerning intellectual self-discrediting, self-doubt and idealization of 'the poor', but by the 1990s Gutierrez had shifted towards the view that through the religion of the poor one can gain access to the faith of the innocent and therefore to the faith of those who enjoy particular 'favour' in the eyes of God. Although there is no softening of the denunciation and prophetic message, this is still a shift in relation to A Theology of Liberation, in which no mention at all was made of popular religious practices. The shift also parallels the trajectory of basismo away from the concern of Marxism and social democracy with state power and towards seeking communion with the people.

Gutierrez' new approach has antecedents, and perhaps also origins, in the sixteenth and seventeenth centuries, when theologians and legal scholars debated the legitimacy of the conquest of the Americas and of the imposition of Iberian rule upon them, the morality of the behaviour of the colonizers, the legitimacy of the seizure of lands and the use of violence, and related issues. Scholars were for the first time coming to terms with a radically different and technologically inferior society: while some idealized it, they argued violently with others who sustained what today would be called a 'Eurocentric' view. This was the birth of international law – in the work of Francisco de Vitoria, of our awareness of 'the other' and even of our very concept of religion as a distinct institution. But for Gutierrez – though he never says so explicitly – the true precursor of liberation theology was the most polemical and controversial participant in these debates, Bartolomé de las Casas, the tireless 'defender of the Indians' and scourge of their conquerors, who preached, argued and reasoned in the Caribbean, in Chiapa, where he was bishop, and at the Spanish court, from the day he abandoned his own conqueror's role in 1515 until his death in 1566 at the age of 82. Las Casas had not even merited a footnote in A Theology of Liberation, and although there are many centres and institutes of the TL school named after him, he is rarely mentioned let alone analysed in the modern theological literature.[23]

Gutierrez' 600-page book on las Casas (1993), complete with a scholarly apparatus worthy of a doctoral thesis, was written at a time of life when others in his position would be settling down to enjoy the fruits

---

[23] His name also still provokes resistance in official Church circles – where his beatification or canonization is not even on the agenda.

of past glories. It is unlikely to have been an academic exercise aiming to make an original historical contribution to las Casas studies, but it obviously went far beyond an attempt simply to bring las Casas to the attention of the modern public. Since Gutierrez is silent on his motives and aims, we can but conjecture, and I think that first he wanted to establish for TL a historical precursor, in contrast with his own earlier work, and that of others, which had drawn its theological inspiration from modern European debates; secondly, for reasons which he might one day explain, he wanted to develop and communicate his own thought, and the change it had undergone, through the interpretation of las Casas; thirdly, it is possible that – in an inverse movement to that of looking for a precursor and placing him on a pedestal – he wanted to put life back into a figure whose reputation had been fossilized, petrified (literally, in the entrance halls of numerous NGOs) and ignored precisely because his name had become a byword, invoked by every good cause but worshipped to the point where the worshippers no longer took an interest in what he actually had to say.

Las Casas, in the 1550s, wrote a History of the Indies, in which the Indians were described as living 'according to natural law', in a state of sinless innocence, almost a golden age. Although he did not invalidate the purely missionary aims of the conquest, he defended the legitimacy of the pre-Colombian states, denied the legitimacy of the seizure of the native peoples' land and denounced the violence perpetrated by the conquerors. The Indians, having a civil society of their own, merited the restoration of land and power to themselves and their rightful rulers. Most controversially of all, Gutierrez gives ample space to las Casas' defence of human sacrifice, which was based on the argument that the Indians loved God and that this was their way of offering up their most prized possession – life itself (1993: 265).[24] Later, in the early seventeenth century, the Peruvian *indio* author Felipe Guaman Poma de Ayala (whose chronicle provides the title of Gutierrez' book: *En búsqueda de los pobres de Jesucristo* – 'in search of the poor of Jesus Christ')[25] wrote a detailed, periodized history of civilization in Peru in order to defend the view that the Indians of old were Christian, since 'although they were pagans, they observed God's commandments and the good works of compassion' (Brading, 1991: 152). Like las Casas, then, Poma did not doubt the legitimacy of

[24] In fact, as we know from Inga Clendinnen's work, *Aztecs* (1991) they sacrificed what was most precious not to themselves, but to their enemies, namely the lives of capture warriors.

[25] It cannot be by accident that Gutierrez has eschewed, or distanced himself from, the standard post-conciliar usage 'the people of God', preferring Poma's phrase for his title.

the pre-colonial order in the Americas, admiring the great institutions of the Inca and the orderly society that prevailed under their rule. Although the conquest may originally have been a legitimate act, freely accepted by the Inca Huascar, and blessed by the appearance of the Virgin Mary and St James at the siege of Cuzco to defend the city against an Indian army (ibid: 153), subsequently the Indians had become a new Israel, oppressed by new Egyptians, the *conquistadores*. These positions − and that of Gutierrez in the recounting of them − are far closer to the current official doctrine of 'inculturation' than might be thought, as witness the commitment in the document of the 1992 CELAM Conference in Santo Domingo to 'promote an inculturation [among indigenous peoples] of the liturgy, welcoming appreciatively those of their symbols, rites and religious expressions which are compatible with the clear meaning of the faith . . .' (CELAM, 1992b: para. 248). Likewise, the same document recognizes that in the religion of the ancestors of the indigenous peoples the 'seed of the Word' was already present predisposing them to the discovery of 'the Creator in all his creation: the sun, the moon, mother earth etc.' (ibid. para. 245).

The inversions continue: Gutierrez follows both Poma de Ayala and Las Casas in defending not only the integrity of indigenous civilization, but even its superiority, when compared with the brutality and greed of the conquerors. The conquerors, acting in the name of the faith, are *fieles infieles* (faithless faithful) whereas the Indians are *infieles fieles* (faithful infidels). The Indians − whom 'we' so despise − may be in greater number than 'us' at the right hand of God on the day of judgement (Gutierrez, 1993: 365).

Gutierrez replaces analysis centred on economic polarization with an account of relations between cultural (not ethnic) groups: by frequently adding 'blacks' or 'Africans' to the word *indígena* (Indian, but also of course 'indigenous' and thus autochthonous) he is saying that what counts is not authenticity or faithfulness to origins, or the distribution of land or capital among ethnic groups, or even ethnicity in the usual sense, but rather the rights of 'peoples' to make their own history and to political and cultural recognition. Gutierrez shifts the meaning of the term 'poor' from a material condition of an individual or group to one affecting an entire people, transcending theological arguments about material and spiritual poverty, and sociological arguments about Marxism. The poor are a people, or peoples, whose culture has been destroyed: through lost lives and property, and also through the corrosive effects of markets and cultural warfare.

This approach leads to the second shock of the book, namely the critique of contemporary liberal conceptions of rights. Las Casas, according to Gutierrez, far from being a 'precursor of a liberal doctrine of human rights', as many have argued, defends 'an evangelical preference for the lost ones of history' (*los últimos de la historia*) (1993: 315), and where others might put the accent on individual human rights, Gutierrez, through his interpretation of Las Casas, puts the emphasis on the relationship between freedom and what we might call the identity of a people. In this reasoning, God did not give the Law to Abraham because at that time the Hebrews were not yet a people. They only became a people after they left Egypt and won their freedom: 'To be a people and to live in freedom are conditions demanded by faith' (1993: 446). The Spanish conquerors in contrast, finding the Indians, who were a people, set about dismantling their institutions and their collective identity. Today, he implies, poverty is as much a destruction of cultures and identities as a material condition.

In *A Theology of Liberation*, the accent was on placing theological issues in a concrete and historical context, rather than analysing them in the abstract: 'love' was not a metaphysical construct or a general principle, but a practical issue in the person's – or the social class's – relationship with particular individuals or groups, obviously in particular with the poor; 'peace' was not an eirenic entelechy but the achievement of concrete goals in a specific time and place. Both required real acts, sacrifices, choices and conflicts. That argument had a profound impact on theology as practised in Latin America. It ripped it out of the academic detachment of Faculties and thrust it into the everyday life of much of the Church, almost literally out into the street. This advocacy is not explicitly denied in the Las Casas study, but it is not taken up either; instead the insistence is on seeing issues 'through the eyes of the poor' – *si Indus esset*. At the same time the very scale of the book and the complexity of its arguments – especially in the lengthy analyses of the terms of the sixteenth-century debates between theologians – are an indication that Gutierrez does not think that it is easy to operate this methodological shift. The 'point of view of the other' or of the poor, is not easy to grasp or convey.

Gutierrez' evolution towards this sort of position has surely been influenced by the events in Peru, and in particular by *Sendero Luminoso*, the organization led by Abimael Guzmán which in its 10-year armed assault both on the State, and also on grassroots organizations and NGOs did not hesitate to murder nuns and neighbourhood leaders. In this context TL's early friendliness towards Marxism, even simply as a 'method of analysis', seemed uncomfortable, while to denounce it would have been to give in to an established order whose spokesmen dismissed any advocacy of structural change as 'Marxist' and subversive. So the subject was put aside.

In contrast, in Central America during the 1980s, to uphold Marxism was to defy bravely but triumphantly that same established order. It was a decade of ascendant respectability, if not precisely political success, for a set of revolutionary groups who became known in the wider world for the pitiless repression they suffered, in El Salvador and Guatemala, or in Nicaragua, for trying to set up an alternative system in the shadow of the United States. The various histories ended in their differing, and in no case remotely successful, ways, but the point is that to sympathize with them, or to be friendly with them, was not something of which an intellectual – and here we are only speaking of intellectuals, especially the priests among them – would have to be ashamed, as would have been the case with Sendero's sympathizers in Peru. Even Archbishop Oscar Romero, who was assassinated in 1980 as he raised the host while saying Mass, could not bring himself to condemn revolutionary violence outright.[26] Nor could Ignacio Illacuria, Rector of the Universidad Centroamericana, assassinated with five other Jesuits and their two women helpers in their residence in November 1989.

In contrast, though by no means total contrast, to the evolution of Gutierrez, we therefore find a 'Central American version' of TL which has kept closer to the programme of Gutierrez' founding text, and which has also perhaps developed in a more internally theological fashion even though its arguments are of a more activist nature. This can be seen in Jon Sobrino's *Jesus the Liberator* (1991),[27] an extended meditation on the gospel and the prophets in the light of the endless violence and war and the increasing material deprivation affecting Central America. The book is particularly insistent on what might be called the counter-intuitive character of Jesus's teaching and action: he prefers to perform miracles for sinners, for the ungodly, and for prostitutes, not for the virtuous. The miracles matter less on account of the cures themselves than because of their message (p. 89) – an interpretation which casts the miracle cures purveyed by modern charismatics in an illuminating light. Jesus's teaching is seen as a challenge to the official religion of the Jewish establishment of the time, and is interpreted as a basis for opposition less to atheism than to idolatry, in implicit opposition to today's official Catholic concerns. The very sub-title of the book (A *historico-theological*

---

[26] According to Sobrino (1993) Archbishop Romero ranked 'structural injustice' as the 'primary and worst of all types of violence'. (p. 212) and while attacking even justifiable attempts to turn violence into a 'cult', defended popular insurrections on the same 'traditional' grounds as a just war.

[27] References will be to English translation, 1993.

reading of the life of Jesus of Nazareth) leads into a discussion of the primacy of the historical Jesus over the Christ of faith. The poor are not individuals whose existence constitutes a summons to charity, and certainly Sobrino's concept of poverty does not fit into the discussion of the distinction between the materially poor and the 'poor in spirit' – rather the poor are a collectivity whose existence violates established religious and cultural norms.

Sobrino does not hesitate to take on directly very sensitive themes, such as that of violence, or to develop searing metaphors such as the 'crucified people'. There is a sense of certainty which was there in Gutierrez' early work but is gone from his later writing. The early TL hostility to 'abstractness', discussed above, is taken up again in Sobrino's hostility to 'alienating images': 'abstraction without specificity, reconciliation without conflict, absoluteness without relation' (p. 17). He does not go as far as some liberationist speech, which seems to express a belief that the Kingdom of God can be pursued on earth, but he comes close to that, for although he describes the Kingdom as 'hope in history' (p. 71) he also describes it as a 'highly positive reality . . . a historical, not an a-historical reality' which will 'not arrive from a *tabula rasa*' but 'from and against the anti-Kingdom' (p. 72).

The most important difference, in comparing Sobrino with Gutierrez, is that in Sobrino's book the identity of the poor is never in question; the text is written on the assumption that we know who the poor are, we know how they experience their plight, and we know the way to solve their problems. They are defined 'economically', as the materially deprived, but also 'sociologically', as stated above, as the prostitutes and the sinners (p. 80). By taking the side of the poor we take their side against official religion: echoing, not without a hint of dissent from the official interpretation, the idea of a 'preferential option for the poor', Sobrino writes that the 'partiality and gratuitousness of God are what cause the scandal, because they upset official religious society', but 'wherever sinners allow themselves to be welcomed by God, there the signs of the coming of the Kingdom are apparent' (p. 98).

Sobrino's book is also the work of a biblical scholar; indeed, it could be interpreted as a struggle within him between the scholar and the activist – in contrast with Boff where the activist won out, to the point where he left the priesthood. There are extended discussions of modern Christology, and of Deutero-Isaiah, which drive home the counter-intuitive message alluded to above: Isaiah's Suffering Servant who suffers for all the sins of mankind, is 'struck down by disease and misery' and 'tortured for our iniquities' (Isaiah, 53: 4–5) but in the end is healed and enjoys long life

(Isaiah,53: 9–12), is likened to the poor in the contemporary world, dismissed as 'subversives, criminals, Marxists, terrorists, even atheists' (Sobrino, 1993: 257), culminating in Illacuria's shocking word 'copro-analysis' – in the Third Word we find the 'faeces' of the rich countries.

Still today, the method of TL preserves the originality which marked its birth, namely its anchorage in a highly conflictive historical process, transcending the rarefied atmosphere of the seminaries and theological institutes where the subject had developed for many decades previously. But these examples show us that we also now see the emergence of different schools of thought: the one groping for points of orientation in a world of multiple identities, obsessed with the identity of the other, the poor, the oppressed, in his and her many manifestations – the other in contrast possessing a dualistic view of the world and seeking by shock and metaphorical inversion to turn the world upside down. As we shall see, although in their frustration *basistas* may call for the overthrow of the established order, their world view is closest to that of Gutierrez, even though they are probably not aware of it.

The Church under pressure

The church as an institution reacted in many ways at different levels to the militancy which its own people, lay and religious, seemed to have unleashed. Pope Paul began to show signs of nervousness in his reference to the dangers of politicization in *communautés de base*[28] in the 1975 encyclical *Evangelii Nuntiandi*. Less than two years after Paul's death, his successor watched carefully over the 1979 Puebla CELAM conference whose conclusions, though frequently quoted by all liberation theologians, shifted the emphasis of Medellín, by placing the word 'preferential' before 'option for the poor' and by introducing the theme of culture as a counterpoise to social justice. By the time the bishops had reached the 1992 CELAM conference in Santo Domingo they appeared, as a body, worn down and worn out by internal conflict: neither the frequently criticized triumphalism of celebrating 500 years of evangelization in the Americas, nor the offensiveness of the commemorative monument built by an ageing and corrupt (but elected) ruler in the Dominican Republic itself disturbed the proceedings. Instead, awareness of the rapid progress of Protestantism in the region, and of the damage done to the Church by its internecine struggles placed the previous 24 years in sober

[28] The text significantly kept the French term even in the English translation, reflecting perhaps perplexity in the Vatican as to how to handle the phenomenon itself.

perspective. The principal problems faced by the Church were the disunity arising usually over political issues, the shortfall in vocations, and the loss of ordained priests and seminarians to secular life.

The trajectory from Medellín to Santo Domingo was, then, a very tempestuous one: all the changes and crises which underlie the account given here took place in a period of less than 25 years. Although it is clear that *basismo* did not emerge triumphant, some of its principal ideas had indeed been incorporated into official doctrine, but inevitably in a dilute form; leading dissenting or radical figures had been marginalized and in some cases had left the priesthood, and sympathetic bishops were replaced on retirement by men of a very different style and persuasion.

We have seen that the Catholic Church is a complex of institutions and that those institutions exist in the midst of a culture whose evolution is not decided from Rome, or indeed from any centre of power. In this vast panorama, *basismo* turns out not to be a major player, and indeed its worldwide repercussions among the intelligentsia are surprising when we set them against the movement's small size 'on the ground' and its failure to secure a position of sustained power in the hierarchy. The movement's paradoxical relationship with the hierarchy explains both its advances and its setbacks. From the writings of Boff, from the conflicts in Nicaragua, and from much else besides, we know that *basismo* is a philosophy which would reduce, if not eliminate, the principle of hierarchical authority, and we know that it works through base communities in which lay people have a predominant role. Yet its relative overrepresentation among priests and even bishops is clear, as is its underrepresentation among the laity as a whole, in lay fraternities and in evangelizing and devotional organizations. This paradox of an anti-hierarchical movement dependent for its survival on the hierarchy itself (noted poignantly by Comblin, 1990) has a two-edged effect: thanks to the support of sympathetic bishops and priests and even to the German bishops' charitable foundations, the base communities and the theology of liberation may have gained a higher profile within the institutions of the church and in the media than would otherwise have been possible, but inevitably their impact has been blunted and the once high hopes of transforming the entire institution have been long since dashed.

That is the story within the Church, but it raises very evidently the question of popular culture: why, despite its derivation from and allegiance to the dominant religious tradition of the region, and despite the commitment of its missionaries to listen carefully to the people and learn from them, has this movement had so much difficulty in its relationship with popular culture? Why have other seemingly conservative

Catholic movements which pay little attention to the pressing realities of life among the poor, and even less attention to elaborating an idea of popular culture, had so much more success, at least in quantitative terms? To deal with these questions we need to go back to the issues raised in the Introduction, and we also need to go to the field and to other sources to understand the way in which *basismo* has projected the people and how that projection has been received and even returned among and by the people themselves.

4

Concepts and Usages in the Texts and Speech of the *Basista* Church

O povo/el pueblo

The peculiarity of *basismo* is the construction of the people by those who do not consider themselves fully of them.[1] Some would say that it is an idealized image projected by intellectuals, and many critics complain that by emphasizing social and political commitment it ignores the 'true' religious needs of 'the people'. In this latter view the satisfaction of religious needs does not lend itself to 'politicization': those who would politicize are either unlikely to gain acceptance among the people for their message, or if they do are guilty of manipulation, of exploitation of the people's innocence or ignorance. Among *basistas* we find two broad views, of which one is not incompatible with this last: some *basistas* do indeed believe that the people's real needs are political and material and that the task of the Christian is to demystify religion in order to raise the consciousness of the people and further their struggle. For them popular religion is a mechanism of mystification which blinds the people to their

---

[1] Exemplary is a former schoolteacher, Aracy, whose life is completely dedicated to the Church-related popular movement. Her mode of being and speaking express, in an extreme form, the struggle of *basista* Catholicism to come to terms with cultural difference. Now in her fifties, she has blonde hair and seems at first to be white, but she says she is a black albino, an identity which some of her associates suspect may be adopted. Her battered VW Beetle is at the disposal of activists of the *basista* Church and of the PT (Workers' Party) – two heavily overlapping categories. At a certain stage of her life, while still working as an official in the State (as opposed to Federal) Secretariat for Education, she went to live in a *favela* and, as she describes it, there were two moments when she really felt she was closing the gap between herself and the people. The details, if reported, would seem trivial, but the point is that by imitating the modes of dress of her neighbours in the *favela* she acquired an enormous sense of satisfaction because she felt that she really had become one of them – one of the people. She wasn't *povão* (lumpen), she said, but she was of the *povo* (of the people) – yet by saying that she was also betraying an underlying fear that she was not one of the people. In the meantime, to complicate matters further, she seemed to have undergone a process of *déclassement*, but her status was preserved by her close association with the priests and activists of the *basista* Church.

true needs and interests and also to the true message of the gospel and the Old Testament. In contrast other *basistas* believe that it is precisely in rituals and celebrations which are barely or not at all controlled by official religious institutions, as well as in the language and celebrations of secular life, that the people give voice – albeit a metaphorical voice – to a suppressed consciousness of exploitation and of the need for revolt.[2] This idea that popular religion – and within it indigenous religion – is a suppressed, subconscious voice has clear affinity with the notion of 'inculturation', currently in favour in the Vatican and favourably mentioned, as we have seen, at the Santo Domingo meeting of CELAM (1992), as it was with Gustavo Gutierrez' interpretation of Las Casas. These interpretations may differ in their political implications, but they share the underlying point that non-Christian or unofficial forms of worship constitute a metaphorical, almost subconscious, type of worship expressing a relationship with the divine and with certain universal principles of humanity.[3]

The practical implications of the notion of inculturation can be seen in ritual innovations such as the introduction, on occasion, of 'African' themes and rituals into the Mass, on the grounds that in Brazil these are close to the world-view and religious spirituality or religiosity of the people – a subject to which we shall return in the context of Pentecostalism. Padre Clovis of the parish of São Jorge in Salvador – from whose '*grupos*' and activists much of the material in this discussion is drawn – said that he was working to '*resgatar a cultura negra*' (to 'recover' black culture), implying that black culture had fallen into a decay or had been suffocated or suppressed by other cultural influences and that he would be contributing to recover this lost authenticity. These approaches to the word 'people' are founded on the same dialectic of authenticity and opacity in popular culture and religion described in the Introduction.

Basistas surround the relationship between themselves and the people with doubt, particularly self-doubt.[4] Far from being a purely psychological or existential state, that doubt is embedded in the 'invention of the

---

[2] This is precisely the idea which Bourdieu views with such distaste; see the discussion in the Introduction.

[3] It has, on the other hand, been played up in writings on 'Afro-Brazilian'; religion, notably by Roger Bastide and on millenarianism by Lanternari (1960) and Worsley (1957), for example, but has also been criticized quite sharply by Maria Isaura Pereira de Queiroz in her work on Brazilian messianism (1977).

[4] Certain varieties of Peronism, in particular the 'national left' and perhaps the '*peronistas de base*' were likewise troubled in the 1960s (Lehmann, 1990).

other' to which *basismo* proceeds — namely the construction of a politics attuned to the specificities of a culture and a tradition by persons who are not part of that culture or feel estranged from it. This is not intended to dismiss the proponents and militants of *basismo* as 'intellectuals' or 'middle-class', but simply to note that in their speech they construct the people as 'other' and themselves as bearers of a message to the people. Indeed, one striking feature of the movement as I observed it in Salvador was the low incomes and status of many of its activists: unemployed students and teachers, ex-priests and religious operating in the networks of Church-related activism and the NGOs, even leaders who had risen from very humble origins and joined the networks of militants.

This element of search and doubt injects into *basista* movements a distrust of institutionalized leadership, and a much weaker utopianism than Marxism, for example, or than many millenarianisms, not to speak of the hopes of eternal salvation promised by Pentecostal preachers. It does not allow for an intellectual elite to provide the privileged reading of history which in Leninist Marxism, at least, would guide the oppressed towards a future with certain definite, albeit highly abstract, characteristics. On the contrary, its constant self-questioning engenders repeated returns to the *base* to discover what the people *really* want, while the watchword *caminhada* emphasizes that the journey takes precedence over the arrival — a radical contrast with the Pentecostal obsession with plenitude, baptism in the Spirit and possession by the Devil, that is, with black-and-white, all-or-nothing relationships, and immediate results. A course in São Jorge parish for people intending to take part in the '*Pastoral da Saúde*' (Health Pastoral) was described by an organizer as valid not so much for the content itself, but for the *acompanhamento da caminhada que a gente está fazendo* — a phrase which, by emphasizing the role of the organizer in 'accompanying' the people's long journey (*caminhada*), places a distance between her and the people, and places the satisfaction of the need for health a long way in the future. The contrast — particularly apt in this case where health is the subject of the pastoral training — with the immediacy of miracle cures advertised by Pentecostals could not be starker. The motto of the community organizations in São Jorge parish, '*um novo jeito de sermos Igreja tomando em conta a realidade do povo na perspectiva da libertação*' (a new way of being Church, in accordance with the reality of the people and moving towards — literally 'in the perspective of' — liberation) — shows how even enthusiastic advocates of the transformation of the Catholic Church into a 'People's Church' still do not claim that it is more than a perspective, a line of work or a process of construction.

Basismo has a deep-running hostility to what activists denigratingly call *assistencialismo*. This touchstone phrase encapsulates a hostility both to what was once known as reformism or social democracy, and to any hint of doing personal favours for the poor or to permitting relationships of personal dependence to develop between leaders and led. It can even extend to agencies and individuals who are seen as well-meaning 'do-gooders': thus Aracy, the former teacher and educational administrator who had gone to live in a poor neighbourhood (see above, note 1), disparagingly said to me that by *assistencialismo* she understood *sopa*, by which she meant the provision of soup to the poor. An even humbler activist, an organizer of citizen's groups on the edge of the suburb of Periperi, spoke of the local politician who likes to show that all that is done is the fruit of his own personal effort, not that of the people, of the community (*sempre mostrar que é ele que faz, não que e o esforço do povo, esforço comunitario conjunto*). In another conversation a priest was criticized in almost exactly the same terms: that he wanted the credit for everything to be his, that he was a 'centralist' (another catchphrase): *A maneira centralista com que ele dirigia o trabalho . . . todo para ele*. The aversion to authority relations was expressed in the conversations I had with activists by a standard array of phrases: not to 'impose' (*não impor*), or to 'centralize': however strong the desire to become a Church on the road (*caminhada* again) to liberation, it could in no way be imposed on the people.

To discover how the religio-political project of *basismo* works itself out in practice we are faced with sources both multiple and difficult to control. This is because the movement is purposefully underinstitutionalized, and also because its manifestations are multifarious and cannot be subsumed – as, say, might be the case in an account of a socialist movement – under any sort of coordinating reference point. Because this lack of institutional definition is an essential characteristic not only of *basismo* as a movement but also of *basistas'* own construction of what they are doing, the word 'fellow-feeling' continues to have its relevance as a description of what holds it together. To sustain the description, therefore, it is not enough to confine oneself to institutionally defined spheres, and the exposition which follows here and in the next chapter will concentrate on three facets and their interactions: the pamphlet literature, which is the product of an effort to 'get the message across' to the people; the organizations I studied while in Salvador in 1991, which are the institutional counterpart to the pamphlet literature, and interviews conducted in Bahia which will further help to construct a picture of the *basista* mind-set.

The pamphlet literature

The grassroots movement in Brazil produces a mountain of pamphlet literature. It varies from biblical guides and commentaries to guides to labour law and accounts of the history of Brazil and of the achievements of the *movimento popular* (the 'popular', or 'people's' movement). It is produced by Brazilian and Latin American NGOs of the sort which specialize in producing materials for grassroots organizations,[5] and is designed usually to be read in study groups. To recount in any detail the subject matter of even a small part of the pamphlet literature would be tedious and probably not very instructive. Instead I wish to convey a sense of the form of that literature and of the illustrative material which the authors clearly intend to be a substantial vehicle for conveying their message.

The first examples were produced by ACO (*Ação Católica Operaria* – Catholic Workers' Action). ACO is a network of priests and activists which runs seminars where activists from various walks of life conduct what St Ignatius called a *Revisão de Vida* – literally a review, or reappraisal, of their life and work, using the 'see-judge-act' method first developed in Europe by Catholic youth organizations after the Second World War, and inspired by the Belgian priest Fr Cardijn. One booklet is a pedagogic guide of 160 pages entitled *Revisão de Vida: Conhecer para Transformar* (knowing as a means to transformation). The cover has a vignette depicting a spanner, a factory, a table lamp and a group of workers. The illustrations consist of simple, occasionally cartoon-like, pen and ink drawings, on every page, numerous diagrammatic devices designed as aids to comprehension, and dramatized scenes with dialogue. The figures, as in ACO books generally, are of three types: contemporary Brazilians; mostly anonymous, biblical figures; and Jesus Christ himself. The contemporary Brazilians are portrayed as clean-shaven – with the occasional neat moustache – mostly white, but some black, both male and female. Factory workers wear a hard hat; rural workers or peasant farmers a ragged straw hat; businessmen/capitalists a top hat, tie and suit. The biblical figures wear striped robes and turbans, with priests in prayer-shawls and women dressed attractively in shawls and decorated belts. The figure of Christ stands out with bare head, long, thick, tousled hair and good looks, and a much more individual expression than usual in such

---

[5] Thomas Carroll (1992) aptly calls these 'grassroots support organizations'.

literature, the work seemingly of a different hand from that which drew either the other biblical figures or the contemporary personages.

The organization of the book bears all the marks of the Franco-Catholic didactic approach: it is divided into three sections – Seeing, Judging, Acting – and each of these has numerous sub-sections which are in turn sub-divided. Each page has questions and answers, interspersed with illustrations, pointers and emphases.

This guide is designed, as are several others in the same series, as a handbook for a group leader or *animador*, and to be used in conjunction with a Bible. Its emphasis on the omnipresent figure of Christ, as well as this use of the biblical text, is a clear departure from the cultural framework of popular religion: the Virgin and the saints, the most immediate objects of veneration in popular religion, providing favours, dispensations or relief, are emphatically absent. Instead the Bible is the source of exemplary figures: Christ and the prophets, portrayed as inhabiting not a faraway place or a distant past, but naturalistic social contexts replete with echoes of modern Brazil: the Pharisees enabled the ruling class to preserve its privileges; the people expected Christ to come as a conqueror, but instead he came as a man of poverty. Indeed in this version the Messiah is not really an individual at all, but a social collectivity, and readers are guided didactically towards this figurative interpretation.

In this text, as in another in the same series on the history of the Jewish people, the Bible is not used as a source of moral tales or sayings for the guidance of one's personal life, nor precisely as a compendium of heroic myths as in the Pentecostal Churches. Yet it is the only text of reference, the only authoritative source of guidance: despite the constant insistence on (non-violent) class struggle, and on the priority of collective over individual identity, thought and action, not one modern thinker or political leader is mentioned by name, whereas the text is littered with references which together include almost every Old Testament prophet.

The references to the Bible are not recounted in biblical language. That is, there is hardly any direct quotation or use of messianic or prophetic discourse. The text does not use the Protestant/Pentecostal technique of enshrining biblical stories or pronouncements in an anachronic or 'dated' language in such a way as to mark it off and preserve its mysterious, or even sacred, quality. (This is consistent with many other aspects of religious practice inspired by *basismo*, in which the thresholds or boundaries between the sacred and the profane are absent – a theme to which we shall return.) There are innumerable examples, as in a drawing of a rabbi, flanked by a Roman soldier, and confronted by people shouting

'*Chega de exploracao!*' (Enough of exploitation!) 'We want liberty!' and '*Pelegos!*' (a Brazilian term to describe dishonest or compliant union leaders).

Similar remarks apply to the second volume of ACO's *History of God's People: an introduction to the reading of the Bible – today*, entitled *From the Exile to the End of Greek Rule*. Although this volume recounts the history as an epic struggle, it does so, once again, in terms drawn from modern radical political discourse, to the point, for example, of conducting a financial analysis of reforms in the Persian Empire of the time (ACO, n.d.: 55). The format, complete with question and answer boxes, cartoons, pen and ink drawings, remains that of an educational pamphlet, but the education offered is demanding: the authors want to resuscitate the sacred and authoritative character of biblical writings, while at the same time asking readers not to read the Bible literally, as an inerrant source in the Pentecostal manner, but rather to treat it as a fount of wisdom expressed often symbolically or metaphorically and elucidated by modern biblical criticism.

It is important to recall that this use of the Bible is a post-conciliar innovation. Although no longer revolutionary, it is still a departure from the religious experience of the previous generation whose contact with the written text of the Scriptures was minimal. In the words of a lady from the São Jorge parish: 'when we were little we only heard (i.e. did not read) the Bible . . . my father read it out loud for everyone to hear'. Today, for the authors of these texts, the Bible is a source of illustrative struggles; for all the obvious influence of modern political doctrines, recourse to the Bible must mean that they believe that those doctrines are in themselves insufficient to 'clinch' a case for political analysis, judgement or action: rather they believe the Bible to be indispensable in some sense for reaching their political conclusions. The cynical judgement that they are using the Bible to conceal their real ends from their audience rests on too many mistaken, dubious or quite simply ill-intentioned assumptions, and the opposed judgement that the use of the Bible as a 'clinching' reference is a product purely of the authors' faith does not account for the particular use which is made of it. To say that the Bible is used as a legitimating reference is no doubt accurate, but also insufficient.

The Bible is a source of identity: in a context where pre-existing symbols of Catholic 'national identity' are falling into disuse or being questioned by various rationalizing forces (not least Protestantism) and in a society where those symbols have not had as deep a cultural implantation as has been the case in the Andean countries, Central America or Mexico, what other sources can a movement at once religious and political have recourse to but a text which enjoys the hegemony of the sacred? It is of the essence of a sacred text that it enjoys legitimacy and authority while at the same time leaving almost infinitely wide margins for interpretation and selection, so that disagreements over interpretation are political matters relating to the exercise of authority. This movement which, on close inspection, can draw on so few strands in popular culture, finds identity in its particular approach to the understanding of the Bible – just as Pentecostals find identity in their 'inerrant' approach.

For *basistas* the Bible is not endowed with a mythical or epic status, in the sense of a myth of foundation or origin: the depiction of biblical stories in 'modern' Brazilian socio-political language does not bear comparison with the Pentecostal preacher saying to his flock '*You* are the children of Israel' and saying so loudly, rhythmically and emotionally, calling upon them to *re-enact* their faith so that God will do for them (and only for them) the same as he did for Israel. On the other hand the activists gathered in ACO seminars, and the *base* groups studying under their guidance, are being invited to compare themselves to the children of Israel, to learn from their story, and also to learn from Christ's approach to the sorts of problems which they face in their daily life, so that they can advance through their own efforts as the children of Israel did. They are not being asked to draw pietistic or moralizing conclusions, in the manner of a privatized Catholicism accompanied by threats of damnation. They are being asked, in the classic phrase, to 'read, mark, learn and inwardly digest'; they are being invited to analyse the Word, and thus to constitute themselves as an enlightened elite of the people, trained to some extent in biblical exegesis.

The trouble, as has so often been said, is that 'the people' seem to have great difficulty in identifying with the oppressed children of Israel, and that this intellectual, analytical Christ figure has little in common with the God (or gods) of popular culture. The movement's religiosity offers no hope save that which the group can create through its own efforts; it is a tall order, and it is unlikely to appeal beyond an activist minority. So the role of biblical reference is to confer upon those who give their time and energy to this cause an identity not so much as the descendants of, or enactors of, the ancient Jews and their epic struggles, but rather as the elect who can read and understand those texts.

The ACO literature described above is one of a wide variety of types of pamphlet literature. Another, produced *inter alia* by the regional branch of the Brazilian National Episcopal Conference (CNBB) in Recife in the days of Dom Helder Câmara deals with quite specific legal and human rights problems. The technique adopted involves recounting an exemplary story, and punctuating it with different types of general or moral reflections: some legal, some socio-political, some theological. Thus the struggle of the people of the 'Coronel Fabriciano' *favela* to defend their land is interrupted by explanations of land reform, of the law governing urban land tenure, of the role of lawyers in society, and of many legal matters besides as well as general socio-political reflections; references to the life of Jesus illustrate how to speak in front of a judge, or how to overcome fear; questions are inserted in boxes in the text as learning aids.

These verse guides are written by educated people trying hard to reduce the distance between author and reader, so their style is contrivedly colloquial. But at the same time they are highly directive: questions are framed rhetorically in such a way that only one answer is possible, a device which surely reconstructs the distance between author and reader. In short, the text claims authority yet at the same time denies, or seems reluctant to acknowledge, that authority.

The opportunity to gain a 'close-up' of the elite-popular culture divide as it affects the character of those texts is given in a booklet designed to support the struggles of *professoras leigas* – 'lay', therefore unqualified, women teachers in state primary schools who have no formal qualifications and earn a minuscule salary even smaller than the official minimum wage. After a lengthy section in much the same style (and probably by the same authors) as the booklet on the 'Coronel Fabriciano' *favela*, the text adopts the format of the *folheto* – a literature of popular poetry[6] which is sold in markets in many parts of the Northeast of Brazil by the poets themselves who pride themselves on their ability to recite and even compose poetry impromptu before an audience.

The long *folheto* poems are written in six-line stanzas with seven-syllable lines, and in a rhyming sequence of ABCBDB (Campos 1959: 12). In one major type, described by Arantes (1977) the protagonists are semi-fabulous individuals: appallingly ferocious landowners; Robin Hood-like figures; devilish individuals, endowed with superhuman strength. Epic struggles ensue. The fables (or myths as Arantes describes them) are divided into two parts: in the first part the forces of evil are supreme, and inflict all manner of beastly humiliations on the poor, or the citizenry in general. At about the half-way point the poet pauses to make some general remarks about the eventual victory of good over evil, and from then on the tables are turned as the superhuman figures of good triumph over the supermen of evil. The dénouement involves a marriage in which class co-existence is re-established under the benign leadership of

---

[6] Also known as *literatura de cordel* on account of the 'chords' on which the pamphlets (*folhetos*) are hung in market stalls in the Northeast of Brazil.

a reformed *patrão*, or landlord, the self-same person who may earlier have been the incarnation of evil (though this is not invariably the case). The *folheto* 'begins by depicting a state of . . . harmony' and progresses 'from equilibrium through imbalance back to equilibrium' (Slater: 1982: 59).

Setting aside differences of verbal usage, the fundamental difference between the 'authentic' *folheto* and the version adopted by the pamphlets of the Archdiocese of Olinda and Recife is that the latter do not contain any story at all: they are purely didactic in content, and thus lose a central feature of the *folheto*. The other very important difference is in the political structuring of the two versions: as Arantes points out, in *folheto* literature the landowner is never eliminated either physically or in his social role: he is either temporarily humiliated, or becomes a reformed character, whereas the *basistas* would regard such an outcome as no resolution at all of an irreconcilable conflict. There are other crucial structural elements, such as kinship, and the opposition of beast and man, which of course are also absent from the didactic version.

The attempt to use the *folheto* style highlights the frequently noted gap between *basista* Catholicism and popular culture, but maybe it should also be thought of more positively as an attempt to create a new pedagogic space rather than simply as a straightforwardly imitative, or carbon-copying effort. After all the *folheto* literature is written by educated members of the popular classes, sometimes even by people employed in institutions; they earn their living by selling their own work or that which they receive in exchange for their own from mean or cash-strapped publishers for resale (Arantes, 1977). They appeal to an existing tradition with its established imaginary and a fixed format. In contrast the aim of the didactic pamphlets, which are institutional products, is to educate, to raise consciousness, and to change traditional habits of thought – so it is hardly surprising if there is a gap between their form and that of traditional modes of discourse on which they draw but which they do not precisely develop or continue. Also they are designed to be used by *animadores*, by group leaders who occupy intermediary positions between the generators of the literature and the uneducated grass roots.

Another example of the 'politicization' of the literature of popular culture is given by Geert Banck (1990) who shows the use made, in pamphlets designed for use by CEBs, of figures from the Apocalypse identical in pictorial style to those reproduced by Arantes and by Campos in their work on *folhetos*. The Apocalypse 'beast' appears in various shapes – that of a crocodile, marked by inscriptions denoting social evils ('misery, egoism, injustice, death, exploitation') or a hydra-headed monster each of whose heads is inscribed with the names of the agents of exploitation ('businessmen, multinationals, the United States' etc.) Now in the *folheto* literature analysed by Campos animals appear in a very different role, namely as personages in fables like those of La Fontaine, so once again we find the mimesis of popular literature in the *basista* form subverting the symbolic structure of the original, and in the process depriving it of the symbolic opacity and ambiguity of the original, depriving the reader of the exercise of interpretative imagination or of a reference to an implicit set of meanings embodied in a shared tradition. The effect is, so to speak, 'flattening', and shows how difficult it is for *basismo* to observe its own injunction not to 'impose'.

Another dimension of the *basista* movement's 'erudite' dimension can be grasped if we come to terms with the more profound implications of its emphasis on the word. We have seen the difference between a *folheto* literature designed to be read or sung aloud to small audiences, and the less formally structured, pedagogic version in pamphlets. We have also noted the very frequent use of the Bible as a source of inspiration and of illustrative stories. This is an attempt to change the identity of a Catholic people by detaching them from a 'popular religiosity' suffused with local cults of saints and messianic figures — most famously Padre Cicero of Juazeiro in the *sertão* of Ceará state (della Cava, 1970) — and to instil instead an identity which makes them heirs to a tradition embodied in universal principles, of which ancient Judaism, the prophets and the gospel are the bearers. In this process, direct contact with the Bible is utterly new, for it has been completely absent from the practice and preaching of popular Catholicism in Latin America. Even the role of the priest is transformed: where once he was the guardian of a mysterious wisdom, in which he marked a boundary between the unlettered laity and the texts to which qualified persons alone had access, now he becomes teacher and counsellor, but also in some ways a more erudite figure, not only because priests are generally more learned than in the past, but also because he relies more on his learning and training, as a source of authority, and less on his ritual prerogatives (which in any case have become less of a monopoly since the reforms set in motion by Vatican II). It is most surprising that popular culture is enlisted to achieve these ends.

Especially when compared with Pentecostalism, the creation of this renewed relationship is slow, frustrating and unsettling. But to criticize it for not reaching the masses on a large scale and at high speed is to miss the point: such a process is bound to occur gradually, and as it proceeds the individuals who join it appear successively and cumulatively as an elect and select group. This does not mean to say that nothing is changing or that the activists are from a pre-existing elite. On the contrary, *basismo* can only advance by creating new elites from among the popular sectors. If we remind ourselves of Paulo Freire's method − whose influence permeates the movement through and through − we will recall that it aims both to desacralize the role of the teacher and to raise the status of the taught by training teachers/*animadores* drawn from among their ranks. The leadership role is not denied: the aim is the creation of a 'popular intelligentsia' educated in modern ideas of Christianity, divinity, and truth. In the process use is made of a popular idiom, but not of a popular religion which in the view of much *basista* Catholicism is marked by the indelible brand of an oppressive social structure.

It is central to the approach to popular culture outlined in the Introduction that terms such as 'authenticity' are ruled out, and that the interaction between the popular and the erudite − the 'popular' itself being a formulation of and a projection by the erudite − be fully incorporated in the analysis. The adoption by *basista* intellectuals and their institutions of these popular forms fits into a broader pattern of 'a more widespread movement originally spearheaded by artists and writers but now involving the middle class at large' (Slater 1982: 37). As early as the nineteenth century Brazilian intellectuals were collecting *folheto* literature, just as their Northern and Eastern European counterparts were collecting folklore (Burke, 1978: chap. 1), and the early twentieth century modernists, in their search for *brasileiridade*, 'had a decided impact on the back-to-the-roots push known as regionalism in the North-East' (Slater, 1982: 38).[7] During the 1950s the *folheto* began to be adopted by the cultural institutions of the State, and not only in the Northeast, from museums and festivals to schools, and this has continued independently of political change right up to the present, involving even multinational corporations. Sophisticated artists and writers have adapted its forms and subject matter in their own work, and among the 'real' practitioners a number of individuals have achieved fame and, very occasionally, fortune in the modern world of mass media and cosmopolitan tastes. The ironies have reached the point where vendors in the markets of Recife and the hinterland of Pernamburo state told Candace Slater that they stock the work of urban middle-class authors in *folheto* style for the benefit of 'educated collectors who can be counted on to buy any story no matter how bad' (Slater, 1982: 52–3).

Thus the minor phenomenon of the use of *cordel* forms in the consciousness-raising pamphlets of *basismo* leads us back once again to the theme of the projection of the popular, and above all to its indissoluble

---

[7] See also the remarks about Mario de Andrade in the Introduction above.

and dialectic relationship with the erudite. The *basista* literature of biblical commentary, consciousness-raising, legal education and the like, distinct and (in a literary sense) impoverished as it might be, is not 'merely' the product of the middle classes but rather one arising from an interaction across boundaries drawn by social polarization. It forms part of a process in which the more educated, or simply more cosmopolitan, sectors, and the mass media, project onto the popular sectors versions and images which those sectors – or in this case their poets and singers – themselves refashion and later 'throw back' in an endless interplay whose subject matter is the very domination which cements and also destabilizes their coexistence.[8]

Organizations and institutions of *basista* Catholicism

We now turn to the institutional forms, habits and contexts in which *basismo* arises 'at the grass roots', and we will be moving away from the realm of the written to that of the spoken word, and also to the practice of activism and militancy, as we proceed from the account of organization at the grass roots to the language and terminology which mark out *basista* discourse, and to the issues of religious practice which *basismo* raises for its followers.

The unstructured character of the Catholic *basista* movement in Salvador – in contrast with São Paulo, Santiago or the Rio suburb of Duque de Caxias which were described earlier – means that it is not feasible to draw up lists of organizations or parishes which participate in it, because there is no 'membership' and, above all, there is no formal boundary delimiting it. This is evidenced quite clearly in the simple observation that when I came to Salvador in 1991 the term 'base community' had fallen into disuse, if indeed it had ever been in much use at all. To seek out the base communities for which Brazil had become so famous abroad was to look for a non-existent institution; but of course there were priests and others working 'in that line': an Italian parish priest in the industrial centre of Camaçari; Brazilian priests in peripheral neighbourhoods of Salvador; an independent Protestant theological college (*Instituto Teológico da Bahia* – ITEBA) which was the only place in Salvador where liberation theology was taught, mostly by Catholics, and especially by ex-priests; ISPAC (*Instituto de Serviço para una Ação*

---

[8] In this connection the notion of authenticity itself, of course, loses its anchorage. Slater herself states that in using the word 'authenticity' she means 'community-oriented' – thus recognizing the problem but succeeding only in shifting it onto another plane. (1982: 53).

Comunitaria – Institute for the Support of Community Action) funded by the German Catholic organization Adveniat, for the training of grassroots activists; a priest in the vast suburban[9] working-class neighbourhood of Periperi who ran numerous schools and education centres in addition to other activities such as a herb garden for alternative medicaments and a vegetable marketing operation. Finally, the Jesuit priest in a different semi-suburban neighbourhood, São Jorge, who supported – but emphatically without taking a leadership or managerial role – numerous community and educational ventures as well as participatory forms of religious observance and leadership through 14 or 15 '*grupos*', including two *capoeira* groups with 300 members each. Apart from these local initiatives, a city-wide institutional mechanism which related members of the institutional Church – but not the hierarchy in any formal sense – to a network of local community organizations had been created in the form of the *Centro de Evangelização da Periferia* (Evangelization Centre for the Periphery of Salvador – i.e. the low-income suburban neighbourhoods), which produced pamphlet literature for the *movimento popular*, again funded from abroad. This last was sustained mostly by the efforts of European priests, missionaries and activists who were long established in Brazil, to the point where their foreign origin was almost irrelevant – except that their experience, erudition and European connections gave them access to sources of financial support for social projects.

These social projects are extremely varied, but whatever the manifest objective of a project or organization, their common underlying objective, over and above the manifest purpose of the projects themselves, is 'critical' reflection by participants in the light of biblical texts or religious rituals, on their lives, on the life of their communities, and especially on Brazilian reality. This type of reflection, with its constant reference from biblical texts or ritual occasions back to the social and political realities of daily life, and its discouragement of private or contemplative forms of religious devotion, is well described by the notion of a 'grounded spirituality' or, as we shall see, '*espiritualidade pelo chão*'. They cannot be described as a movement in any standard sociological sense because they are not linked together either by centralized leadership or even by a coordination of local leadership: the 'networking' feature prevails, as does the 'fellow-feeling' among participants and activists bound together by a common cause, a struggle, a *caminhada* (long and painful journey), an idea of community Church, and the like. These are not membership organizations, in which

---

[9] In Salvador the term '*suburbio*' was used to refer to a particular area around the bay opposite the Penha peninsula, and distinct from the term '*periferia*' more generally used to described outlying areas of large Brazilian cities.

people pay a fee or place their names on a list; they are not bureaucracies, since there is little formal authority apart from tiny secretariats – and even these often operate on a voluntary basis. They are even less institutionalized than the NGOs on which they may rely for funding, in part because they are issue-centred and project-centred, and one organization may give way to another as fashions change and projects reach completion, and in part simply because of the difficulty they experience in creating enduring leadership due to the emphasis on 'not imposing', on preventing any opacity from arising between the true desires of the people and their organized expression.

ISPAC, the Institute for the Support of Community Action, exemplifies the ways in which the *basista* message is diffused. Originally created in 1968 by the regional branch of the National Episcopal Conference, to offer university-level courses to Church personnel involved in religious education, by 1991 it was largely staffed by ex-priests and ex-religious, had changed its name, had become independent of the hierarchy, and now asked of its prospective students, most of whom were lay people, no academic qualifications, but only that they had two years' experience in *trabalho popular* (work with the popular movement).[10] Beyond the courses themselves, the ISPAC staff were involved in projects, and were linked to parishes, thus maintaining the relationship after the course is over.[11] The course content was described as centred on the role of human beings in historical transformations, in the light of biblical texts, with some emphasis given to the role of blacks and to women. Among former students I met women involved in organizing kindergartens, neighbourhood associations, and washerwomen's associations. Emerging from the course they were equipped with a language of resistance, a set of epic historical referents such as the history of the early Church, and a network of contacts.

These efforts interlink with others which take place at the level of the parish, and whose existence and success depend critically on the support and leading role of the parish priest. The priest may have few material resources at his disposal, but his power of initiative remains substantial as, presumably, does his power to prevent others taking initiatives. Despite

[10] Those attending sometimes obtained small grants for funds ISPAC had raised from Adveniat, and even from individual parishes in Germany.

[11] A member of the ISPAC staff gave me an illuminating account of a visit he made with a colleague to a partner parish in Germany, and the ensuing interplay of mistaken perceptions and expectations. The two visitors were housed with separate families so that they would learn German and not speak Portuguese all the time; they were asked not to wear sandals while celebrating Mass, and they had to explain that their visit was not to give an account of themselves, as they might to a sponsoring body.

the contestatory theses of some of its most noted spokespersons, *basista* Catholicism remains reliant on priests, and it is therefore not surprising that in the period of tenure of a Pope so hostile to this tendency, the movement has, by common consensus among the priests, religious and activists with whom I came into contact, lost the momentum it once had. Was it not now (in 1993) 15 years since a new priest had been incorporated into the work of the Centre for the Evangelization of the Periphery?

The idea of a 'project' is central to the life of these organizations: a kindergarten, a primary school, a *capōeira* academy where young people learn the stylized, dance-like enactment of a form of unarmed combat associated with the life of slaves on the plantation; employment-generating schemes often related to the sale of food in one form or another; a health project staffed by volunteer doctors and trained lay (always female) volunteers from the community. These activities invariably generate employment, though at negligible rates of pay, and when funding fails or terminates the employees may continue to work as volunteers. In the Periperi neighbourhood a parish priest was devoting his time to buying and selling vegetables in the (no doubt illusory) hope of 'cutting out the middlemen' and also running a herbal medicine project. In the Parish of São Jorge, an Italian doctor and lay worker, who seemed to have settled in Brazil to devote their lives to working with the poor, organized a health centre, trained the volunteers, and raised the funds to build it to a high standard of construction.

The explicit rationale for these projects is both developmental and educational. The young people working in what they called a 'community school' supported by Padre Clovis were at pains to emphasize that, despite precarious funding, the quality of the school met with the satisfaction of parents and staff. An unemployed volunteer student teacher contrasted the chaos reigning in the municipal primary schools – their state of terrible disrepair, the ever-present threat of strike action by underpaid staff – with the ethos of the parish school, to which parents preferred to send their children. Their approach to education was more 'critical' – 'we don't want to turn the children into robots' – and less competitive.

There is an implicit rationale also: the generation of employment for the activists, even at extremely low rates of pay, on occasion even below the official minimum wage. The observer may go one day to a meeting of health centre volunteers, and then meet the same faces the next day working in the office of the primary school next door. In circumstances where young people in low-income neighbourhoods had given up any prospect of employment, a job in a respectable organization linked to the

Church and funded from abroad at least offers social status and a leadership role in the popular movement.

The activists and primary school teachers were often university students who had interrupted their studies or were unemployed, while older, mostly female participants became involved in projects, like a health project, which gave them a role and a meagre intermittent wage. [12]

Apart from projects, the network encourages all sorts of self-managing activist and educational groups. The Jesuit priest in São Jorge, Padre Clovis, said that some 1,200 people were involved in activity groups in his parish: visiting the sick, prayer groups, the defence of human rights, education, health and so on. He also organizes retreats for young people, in the parish itself and at locations elsewhere: when I spoke to him he was working on St Ignatius's *Spiritual Exercises* in preparation for one of these retreats. [13]

These examples reveal a network of institutions which are forming community leaders who can accumulate positions of leadership within the world of the *movimento popular* on the basis of knowledge, connections, trust — among which connections with and the trust of international charities is particularly valuable. At the humblest level we find a lady who, having been Secretary of the *Pastoral da Juventude* (Youth Pastoral) in her parish (Periperi) for two years, then 'moved on' to become the leader of the neighbourhood association. We find Aluysio, the former Marian friar who, in a small working-class neighbourhood area ran a neighbourhood association, a little popcorn-selling project, a community school with 'well-paid' teachers, an adult literacy programme, a cultural centre with cooking facilities, a building, a *grupo de futebol*, a *capoeira* group, and a community cafeteria (*cantina comunitaria*). [14] Aluysio has the European connections which make all these ventures work. Padre Clovis, in contrast, who also has the connections, is, as has already been noted, very concerned not to hold on to the reins, and also to prevent the rise of figures concentrating power in their hands, in whom he sees the danger

[12] It is important to remember that those who are above the average income in a working-class suburb, especially after the economic shocks of the 1980s, are still far below the average income in a country like Brazil, so one should not rush to dismiss them as an elite, simply because they can read and write.

[13] The retreat was to take place on the island of Itaparica in the Bay facing Salvador, a place noted for its tourist attractions. I said to Padre Jorge that the young people would have a good time swimming between their spiritual exercises, but he replied, 'no swimming'.

[14] This does not mean he is formally in charge of all these ventures, but according to my informant, they all depend on him for their management and survival. Aluysio himself did not project a power-hungry image at all, and it would be wrong to interpret this list as a reflecting pursuit of power: rather a relaxed exercise of community influence.

of petty dictators.[15] Like another Church-trained activist, he sees the problem of leadership at the level of the base organizations themselves: *aquele lider carismático que não deixa as pessoas crescer* ('the type of charismatic leader who does not allow people to grow'). But then Padre Clovis has the security of his parish, and maybe he can afford to take such a relaxed view of his role.

The role of priests in *basista* organizations leads us back to José Comblin – the famous theologian of liberation – and his agonizing reappraisal of the Catholic Church's efforts in the field of popular mobilization, especially CEBs, in the Northeast (Comblin, 1990). He criticizes CEBs for their reliance on the representatives of a hierarchy which they should in principle be combatting, for their inward-looking, stagnant character, and for the defensiveness of their activists – secular and ordained – who hold back potential leaders from rising from the rank and file. These *animadores* and pastoral agents, in Comblin's analysis, take refuge in the security of their positions of hierarchical approval and superior education, and then exclude the rank and file from acquiring knowledge on the grounds that to do so would be 'bourgeois' or unnecessary, and that the people already know what is needed. This adds a new twist to the *basista* projection of popular culture, by claiming that such projection and idealization in fact enables those who proclaim it to exclude the people from ever rivalling their own learning. Thus Comblin adds yet another tier of projection, accusing the *basista* activists of being yet another elite, and then – as if to add insult to injury – turns aside to proclaim his jealous admiration for the Pentecostals, who are able to overcome these problems.[16] This may be a realistic assessment of his experience in Pernambuco, but the evidence offered here from Bahia shows first that such a judgement might be too hard at least if applied to Bahia – I have not heard of pastoral agents or activists in Bahia actively discouraging, yet alone excluding people from studying or acquiring knowledge from the erudite culture – but secondly

---

[15] The context of the discussion was the following story, which I discussed with Padre Clovis, as recounted to me by a man in a bar in the Sussuarana *favela*, who came from another neighbourhood, Tancredo Neves, previously known as Beirú. In Beirú the family Pereira used to exercise absolute power: they would rape your wife or your daughter, grab your watch, in short do as they pleased. Then one day a *criolinho* moved in and said 'I won't have any of this: I might just as well dress in a skirt if I am going to allow my women to be messed about like this.' So the *criolinho* organized the people, organized an association of some sort, had himself elected to the town council and overthrew the Pereiras. Now he has a nice house and although he does not steal you have to make an appointment to see him, there is a guard and a fine car in front of his house and so on. Conclusion: '*criolinho virou criolão*' (the little black man became a big black man). To which Clovis replied 'precisely – we don't want to allow the rise of the *criolão*'.

[16] Comblin's conclusion is that the Pentecostals practise the only authoritarianism the poor know and understand, namely the 'authoritarianism of love'.

also that it is necessary to keep in proportion the extent to which the activists really are an economically or politically privileged group.

Basismo is, nevertheless, a movement in which informal and unstated complicities play an important role. Its culture consists of a ready-made set of assumptions, unthinking reactions and linguistic usages which enable both outsiders and insiders to realize that they are in the presence of adepts of the movement. The data required to describe that culture are more likely to emerge from conversations than from interviews, from incidental remarks rather than from carefully formulated ones, and from turns of phrase rather than from sentences or propositions. In the following chapters I analyse the presence, absence and fields of association of what I regard, on the basis of experience, as key terms and turns of phrase which came to the surface during my conversations in Bahia.

5

Discourse

The conflict between individual and collectivity, and the conciliation of faith with real-life commitment

In late September 1991 I took part in an ACO seminar for activists from Bahia and from the neighbouring state of Sergipe. Such seminars form part of ACO's continuous educational, consciousness-raising and networking activity and, as a community leader said, they provide opportunities for participants to learn to speak in public, and to manage meetings – essential building blocks in a process of popular mobilization. This seminar was attended by 40 lay activists, of whom 23 were women, plus four priests (two of whom were French) in an advisory/leadership role. Some 40 per cent had secondary school education, and the rest had completed primary school. Many were unemployed or had a negligible income. The presence of a number of ISPAC graduates, and of course the common affiliation to ACO, which has some one hundred groups around the country, contributed to an atmosphere in which people felt at home with each other; indeed some of the time was spent discussing quite personal matters. [1] Another element of this atmosphere was the frequency with which the Workers' Party (PT) was mentioned, reflecting an implicit understanding among all participants that it was the only party whose aims coincided with, and indeed were conducive to, the achievement of the aims of ACO.

The proceedings were organized around the See-Judge-Act method, which fitted well the Cartesian proclivities of Bernardo, a French priest

[1] Thus one young person said she loved ACO like her son, like her family.

who struggled all day, not without some success, to impose intellectual coherence on the discussions. (At one point he expressed his disapproval of a colleague for his 'Brazilian' habit of 'mixing faith and life'!)[2] After an initial reading from the Bible, the seminar proceeded to study a section of the ACO book *Revisão da Vida* (see above) and subsequently divided into groups, each of which studied a biblical passage (again with the 'See-Judge-Act' method) and later returned to the plenary with their conclusions.

The tenor of the meeting was one of strenuous introspection, both personal and collective. The participants were constantly urging themselves and each other to think very hard about issues, to look into themselves, and to take risks by talking about themselves. The complacency of *comodismo* (self-satisfaction, or taking the line of least resistance) was denounced. Participants were called upon to think hard about oppressed groups in society, in particular the *lavadeiras*, the washerwomen. The Catholic left in Bahia had made much of the plight of these women and of the efforts expended by activists to organize them into a union, and to draw up with them a price list for their services. By mid-1991 the *lavadeiras* had become icons in local *basista* talk of suffering and exploitation.[3] Fr Bernardo spoke of the washerwomen representing the face of innocence and the unblemished concreteness of suffering, exemplifying the sense of awe often experienced by the observer/activist/ believer when contemplating the true face of suffering.

In stark contrast — as shall be amply demonstrated — to the Pentecostals, *basistas* are given to unease. If the relationship between themselves and the poor gave rise to an uneasiness expressed in the anxiety to get ever nearer to the pits of poverty, and a nagging sense that those pits are unreachable, so did the relationship between their secular or political concerns and their faith. In the words of Fr Bernardo: '*será que nos damos o tempo e o espaço suficiente para aprofundar a fe em função da luta?*' (do we give ourselves the necessary time and space to deepen our faith in the light of the struggle?). A lay participant affirmed, defensively perhaps,

---

[2] In the second plenary session when the discussion groups reported back I was designated as the *rapporteur* – that is to say I listened to the discussions and then wrote a summary of the proceedings on a blackboard. On taking the lead in the subsequent discussion Bernardo praised the '*capacidade de sintesis*' of the *rapporteur* and I reflected that at last a privileged British education had found favour in the eyes of a product of its *outre-Manche* equivalent. Fr Bernardo fell ill with cancer in 1992; he was taken to France but returned to Brazil when his condition was incurable, to die in his adopted homeland.

[3] This iconization has been seen elsewhere: in the south of the country in the mid-1980s a group of country people, victims of various struggles for land, set up a *campamento* (encampment) in Ponto Alto in the state of Rio Grande do Sul which became a place of pilgrimage for *basistas*.

that involvement (*militancia*) in the movement was a matter of commitment not to society but to Christ. Another talked of their 'social interventions – the 'act' phase of see-judge-act – as inspired by the 'acting' of Christ. (*Nos alimentamos o nosso agir com o agir de Jesús Cristo.*) An apt phrase synthesizing these opposing demands was '*a espiritualidade pelo chão*' – literally 'spirituality with your feet on the ground' or, in a phrase I have already used, 'grounded spirituality'. The critique of the separation between faith and daily life – but especially public, *collective* life – and a concern to hold the emotional and more personal, private aspects of religious life in check, was a constant theme, not only in the language used but in relation to quite pressing problems. Thus various women explained how involvement in the movement had wrecked their marriages,[4] but also expressed their satisfaction, even pride, at having chosen the movement and thus having not merely made a political choice, but also found a path towards self-realization. (The Pentecostal Churches likewise offer women in particular a strategy and even an opportunity for self-realization, though they definitely do not encourage separation or divorce.)

A parallel source of anxiety was the worry about the relationship between individual and collective motivations and even modes of thought. Fr Bernardo remarked that *Revisão de Vida* was undesirable when conducted outside a formal group framework – hinting at the importance of mechanisms of clerical or at least 'expert' control in Catholic lay groups. Referring to social and political conflicts, it was said that if people 'see' only through their own eyes ('*se a gente ficar só com o seu olhar*') their seeing does not produce results, but when they look through the eyes of the collectivity ('*mas quando ficar com o olhar coletivo*') then it produces results: '*a revisão de vida nao é completa se e feita a sós – a revisão em comunidade permite a confrontação*' (*Revisão de Vida* is never complete when one does it alone – conducted in community it permits confrontation). This referred to an analytical, not a physical, confrontation, though a painful one, in which people look through the eyes of their social class and also through the eyes of a Christian. And likewise, when people have personal conflicts – as they often do, especially with their husbands – as a result of their participation in the movement, these can be overcome if the *caminhada*, and the faith which appears as synonymous with it, is a shared one. This insistence on the collective dimension of this modern, lay and collectivist version of the

---

[4] cf. a reference to '*mulheres que chegam até a se separar pelo envolvimento na luta*' – women who go as far as to leave their husbands on account of their involvement in the struggle. But a woman from a very poor neighbourhood responded by describing such behaviour as an 'exaggeration'.

Spiritual Exercises is complemented by the idea of *caminhada*. A lay activist described *Revisão de Vida* as '*o caminhar junto, a fe junta, a revisão de vida em comunidade*' (moving ahead together, practising the faith together, practising the review of one's life in communion with others),[5] illustrating the multiple allusions contained in the ubiquitous word *caminhada*. As has already been noted, it is a reference to the wandering of the Children of Israel in the desert, but it also recalls that whereas the wandering in the desert had an objective – the Promised Land – in the modern context the *caminhada* is a long drawn-out, burdensome and troubled wandering in pursuit of an ill-defined goal. Fr Bernardo expressed this uncertainty in a sentence in which the shift from certainty to uncertainty was unmistakable: '*o Reino sera de justiça . . . mas também de participação e de plena comuniao – a gente nem sabe como vai ser*' (the Kingdom will be one of justice . . . but also of participation and full communion – we don't really know what it will be like). Others offered a straightforward conception of a Kingdom to be constructed collectively in this world anyhow: '*construir esse Reino – o problema tem que se resolver juntos em nosso meio,*' and, finally, the late Fr Tonucci, parish priest of the industrial town of Camaçari, and an active member of the ACO network, stated that if the Kingdom of God is a gift of God, it is also *construção da gente* – it is 'for us to build it'.[6] Thus, not infrequently, while the opposition of the individual and the collective is expressed clearly enough, in spiritual as well as political language, the division between 'this world' and 'the Kingdom' was played down.

The ACO meeting also revealed usages which underpinned the hopes of participants that their commitment would help them and their followers to achieve citizenship at a personal level. The word *gente* was used in the distinctively Latin American (Spanish and Portuguese) sense not just of persons, but of personhood, respectability, honour and integrity when people described how the movement might satisfy their aspirations, thus illustrating that the theologico-political reverence for poverty and the poor did not exhaust the motivations of activists.[7]

---

[5] Yvon Le Bot (1993) has written disparagingly of how the confession could be turned into a political and public self-criticism among the Guatemalan guerrillas, and it is not difficult to imagine that when the 'revision of life', derived from St Ignatius's *Spiritual Exercises*, becomes a group activity it could, if not properly managed, be destructive. However I heard nothing of such resulting tensions in Brazil.

[6] Such discussion can reach humourless extremes – as when people are warned against 'individualist distractions' during boring meetings (*se sair uma brincadeira muito individualista . . .*).

[7] cf. Adam Smith: 'Under necessities, therefore, I comprehend not only those things which nature, but those things which the established rules of decency have rendered necessary to the lowest rank of people' (*Wealth of Nations*, ed. Campbell and Skinner, p. 870).

A popular structuralism

Ever since Medellín, Latin American bishops and priests have had to deal with the idea of 'structural sin'. The inspiration of this has been twofold – a modernist attempt to escape from the guilt-ridden Catholic obsession with personal morality and in particular with sex, and a critique of personal, individualized charity as the Christian response to poverty. The emphasis on sin being embedded in the structures of society contains a critique of the established responses to poverty which have led Christians to patronize, even dehumanize, the poor, while simultaneously exalting their condition and making a virtue of their misery.

In *basista* discourse the traditional idealization of poverty has been replaced, almost subconsciously, by the complex, ambiguous, self-conscious almost uneasy idealization of 'the people'. *Basistas* do not want to forego the notion that the poor are the People of God, in the phrase consecrated by Vatican II, and are the bearers of a spiritual truth, in the tradition of Las Casas described above, yet at the same time they want to do away with poverty and the exploitation and injustice suffered by the poor. Hence the insistence on the structural character of poverty and the sinful nature of social structures.

The discourse of *basista* activists is therefore littered with phrases expressing a search for underlying – therefore structural – causes and remedies in implicit opposition to explanations in terms of human agency and remedies based on varieties of *assistencialismo*. Thus when problems of crime, violence or drug addiction are mentioned immediate reference is made to underlying causes. To quote the former Marian friar (*irmão marista*) Aluysio, prime mover as we have seen of all community activities and organizations in the *bairro* of Alagoados: '*o pessoal mais consciente procura as causas, as raizes . . . a realidade*' (people with the most awareness seek out the roots, the causes . . . the reality). He was speaking about crime, an issue which obviously attracts many comments of this sort, but the words used, almost exactly similar to those used by Fr Clovis in the context of a discussion of drugs, more than merely a desire to forgive the poor for their crimes, betray in the use of the word 'roots' a search for ever-deeper explanations. Likewise the use of the word *realidade* conveys the notion that by touching the reality, by living it, by drawing as close as possible to the everyday life of the other – the *povo* – those who are not of the people will, in a palpable sense, apprise themselves of their reality and of the true causes of social problems.

The idea is stated in slightly more everyday terms by Dona Luisa, a woman from the interior of Ceará who came to Salvador and made a living by selling household goods door to door. Eventually she became involved in the washerwomen's movement, and thus with the *basista* Church; in accordance with the pattern described in preceding pages, she followed the ISPAC course, is involved with ACO, and also writes songs. Of crime she says: '*a gente não faz uma coisa errada porque a gente quer . . .*' (people do not do wrong because they want to . . .) but because society forces them to. The message about analysing deep causes eventually has reached the activist working on an everyday basis with organizations at the neighbourhood level.

If the causal mechanisms underlying social problems are not located at the level of the individual, but arise from deep-seated structural problems in society, then measures designed merely to alleviate existing structures, or to help individuals, are unlikely to improve matters, and, by making the current situation slightly more tolerable, may even prolong the life of the unjust structures in the long run. It is an old argument against reformism, and *basista* discourse uses the word *assistencialismo* to define such measures as individually targeted and clientelistic, as well as non-participatory. In the words of a CEB activist in Recife in the 1980s, quoted by Mariz: 'Assistance is this: you make and give to the other, then they do not participate in anything. They just receive, they thank you and it is finished . . . It is not to do *for* the people that helps them to improve, but to do *with* the people' (1989:151 – emphasis added). In a conversation with me in 1991, a former nun aged 24, jobless and apparently somewhat depressed, described the Pentecostal Churches as *assistencialistas:* '*a pessoa vai porque de inmediato sabe que vai receber o que precisa*' (people go to them because they know they will immediately receive what they need). Immediate satisfaction is contrasted here with the long haul of popular organization, and with the deeper, and collective needs of the people – in particular their 'thirst for liberation' ('*sede de libertação*'). For Aracy, from whom we have already heard, ladling out soup to the poor is demeaning to the poor and reflects the cynicism of those who wish to fob them off or buy them off or merely salve their own consciences. In this world-view, there is little to distinguish well-intentioned charity from the activities of a self-seeking politician always trying to show, in the words of a neighbourhood leader similar in background to Dona Luisa, '*que é ele que faz, nao que é o esforço do povo, esforço comunitario conjunto*' (that the achievements are *his*, not that they come from the people's joint effort from the community as a whole). Yet that same leader still recognizes that to try to organize the people without 'offering something' is to invite failure (*quando a gente vai organizar o povo sempre tem que oferecer alguma coisa*). Dona Luisa, likewise, speaks approvingly of people's emotional reactions to an *agente* (religious or socio-religious activist) or priest but says that such an attitude should not dominate.

Consistent with a strong structuralist position, Padre Clovis, the parish priest of São Jorge, does not use his position to intercede with authorities 'in personal cases'. He visits people when they are sick, but does not regard it as his job to help solve their personal problems. Consistent with a strong *basista* position, he also says that people like himself must take care to prevent the rise of domineering leaders in base organizations, though sometimes such remarks could be interpreted as meaning, at least in practice, that no leadership at all should be allowed to develop. The Associação de Bairro (Neighbourhood Association) in Aluysio's neighbourhood takes this even further: their *pratica de grupo* (practice of working in groups) forbids them from having a president at all. In Aluysio's words, 'a structure should be at the service of man's liberation' (*uma estrutura é instrumento de libertação do homen*) so long as it is not misused — implying that since structures are prone to misuse, a temptation to our desire for power and wealth, it is better to do without them.[8] This distrust of leadership is the counterpart to the great importance attached by *basismo* to consciousness. It should not be forgotten that one of the original inspirations of the movement was Paulo Freire who, in his works on education published in the late 1960s and early 1970s propounded the concept of a 'critical consciousness' as opposed to the submissive consciousness which traditional education had encouraged (Lehmann, 1990:96–101) If there is no leadership, then the way forward to liberation would have to be based on the self-activation of the people driven by their own consciousness — that is, by an awareness of the true nature and causes of their oppression.

The critical consciousness

If leadership must be preserved at all costs from the taint of corruption by power, even at the cost of having no leadership at all, then the consciousness of the people must with even greater reason not be

---

[8] Others might add, though, that Aluysio, who is of course a member of the Association's Coordinating and Finance Committees, remains a very influential figure.

abandoned to a fate of permanent passivity. Education therefore is a pervasive feature of the *basista* movement: no project is complete without an educational component, and establishing a kindergarten or primary school is, as we have seen, a frequent option among community projects. In comparison to the official municipal provision, the teachers at the infants' school in São Jorge were proud of their own commitment and of the more orderly and friendly atmosphere of their school, but they also emphasized the content of their teaching: so as not to turn the children into 'robots', they tried to develop the children's *senso crítico* (critical awareness). This in turn required that schoolteachers be rooted in the same *realidade* (reality) as the children. A teacher complained that when they sought collaboration from the municipal educational authorities the latter would not contribute the money or materials which were so sorely lacking, preferring to contribute by sending in teachers from a 'different reality' (*outra realidade*), illustrating the disinterest, even hostility, of official educational authorities with respect to the development of the children's critical faculties.

In addition the teachers wish the children to develop cooperative rather than competitive personalities – they should not '*trabalhar a nivel de competição*' (literally 'work at the level of competition'): the classroom competition encouraged in official schools, by analogy with the competitiveness of a market economy, is not encouraged in community schools.

ACO itself is also in many ways an elaborate adult education exercise. The See-Judge-Act routine, under the guidance of experienced activists (*agentes pastorais* – 'pastoral agents') is not unlike group therapy and in describing it Dona Luisa uses an apt phrase to convey the pain of critical thinking: ACO, she says, teaches us to *avaliar* (evaluate), '*ahi da briga . . . mas aquela briga constructiva*' ('that really provokes fights . . . but a constructive type of fight'). Having become an activist to the point where most of her social life is involved with the movement in its various guises (the washerwomen, the neighbourhood association, ACO, visits from colleagues) and also earning something from one project or another, Dona Luisa is fully attuned: the movement has transformed her from a struggling migrant into a popular intellectual.

The insistence on a *senso crítico* leads us to ask how *basismo* then confronts popular culture, which does not contain this critical stance in any usual sense of the term; indeed Vainilda Paiva (1980) has shown that Freire's aim was to bring about a transformation in popular consciousness from traditional, irrational, submissive ways of thinking towards more modern, more rational and in that sense more 'critical' ways. In the early 1960s his was a modernizing project rather than a radicalizing one, in tune with the thought of mainstream modernizing (not Marxist, or even *marxisant*) nationalism.[9] This reminder, together with the descriptions above of the efforts of activists and teachers 'on the ground', illustrates the ambiguities and role confusions surrounding the relations between activists and 'thinkers' and between both of these and the 'people' among whom they find their following. *Basistas* look to popular culture for a tradition of resistance – a tradition which they themselves may have discovered or even invented. An example is the renaissance of *capóeira*: a stylized, dance-like version of unarmed combat[10] whose roots are said to lie in slave culture and in Africa. In São Jorge's Academia de Capóeira, a master supervises training by a wide variety of young people, significantly both black and white. He explains that *capóeira* acquired the name because it used to take place in a field secretly, away from the eyes of the slave-owners.[11] But then, the master continues, the slaves realized that the dance movements could also do harm and used it against their owners. In recent years, he said, *capóeira* was associated with crime and violence, but this is changing with the establishment of schools like his. The reaction of a young activist, who has a degree in social work, when I reported the conversation, was to pick out the way in which the master had presented *capóeira* in terms of race and marginality. He too was looking for the element of resistance in popular culture. Aluysio (the community leader and former Marian friar) had, in the same vein, described *candomblé*, the *religião do negro* (black religion) as *resistencia negra* (black resistance).

These are the views of intellectuals, albeit 'popular intellectuals' without a university education. It would be wrong to dismiss them as coming from people with no contact with the *base*; on the contrary these are people who make it their business to have regular, even daily contact. But others take a different view, namely that popular culture resists the politicization of religion by this type of activist, and that 'what the people

---

[9] Only after his exile and his contacts with international radical circles did Freire's use of the word 'critical' shift towards signifying hostility towards the established social structure (see Lehmann, 1990: 96–101).

[10] Lewis (192:xxiii) says that it is 'a martial art involving a complete system of self-defence, but it also has a dance-like, acrobatic movement style which, combined with the presence of music and song, makes the games into a kind of performance . . . .'.

[11] The origins of the term are mysterious, and debate about them itself affected by the search for legitimating origins and authenticity. Lewis has doubts about the derivation from the same word *capóeira* meaning 'secondary growth (usually grasses and shrubs) that appears after virgin forest has been cut down' (p. 42). This is the most popular version and is reflected in the master's interpretation quoted here, but conflicts with the historical evidence that *capóeira* dancing is an almost exclusively urban practice. So he prefers a derivation linked to the word *capão* (capon) and thus to cock-fighting. (p. 43).

want' is 'mysticism', emotion and the satisfaction of their spiritual needs. The next section examines how the political and the religious are experienced in relation to one another by people who take part in the *basista* movement.

A post-conciliar religious practice

In a conversation with several (middle-aged or older) women involved in the health project in the parish of São Jorge, I raised the issue of the theology of liberation (TL), in the context of changes in the Church in their lifetime. Their answers showed a surprising indifference to changes and disputes peculiar to the Latin American and Brazilian Church; in their experience the main changes in their lifetime had been those inspired by Vatican II − bringing the Church 'up to date' with modern times (*aggiornamento*) and devaluing the cult of the saints and associated forms of popular worship. Despite the enthusiastic adherence to TL of their priest and many of the young activists who worked with him, TL occupied a secondary place in their description of their own religious life and also in their description of Church life. If the activists thought that the undoubted collaboration and involvement they had elicited from the ranks of the church-going faithful − namely, women, and in particular older women − reflected enthusiasm for the TL message, they would be wrong. The women were not hostile to TL; rather they regarded it as an irrelevant ideological indulgence, laughing it off in one case as *esse grande socialismo* (just one big socialism).

The deep changes in the Church described by this group could be divided into three types: the devotional, the 'atmospheric' and the political. The *cassação* (literally the suppression of rights − the same word as that used when an individual is deprived of his or her political rights) of many saints by Pope Paul VI had a 'very strong impact' but was not resented: '*nos sabemos que nao devemos ser adeptos à idolatria*' (we know we must not practise idolatry) − idolatry being the adoration not only of images, but also of money and gold. Saints are nowadays to be seen as an example, not as intermediaries before God. The conclusion was stated as (I suspect) it had been learnt in a classroom by two women, the one as if echoing the other: 'The Bible says that we must not worship the saints (*adorar*) . . . rather that we should venerate them' − although some people had not accepted that, and one of those present admitted that she still prayed to Santo Antonio '*para que interceda para mim ante Jesús Cristo*' (to intercede for me before Jesus Christ), adding inimitably: *tem que arranjar um pistolão* (one has to arrange a connection).[12] To this a companion rejoined, as if bridging the gap between popular religion and post-conciliar orthodoxy, saying that *'Deus ouvia ela pela inocencia dela'* − (God will have heard her on account of her innocence).

The dialogue shows that these women have experienced a change in their devotional practices, but there is nothing in the conversation which goes beyond mainstream post-conciliar practice, such as the more conflictive practices reported from among some Central American revolutionary organizations where it is said that priests would use two rifles to construct a cross and officiate before it. Thus one of the most significant changes for them had been the opportunity to read the Bible, and also to understand Mass, now that it was said in the vernacular. When asked to date the changes they referred to Pope John XXIII, the Pope who summoned the Council − not to Medellín.

They also described a change in atmospherics − in their relationship with the priest and with the physical environment of the church itself, both previously forbidding and distant, now much more accessible: the abandonment of the custom whereby the priest said Mass with his back to the worshippers was specifically and significantly mentioned, as was the opportunity offered to lay people to *programar missa* − to organize and lead Mass. In short there is more openness, tolerance, informality and this is identified with *paroquias de comunidade*, the word used in Salvador to describe parishes where a *basista* style of leadership and participation prevails, in contrast to conventional parishes in middle-class areas.

'antigamente era uma coisa segura, fechada, limitada . . . a gente ficava sempre com resguardo, não tinha coragem de se aproximar de padre . . . agora tem facilidade de se encontrar, de entrar em cualquer congregação'

(Previously Church was a secure, closed and limited affair . . . people always regarded it with a certain amount of trepidation, they did not dare go up to the priest . . . now it is much easier for people to meet, and one can enter church during any service . . .)

These words then gave rise to the following reflections in the group:

'Eu dei expansão à fe que tinha adentro . . . eu tinha medo até para falar . . . não tinha educação'.

(I allowed the faith which was within me to express itself freely . . . before I had been afraid even to open my mouth . . . I had had no education.)

---

[12] *Pistolão* is the slang for an outside connection which obtains a person a job or other favour, usually in the government bureaucracy. Saint Anthony of Padua is Bahia's favourite saint, a follower of St Francis and much venerated for his preaching all over the Portuguese-speaking world.

The women remarked also on the informality of modern Church celebrations: people even attend services in shorts; and they welcomed this openness to the young, felt to be bringing renewal despite the outlandishness of some of their message.

Whereas this conversation betrayed no assimilation by the women of the combative themes of TL, they did express clear commitment to the collective, or communal, character of certain innovative practices – such as confession in community (*confissão comunitaria*),[13] or indeed their own health project – and of consciousness-raising activities in the parish more generally. In contrast, they described the 'old' style summarily and dismissively as *cada um individual* (everyone for himself, or on her own).

If these conversations do reflect a broader trend, then clearly religious practice has undergone change, less in the direction of politicization – as devotees or, alternatively, opponents, of TL might have expected or feared – than of a reorientation of its symbolic forms and referents. The reorientation shifts the focus of ceremonies and devotions away from the cult of the saints, shifts the focus of the 'atmospherics' away from the supernatural, and shifts the relationships with officiants away from an individual towards a communal relationship. It is clearly very different from the Charismatic Renewal, for example, but it is also very different from the way of being a Catholic which these people had known in their childhood. The next section asks whether this way of being a Catholic has not also eroded the boundary between religion and the secular domain.

Form and content in religious life

Not surprisingly, the young activists who have not lived through the original liturgical changes set in train by the Vatican Council develop their ideas differently, and although one could insist on differences in politicization, a more profound difference in the treatment of religious themes between them and the conversation just reported is that they are far more concerned with content and less with form, especially ritual form. Those who attend retreats under the guidance of Padre Clovis do not necessarily go to church or even express conventional Catholic belief. The phrase which encapsulates their concept of a religious life is *celebrar a vida, não a missa* – 'to celebrate life and not (just) Mass'. On three different

---

[13] Another activity which, if badly handled, could go wrong – and indeed I have heard the view expressed that this 'community confession' can degenerate into a Stalinist-style 'self-criticism'.

occasions I heard very similar phrases which had a common origin in the dissemination of liberation theology.

From Aluysio, the former *Irmao Marista* already quoted: '*a gente vive mais a fe da gente na vida* . . .' (we live our faith more in our daily life . . .). The clear implication was that it was more in daily life than by attending church services.

A young teacher in the community school of São Jorge, studying on a teacher training course: '*Não vou a missa mas no momento de celebrar a vida ahi eu acredito.*' (I do not attend Mass, but when it comes to celebrating life then I am a believer.)

The same teacher: *Eu acredito na liturgia, mas a liturgia que é ligada à vida.* (I believe in the liturgy, but in that liturgy which is related to life.)

The opposition *missa/vida* (the ritual of Mass *versus* the reality of life) is clear, and can be subsumed under a wider form/content dichotomy. It is linked to other oppositions: between quality and quantity, for example, when a person says that what counts is not the number of people attending a church service but the depth of their faith. It is linked to the policy of insisting that people proposing to go through a routine Church sacrament such as marriage, baptism of their children, confirmation (*crisma*), should take a course and last it out – which in the conditions of low-income neighbourhoods in Northeast Brazil is a demanding requirement. (In the São Jorge parish, the *crisma* course lasts a whole year: I was told that out of 20 who had started the course in 1990–1, only seven lasted to the end.) If religion is so insistently and exclusively about belief, then is it any longer religion? Conversely, if people follow a cause which is, by its leaders' own word, a religious cause, and do so out of solidarity or because they find in it fulfilment or an expression of a collective identity, who is to deny that it is religious?

Religious practice is ritual practice, and ritual depends on forms which are enacted and reenacted at times and in places which conform to certain consecrated criteria of appropriateness or, as it is more usually known, sanctity. Political involvement in religion as practised by *basismo* emphasizes substance and belief at the expense of ritual form, and therein may lie a weakness of the grassroots movement as a religious renewal in Latin American Catholicism.

The same person who downgrades attendance at Mass in favour of the 'mass' or the 'liturgy' of life itself will most likely advocate a metaphorical interpretation of biblical texts, as in Sobrino's interpretations of New Testament miracles described above. He or she will also hasten to shift from an individual to a collective register by a metaphorical device, as when a preacher (and ex-Franciscan) reminds his listeners that the illnesses which really count are not those they suffer in their bodies, but those of the neighbourhood – misery, crime, and so on. The common feature in these shifts and oppositions is in favour of the epic qualities of the biblical stories with which the people as a collectivity today might identify, at the expense of activities or interpretations in which the distance between the Bible – no longer epic and therefore no longer history – and the individual is abolished. It should once again be emphasized that the prominence given to the Exodus story, and to the Old Testament prophets by TL and *basismo* is something quite new in Catholic life. In this identification with the epic struggles of the Old Testament the *basistas* have much in common with the Pentecostals despite their many differences.

Though that similarity may be surprising, in the light of the very long term (20 centuries) it is less so. Has not even a liberal Churchman like Yves Congar written about the 'Protestantism' of a Church without hierarchy as advocated by Leonardo Boff (Lehmann, 1990:131)? Is the critique of the cult of the saints not a belated assimilation of the teachings of the Reformation? This way of relating to the religion's past, by abolishing the time distance and creating a direct relationship with the spirits of the dead is of course deeply rooted: Peter Brown some time ago explained the revolution in culture represented by the early Christians' removal of the location of dead bodies from beyond the confines of the city to tombs, which immediately became shrines, in the urban centre (Brown, 1981). The healing, possession and exorcism which surrounded the shrines were the (far from unintentional) prelude to personal dependence and patronage, and the patronage relationships extended to the saints, described by Gregory of Tours (538–94) as friends of the Lord (*amici domini*). Through all the meanderings and crises of Christianity and history, of conquest and the enmeshing of indigenous cultures, these elements survived in many of their essentials until the second half of the twentieth century, when Vatican II, reflecting and catalysing change, paved the way for an official post-conciliar Catholicism, of which *basismo* is a sub-product, perhaps merely a by-product.

In this post-conciliar Catholicism the Bible is among other things an epic and thus a source of identity. The text is historicized, made accessible as epic history, no longer a compilation of timeless morality tales to be interpreted by authorized persons. A second feature is the 'delisting' of saints, and the discouragement of the patronage relationship which their intercessionary role had sustained for so many centuries. A third feature is the propagation of the idea that the People of God play a role in history, and do so as a collectivity, in contrast with the idea that individuals, if they reach the proper state of virtuosity, can somehow re-enact the lives of the saints and heroes, or simply the beneficiaries, of Biblical miracles and other divine interventions.

Whether this post-conciliar Catholicism is now becoming the dominant tone of the Church and of Catholic culture is another matter. The descriptions at the beginning of this section indicated that there are powerful forces ranged against it, and it is possible that the Council will in retrospect be seen as a momentary deviation or as the birthplace of a respectable minority tendency. It might also come to be seen as a watershed after which theological reflection and religious practice, and similarly professional theology and the institutions of the Church, became separated by a permanent and almost unbridgeable gap.

In Brazil, these elements have combined with the tradition of Catholic Action, with liberation theology, and also with certain traits which are possibly peculiar to that country's cultural complex, to produce the mind-set described in the latter parts of this chapter. Those traits have to do with the relationship constructed in the imagination of the educated between themselves and the people – the construction of the other. The People of God emerge here as bearers of a virtuous and innocent religious culture of their own, and are invited to emulate the epic struggles of the Children of Israel. The following chapters on Pentecostalism will carry forward an analysis of this relationship between erudite or official culture and a projected culture of the people, and we shall see how the cultural change wrought by Pentecostalism can be interpreted in terms of a popular/erudite dialectic which seems to be peculiarly Brazilian, but may one day turn out to be a particular case of a much more widespread and pervasive phenomenon.

6

Conclusion

This account has analysed *basista* Catholicism from several different points of view: it has been situated in the modern history of movements inspired by the social doctrine of the Church; it has been contrasted with other Catholic movements of evangelization in Europe and Latin America following very different strategies and ideologies but achieving far greater success in terms of the numbers of their followers; its discourse has been analysed through the texts of the pamphlets it produces and through the words of activists in grassroots organizations and projects; the forms of its organization have been described for different places in Brazil and Latin America.

If the multiplicity of these perspectives distinguishes this study from others, it also has served to dispel a few widely held misapprehensions. For example we have seen that although in many, if not most, dioceses CEBs are far less institutionalized than is sometimes thought and are heavily dependent on the support from bishops and priests, where they are institutionalized CEBs are in effect a form of parish, since the extreme shortage of priests leaves a void in the proliferating suburbs of big cities to be filled by this innovative form of organization. That was not quite the intention but it is occasionally the outcome. The multiple perspectives have also served to highlight the small scale of *basismo* in Catholic culture as a whole despite the high profile of the conflicts pitting some of its most outspoken advocates against the Vatican and despite the influence it undoubtedly enjoys in secular circles such as the development community.

We have seen how the intellectual genealogy of *basismo* is more diverse than is usually thought: a distinction must be drawn between the activist tradition of Catholic Action and the more purely intellectual school of liberation theology, itself by now a tradition spawning divergent tendencies. Likewise, those who would point out the lack of mass adherence to *basismo*, criticizing it for its intellectual bias, should take note of what I have called the popular intelligentsia which has grown up in these grassroots organizations linked in to Catholic activism.

Returning to the framework set out in the Introduction, the distinctiveness of the account lies in the analysis of discourse and in particular of the ways in which the category 'the people', side by side with popular religion and culture, figures in that discourse. The word discourse is much abused, but, like other terms – 'fundamentalism', 'populism', 'peasant economies' – it has infiltrated our language to the point where it is both undefinable and indispensable. I have used it in a way that certainly does not conform to that spelt out by Michel Foucault's *L'ordre du discours* in which discourse is present in many spheres and forms, but always embodying the authoritative, a system of exclusion, whether linked to a criterion of good behaviour, of sanity, or of rationally established truth. Instead, I have used the term loosely to describe a collection of phrases which repeatedly appear in the language of individuals – perhaps indeed because of an authoritative, but now forgotten, origin – and are distinguished by metaphors or allusions which people of a certain sort will understand. Words such as *caminhada*, *realidade*, *vida*, or *olhar* (the 'approach', or 'looking through the eyes of . . .') as used by *basistas*, contain within them a 'charge' associated with particular commitments familiar in the network. Taken together these words and their fields of association amount to a renewal of the long-standing dialectic between the erudite and the popular within the fields of politics and religion and a resistance to the neo-liberal spirit of the times.

We have seen that, observed in the community or neighbourhood, in its projects and meetings, Catholic *basismo* is characterized by an inward-looking disposition, concerned with quality, not quantity, and unwilling to compete with the Pentecostals head-on in their (literally) wholesale methods of gaining converts. Yet observed from above, and as part of an infinitely broader *basista* movement, we can see that the extent of its influence is out of proportion to its quantitative weight, and is much greater in the official and non-governmental development community, in international Catholic networks involved in social support of various kinds, and even in the social interventions sponsored by governments to palliate the effects of structural adjustment policies. To be sure, this last is the 'tepid' version of the message, and also the 'elite' end of policy-making where its influence is more visible than it is at the grassroots, but taken together we see that the language of participation and citizenship has now penetrated a wide variety of political and institutional contexts and has thus acquired a legitimacy which may inhibit, in the future, a repetition of some of the more egregiously authoritarian political and developmental episodes which Latin America has witnessed during the post-war period. It remains, nevertheless, ironic, that the observable impact of this discourse of popular participation and activation is at the apex of decision-making, while among the poor themselves its impact, though real, is restricted to small pressure groups and institutional niches.

Basismo is a language of opposition to the grandiose and oppressive, to inhumanities of scale. Today, however, the threat to livelihoods comes less from the exaggerated dreams and pharaonic projects of development planners, now reined in by fiscal austerity, than from the unchecked interstitial dynamic of markets and the abuse of market power in the guise of structural adjustment and policy reform. In the next Part I we shall describe in some detail the wave of Pentecostalism which seems so eerily appropriate to the new circumstances.

PART TWO

Pentecostals

7

The Organizational Dimension of Pentecostalism and Neo-Pentecostalism

Managing growth and marketing

It is clear from the semi-reliable numbers extracted from censuses, as well as from the visual and aural evidence of both marginal or peripheral urban neighbourhoods and remote villages in most of Latin America, that the following of the Pentecostal Churches is growing vertiginously. The fastest-growing especially have achieved this despite – or because of – a message often described as politically conservative, socially individualistic, and very pro-North American. Their religious practice seems to be a 'throw-back' to superstition, with its emphasis on healing and exorcism, and to the days when the Catholic Church lived off the tithes of the poor: their use of high-pressure tactics to persuade their followers to make financial contributions is described even by 'people in the street' as a shameless 'exploitation of the people' for the personal gain of their leaders and pastors. Unlike *basismo*, which painfully inches its way towards communication with popular culture, these Churches seem to have no problem in speaking the language of the people, even while simultaneously denouncing almost every facet of the cultures which over centuries of syncretic Catholicism have shaped the identity of the people and made their history present in their daily lives. All this while making what appears to be undiscriminating use of the same techniques as those applied in the same cause in the most diverse cultures and societies right across the globe. The following pages will refine this stark and counter-intuitive picture and will attempt to clarify the many questions it raises.

The first nuance distinguishes among the different Pentecostal Churches, and more generally among Protestant Churches, according to the duration of their existence, the degree of institutionalization of their organization, the prominence of healing and exorcism among their practices – in short, their more or less intensely charismatic character. A well-established literature, beginning with Troeltsch, distinguished between 'sect' and 'denomination' and described the process whereby the one gradually evolves into the other, but came under sustained criticism in the 1960s, especially from Bryan Wilson (1961). Nevertheless, it proved neat and therefore resilient, and found its way into the parlance of the actors themselves. But as we shall see, the latter part of the twentieth century has seen the rise of what might be called neo-Pentecostalism, a new version of Pentecostal sectarianism, and although many of the organizations which could be thus labelled may one day become institutionalized denominations indistinguishable from their predecessors, their many distinctive and novel features strain the boundaries of the category 'sect' in its usual sense. Compared with senior, more established (but still Pentecostal) Churches, the newer ones have more personalistic power structures, use more intense and more public pressures to persuade their followers to make donations, and are less tolerant of outside observers. In this section the contrast between the Assemblies of God and the much younger Universal Church of the Kingdom of God will provide a framework of analysis, based on information from secondary sources and primary research referring to the Northeast of Brazil and to its two principal cities – Recife in the state of Pernambuco and Salvador.

The Pentecostal, or *evangélico* churches as they are usually known in Latin America, are innumerable, especially if local independent chapels and prayer groups are counted individually. Even the large-scale national or regional Churches are counted in their tens, ranging from highly centralized organizations to loose federations. In Brazil the largest are the Assemblies of God, followed, in no particular order, by the *Igreja Quadrangular* (Four-Square Gospel Church), *Brasil para Cristo* (Brazil for Christ), *Casa da Benção* (House of Blessing), the *Congregação Cristã* (Christian Congregation), the *Igreja Universal do Reino de Deus* (Universal Church of the Kingdom of God), *Deus é Amor* (God is Love) and so on. The two Churches which I shall refer to most frequently are the Assemblies of God and the Universal Church of the Kingdom of God. The Assemblies originate in the now legendary efforts of two Swedish Baptists who came to Brazil from Chicago in 1911. They were not the founders of Brazilian Pentecostalism but they founded what became by far the largest Pentecostal body in the country and they were the founders of Pentecostalism in the North and Northeast of the country, whereas the earlier *Congregação Cristã* was founded by Italian immigrants (also from the United States) in the

South, which at that time was not yet even connected to the Northeast by road or air. Despite the shared name, and a shared theological and ideological genealogy, the Assemblies should not be thought of as a transplant of the North American Assemblies of God: they are a completely independent organization, and within Brazil the various State Conventions (*Convenções Estaduais*) which govern the Assemblies themselves operate almost as independent entities. The Assemblies' success in growing to be Brazil's largest Protestant Church owes much to their independence and lack of reliance on foreign missionaries (Pepper, 1991).

The Assemblies account for 63 per cent of Protestants in Brazil (Pepper, 1991: 132), and the North and Northeast are their strongholds.[1] In Recife, once the dominant economic and political centre of the Northeast, but now overtaken, at least demographically, by Salvador, the number of full members of the Assemblies rose from 1,000 to 34,000 between 1940 and 1975, and three-quarters of this was new recruitment, as distinct from transfers of membership from other congregations outside the city (Hoffnagel, 1978), while Pepper provides a figure of 18,000 in 1968, which would imply a very rapid growth in the subsequent six years, and also shows how vague these numbers really are. According to Vasconcelos (1986) they had grown to 60,000 and 166 churches by 1986, and 500 in the state of Pernambuco as a whole. In addition to problems of validity, these numbers also pose serious difficulties of statistical interpretation: there are large numbers of departures, some on account of migration, some on account of death, and some on account of expulsion – though many, if not most, of those expelled will subsequently return to the fold ('reconciled' is the term used). We shall return to the degrees of belonging.

The Assemblies have a nationwide presence, but it is the state-level structure which dominates. The *Pastor-Presidente* who presides over a State Convention of the Assemblies, can occupy the position not only for years, but for decades: the last President in Bahia held office for 25 years, and in 1991 in the state of Rio Grande Do Norte the incumbent had beeen in office for 40 years. In Hoffnagel's account the *Pastor-Presidente* in Recife

[1] The numbers game is endless: Freston (1994) quotes the 1980 Demographic Census as giving 8.9 million Protestants in Brazil as a whole, and the National Sample Survey (PNAD) of 1988 as raising their share from the 6.6 per cent of the Census to 10.8 per cent. His regional data are present in percentage terms which hide the absolute numbers, but all the sources coincide in a rising rate of growth throughout this century of Protestants, above all of evangelical and Pentecostal churches. Freston produces evidence based on censuses showing this rate rising from a 10-year rate of 25 per cent in 1890–1910 to 64 per cent in 1970–80, and even further in the 1990s. The increase in the *rate*, not just the absolute figures, is striking and probably correct.

and its state Pernambuco is the object almost of a cult of personality: the faithful keep his photograph in their houses, send him birthday presents, turn out *en masse* to welcome him at the airport (Hoffnagel, 1978: chapter IV), and quote his words in tones of awesome respect.

Since the Convention's members are all drawn from the ministry, although they formally represent different towns or localities, they form first and foremost a body of pastors. The *Pastor-Presidente* is therefore above all the head of a religious hierarchy and, at least in Bahia, a Vice-President is responsible for administrative and financial matters. Like politicians, their offices attract a constant flow of petitioners. The number of fully qualified pastors in a state is small, for many stages and tests must be passed before acceding to that rank. According to Hoffnagel (ibid.), in 1975, the state of Pernambuco had 13 pastors, 27 'evangelists' and 65 'presbyters', which would appear derisory for its 34,000 members in Recife alone until it is realized that there are further categories of deacons (77), auxiliaries (250) and simple 'helpers' (*cooperadores*). In the years after Hoffnagel did her research some of these numbers grew rapidly. Vasconcelos (1986) writes of 16 pastors and evangelists in Recife alone, plus 110 presbyters and 300 deacons chosen by their 'local' churches.[2] Differences between the two accounts are evidence of the fuzziness of the information received by outsiders. In Bahia, likewise, titles begin at *auxiliar*, rising through *diácono* (deacon), *presbítero* (presbyter) and *evangelista* (evangelist), to full pastor status. Similar titles, as we shall see, are used in the Universal Church (and no doubt others). The apparently elaborate formality of these categories must be balanced by the strong evidence of the personal exercise of power in these organizations.

To rise above the 'lowest' level a man (and it always is a man, even though 63 per cent of the members of the Church in Recife were women) must be married and live with his wife. He becomes *separado e congregado*, 'picked out' or 'chosen', yet he is unlikely to become a paid employee (Hoffnagel, 1978). Only eight of the members of the ministry in Recife were salaried in 1975. However, the Assemblies do have a sizeable administration staffed by paid employees, many of whom, to judge from what I observed in Bahia, are also members of the ministry.

If this apparently hierarchical structure has little of the participatory content often attributed to Pentecostalism, that is due to the radical and carefully managed separation between those gifts defined as spiritual and

---

[2] The phrase 'local' almost certainly still refers to a *matrix* rather than to a 'rank and file' *congregação*; the *matriz* is the seat of the Assemblies in an area – for example one *matriz* is in charge of the whole of Recife or Salvador and administers all matters concerning personnel, finance, membership, and so on.

the training offered by the Church. A 'call' (*chamada*) to 'accept Jesus', like the milestone of 'spiritual baptism' could happen, in theory, to anyone anywhere. In practice it happens only under certain ritual conventions – though it cannot be said to be, precisely, programmed. The acceptance of Jesus is signified by a gesture; a person feels moved to raise a hand or to step forward and kneel at the front of the congregation, and thus exhibits a preliminary adherence to the Church, which may, or may not, be followed up by further involvement. 'Spiritual baptism' is an event of more profound significance, which, to be recognized, must be properly witnessed: it is signalled by speaking in tongues (glossolalia) and is evidence of 'conscious experienced power'. Some people pray for spiritual baptism, or baptism by fire, for years (42 years in one case cited by Hoffnagel) while others may have received it before even joining the Church. It only ever happens once, but it confers the 'nine charismatic gifts of the Spirit' for ever.

Such spiritual status does not necessarily lead to a position of administrative responsibility in the Church. The positions, all filled by appointment, not election, can be divided into those of purely local character, confined to the administration of a particular congregation (for example in Bahia as superintendent or vice-superintendent), and those with a wider responsibility conferred by the *matriz*, or 'mother Church' which retains authority over pastoral appointments, the issuing of official membership cards, finance, building projects, and much else besides.[3] The preachers and teachers who lead services and study sessions are often sent to local congregations by the *matriz* and perform anonymously: the congregation does not develop close ties with them and may not even know in advance who they are. Although this is an indication of the centralization of control over the management of the Assemblies we shall see that the centralization seems to be less than in some other, younger, organizations.

Hoffnagel also describes the care which is taken in the recruitment and training of members: young people are organized in groups and encouraged to speak in public, to sing in choirs, to recite poetry, to organize elaborate festivities, and to go out on recruitment campaigns. Likewise in Salvador in 1991, the *Grupos da Mocidade* (youth groups) were organized into activities such as drama and choir singing, the latter to a

---

[3] In 1975 the city of Recife had a single *matriz* for a population of two million and a membership of 34,000; in Salvador in 1991, the *matriz* served 143 churches, some 20,000–23,000 baptized members, and a further 7,000–10,000 *congregados*, that is, members as yet unbaptized. In Belem, further north on the mouth of the Amazon, 153 *Casas de Oração* (as they call congregations there) served 40,000 members. The Four-Square Church had 90 churches in Bahia, and a national membership of 600,000 not including 200,000 people who attend but are not members.

high standard in the *matriz*. The activities in turn are divided by age and sex categories, the young, the old, women, men, each having their own choirs and so on.

The Universal Church is a much younger organization, more brazen, more of an affront to the established ways of being Christian, even in Brazil. There are few written accounts of its short history, and what follows is drawn from a lengthy interview with Pastor Rodrigues, who in 1991 headed its operation in all eight Northeastern states as well as Amazonas and Pará. The Pastor, a man of 33, divides his time between a myriad of tasks: he leads services, attending to long lines of faithful asking for counselling both before and after; he is the Executive Director of a radio station – Radio Bahia (owned by the Church); he manages the financial affairs and business transactions of the Church very closely; and keeps a close eye on all personnel matters.[4]

Rodrigues told how his Church's leader Edir Macedo started out in the early 1970s as an activist in an elite (or at least middle-class) evangelical Church in Rio – the *Igreja da Nova Vida* – but entered into conflict with the Church's leader, Pastor McAlister, when he and a group of like-minded members wanted to take the message to the *morros* (literally 'hillsides').[5] The mixture did not work: 'If you fill a rich man's Church with poor people the rich walk out' (*se encher uma Igreja de rico de pobre o rico sai*). Thereafter they joined the *Casa da Benção* Church, in which two of their number were ordained, though again they separated (apparently amicably) to pursue their own project, mostly in the street, as the *Cruzada do Caminho Eterno* (Crusade of the Eternal Way) in 'about 1975 or 1976'. The account then mentions two points: the realization that once converted, people needed *acompanhamento*, (literally, 'accompaniment', more properly 'guidance'); and the gradual emergence of Macedo from the obscurity of being one among many, to a position of authority in another breakaway Church (this time the Universal Church) based on his burgeoning success as a preacher. It seems that eventually Macedo himself was also ordained by pastors from the *Casa da Benção* and in 1975 he established the *Igreja Universal do Reino de Deus*.

---

[4] During our interview he was advising a distant colleague by telephone on how to avoid tax by conducting a financial transaction in a certain way and on what sort of transmitting equipment to buy for his radio station; he signed a cheque for US$ 17,000 in payment for a church he was taking over, and conducted various other real estate transactions. All this with a keen eye for legal and financial detail worthy of a dynamic business executive.

[5] A generic term used for the poor neighbourhoods of Rio, referring to the hillsides where *favelas* were first built. A BBC documentary broadcast in 1992 on the subject of Brazilian religion, in which Pastor McAlister figured quite prominently, gave intuitive confirmation to this account of the social base of his Church.

This is not a history, of course, more a myth of origin – just as the Assemblies' history starting with the Swedish missionaries and their visions (Pepper, 1991) is a myth of origin – whose status as legend is underpinned by interspersed biblical references: Macedo is compared to David, the youngest who was chosen; ordination – termed 'consecration' by Rodrigues – is illustrated by a reference to the blessing of Isaac by his father Abraham, and another to the New Testament: 'If two or three of you are agreed on earth ye shall be tied in heaven'.[6] It also tells us how the culture of Pentecostalism accomodates driving ambition such as is evident behind Macedo's successive breakaways and his subsequent meteoric career. The Evangelical Churches are portrayed as a single movement in which ordination is, so to speak, transferable, and a pastor's departure to form a rival establishment is not a sign of fundamental disagreement, as it would be in Catholicism, and as it was in the intricate disputes among American sects in the early twentieth century (Anderson, 1979).

Continuing the entrepreneurial analogy, Pastor Rodrigues describes the Rio neighbourhood where the Church started operating as 'Social Class C'. In 1991, 16 years after its founding, it had an elaborate nationwide organization which in the state of Bahia alone involved more than 10,000 unpaid volunteer workers plus a small corps of some 135 paid pastors, co-pastors and assistant pastors. This structure was responsible for an aggressive and continuous conversion campaign and for sustaining some 100 churches – area organizations which contain various meeting places – which continuously spawn 'nuclei' (based in a private house) and 'campaigns' – defined once again with the help of an entrepreneurial analogy as a group well enough established to meet in rented premises.

The organization's personnel are classified in a hierarchy, though since they are mostly unpaid (and probably contribute to the Church substantially more than rank-and-file members of similar economic means) they are not a hierarchy in the standard ecclesiastical sense. The nearest parallel is the Leninist model of a political party built on democratic-centralist lines: a core of full-time cadres form the spinal cord; a large number of full members of the organization, equivalent to the 10,000 unpaid workers in Bahia mentioned above. Beyond these there is a penumbra of sympathizers who attend services regularly, and 'fellow-travellers' who attend occasionally, said in Portuguese to *frequentar* the church. Continuous contact with the 'rank and file' members is maintained by *obreiros*

[6] The reference is to Matthew 18:19: 'if two of you agree on earth about any request you have to make, that request will be granted by my heavenly Father. For where two or three have met together in my name I am there among them'. It is not a passage which has any direct reference to ordination.

and the *presbíteros*, while *missionarios* go out to proselytize, at the cutting edge with the unconverted masses, and *evangelistas* seem quite frequently to be the preachers officiating at the front of a prayer meeting. The *obreiros* are to be observed patrolling the prayer sessions, dressed in a uniform which for women (the majority) consists of a blue skirt and white striped blouse, while the male *obreiros* wear a cream short-sleeved shirt and black woven tie with grey trousers. Under the direction of a (male) *evangelista*, or other personage who is orchestrating the proceedings, they signal members of the congregation to stand up and sit down, console the depressed, and lay on hands to conduct instant exorcisms.[7]

Above all these unpaid ranks are the *diaconos*, who in Rodrigues' account have the job of organizing day-to-day Church life: communion, the church premises, discipline, choir practice, youth groups and hospital visiting. Still unpaid, the *diacono* appears to be a crucial figure between the fully-fledged, salaried *pastores* and the other grades.

There is in addition a parallel administrative structure of paid employees, many, if not all of whom, are also religious activists. The Church's operations, ranging from property and financial management, training, and construction to the production and distribution of church benches (which are absolutely uniform) require a substantial staff, but precise information on this administrative side is not available – either from the Universal Church or from the Assemblies. *Deus é Amor* is the most secretive of all: staff are evidently forbidden from answering questions on any subject, secular or spiritual, and members of congregations are equally unwilling to do so.

If the Universal Church really is as distinctive as its media image and political notoriety lead us to believe, its distinctiveness may lie more in this structure, in the method of organization for expansion, than in its beliefs and practices, many of which are little different from those observed in other neo-Pentecostal Churches such as *Deus é Amor*, or the *Brasil para Cristo* Church (Page, 1984), or even in other parts of the world such as Nigeria (Marshall, 1991). Pastor Caio Fabio d'Araujo, the President of the Brazilian Evangelical Association, which was formed in 1991 in part in response to the press focus on the eccentricities of the Universal Church, emphasized to me (in 1991) the distinctiveness of its organization in his description of Edir Macedo's close attention to the welfare of his staff: in the manner of a company sales force, he gathers his pastors in hotels with their wives for morale-raising meetings, and takes

---

[7] The *Deus é Amor* church uses a similar method, though in a more low-cost vein, in accordance with its lower-income following: instead of skirts, aprons; the men's suits, even their after-shave lotion, are cheaper.

them on tours to Europe and Israel. In Pastor Caio Fabio's view their material and even sexual needs are the subject of close concern on the part of their Church. The originality of the formula is further underlined when to the commercial character of this motivational system is added the Leninist mobilizational dimension: extreme secrecy with regard to internal authority structures and financial affairs, and a very heavy emphasis on proselytising.

These differences are particularly evident in the sphere of organizational method. Beyond that sphere, the differences between Pentecostal and neo-Pentecostal Churches – the second and third wave in Freston's parlance – are a matter more of degree than of kind. Pastor Caio Fabio explained that the Universal Church had not been willing to open up its books to the Brazilian Evangelical Association, and for that reason had not joined, but that is hardly likely to be the main reason for excluding them, or indeed for the lack of interest in joining this mainstream organization on the part of either the Universal Church or *Deus é Amor*. In other respects, for example the centralization and personalization of power, the Universal Church is by no means unique as Hoffnagel's account of the Assemblies in Recife and Freston's references to *Deus é Amor* show. The Universal Church's practice of somehow sharing the contributions of the faithful with its officers, employees or representatives or rewarding them for proselytising success, is standard practice in Pentecostalism – indeed it may allow its local representatives a narrower margin of managerial freedom than the Assemblies or the Four-Square Gospel Church. Thus the pastor of a chapel in a very poor *invasão* in Periperi was allowed to keep his congregation's contributions and spend them on building a chapel.[8] The glaring and self-consciously scandalous handling of the themes of the Devil and of financial contribution by the Universal Church and, less flamboyantly, by *Deus é Amor*, contrasts with the much more discrete style of the Assembly in this regard, but as we shall see fear of the Devil and belief in the powers of exorcism are equally a feature of the culture of the Assemblies. There are also differences among neo-Pentecostal

[8] According to Freston (1994), in the Universal Church all takings are passed on and preachers and pastors are paid from a central source. At a Northeastern convention of the Four-Square Church (*Igreja Quadrangular*, originally an American breakaway from the Assemblies of God but for many decades now an established Brazilian organization in its own right) I listened to a pastor's address which clearly implied the relationship between his well-being and that of his parishioners. In a membership drive in Recife a pastor of the Four-Square Church issued t-shirts inscribed with his name. Both spoke of leaving a comfortable situation in São Paulo, in prosperous congregations, to come to the more missionary territory of the Northeast. The leader of a small chapel of the Four-Square Church in the Liberdade area of Salvador told me how he was being funded to take seminary courses, with a view to ordination as a full pastor, with help from his congregation, and also how he had obtained bricks with which to build his chapel from a local politician.

churches: the obsessive prudishness and austerity of *Deus e Amor* is a slightly exaggerated version of the rules observed by *Assembleistas*, but stands in contrast to the more tolerant approach of the Universal Church.

The outsider, in short, can be misled by appearances both of difference and of similarity: the Assemblies and the Universal Church, and the many others which share a Pentecostal identity, form part of a single, though broad, movement in which different Churches share many doctrinal and organizational features, in which new Churches are constantly appearing (and almost as often disappearing) borrowing features and techniques from those already established, and indeed usually having no new features at all except the fact of a different leader. There are myriads of smaller ventures in cities, towns and neighbourhoods, started up by adventurers and preachers and entrepreneurs for myriad motives. For example, in a very new *invasão* (a piece of land seized, marked out and built on by illegal or semi-legal occupants) in the Periperi area of Salvador a man had started up a Church called the *Igreja do Pronto Socorro de Jesús* (literally 'Jesus's First Aid Church'), changed to '*Tenda dos Milagres*' (the 'Tabernacle of Miracles'), and then, in response to protests from the neighbours on account of the similarity of its name to the title of a popular *telenovela* (soap opera), changed it to simply *Igreja Pentecostal Unido* (United Pentecostal Church). In the same area a pastor told me that he had disaffiliated from a small nationwide Church because its headquarters were in Rio de Janeiro and had affiliated instead, together with his congregation, to a local Church, the *Igreja Monte Hermon*, simply because it was less inconvenient.[9] The founder and head of *Monte Hermon*, which has several affiliated congregations and pastors in Salvador, was, in his turn, affiliated to the National Baptist *Council*.[10] This affiliation embodies a stamp of approval, and a service relationship rather than one of authority, in which the member Church uses the liturgical and other material published by the national body, but remains an independent Church.

Individuals migrate between these Churches for all sorts of reasons, which often may tell us more about their convenience than about some dramatic gesture of separation or dissent. Thus Raimundo, an activist in evangelical causes, tells how he moved to the Universal Church from a small chapel called Philadelphia, affiliated to the 'Second' Baptist Church in Periperi

---

[9] By 'Church' affiliation is meant, in this context, allegiance to a superior pastor and acknowledgement of his authority, and also reliance on that pastor to legitimize what the satellite congregation is doing — yet at the same time the migrating pastor clearly retained his 'own' congregation.

[10] Which follows the *Baptista renovado*, or 'renewed Baptist' current and is not to be confused with the more 'historic', less charismatic National Baptist *Convention*.

(affiliated to yet another evangelical Baptist grouping) but later moved back again because Philadelphia was in trouble, with low membership and few resources. People may move to a new area and find it more convenient to join a congregation with a different affiliation from their previous one.

Likewise, new Churches are not necessarily or even usually frowned upon, nor are they thought of as schismatic in any but the weakest sense of the word, since they do not express doctrinal differences. Members of more established, more respectable Pentecostal Churches, like the Assemblies, or individuals like Pastor Caio Fabio of the Brazilian Evangelical Association, look upon their younger, more aggressively charismatic cousins with almost avuncular benevolence: they see them as taking over where they themselves have left off, or simply as having found the right marketing technique for a particular market 'niche'. Thus a senior religious educator in the Assemblies in Bahia explained that there are different 'levels' of message for different 'levels' of culture, education and income and that the 'sorts of people' who joined the Universal Church 'needed' more emphasis on exorcism on account of their cultural background. A pastor in the *matriz* of the Assembly in Belem (whose vast modern church can hold 8,000 people) spoke of the newer Churches as an 'awakening to the Bible' (*despertando para Biblia*) which had been hidden by the hierarchies of older Churches. He expressed some reservations concerning the Universal Church's excessive concern with the material side of things and said that Church could not offer salvation, but he also said that its miracles 'work' because people have faith, and he emphasized that the Universal Church, though different, was not in error.

Thus the widespread opinion that the Churches compete fiercely was not confirmed by my observations. Pentecostals speak of themselves collectively and inclusively as *cristãos* (Christians) but of the Catholics as just *católicos* – they do not acknowledge the Catholics as Christians. When pressed on this point, rank and file followers reply with the same incredulity as one might expect to a question asking whether whether Muslims are Christians – it is a matter of categories, without necessarily even a pejorative connotation and implying there is no exclusion because inclusion never arose in the first place. This may be merely a usage which has grown up, reflecting the complete lack of religious education among the mass of the people, who have never been taught that Catholicism is a Christian religion rather than a collective identity, or one of the many available apparatuses offering cures and marking the passage of life crises and the annual calendar; but the categorization may also reflect a conscious affirmation that Catholics are not Christians but pagans, just like the adepts of *umbanda* and *candomblé*.

Large-scale 'neo-Pentecostal' religious organizations do not suffer major breakaways and place a very strong emphasis on the solidity of their organization. They are for the most part modern charismatic organizations. At the apex religious and administrative authority is united in a single charismatic leader, but beneath him there is a separation of religious from administrative functions, which keep their administrative and financial dealings very secret, and which apply to the mobilization and control of the rank and file techniques similar to those of democratic centralism: pastors and other preachers are rotated or 'parachuted' as anonymous figures into congregations, and are not encouraged to develop close personal links with the following, so as to reduce the risk of schism or the growth of personal followings; there is a clear division between the functionaries of the organization – though these are not usually employees – and the rank and file.

The rotation principle operates at the nationwide level in the Universal Church, so that it would not be possible, under its present system, for an individual to hold office at the head of a state organization for decades as has been the case in the Assemblies. At the level of individual congregations the anonymity of the preacher is more pronounced than in the Assemblies: in the Universal Church the preacher is 'sent' from the main Church and could change from one week to the next, whereas in an Assembly congregation a local President or Superintendent (appointed by the *matriz*, or else elected consensually with the approval of the *matriz*) provides continuity and a contact point for transmitting local concerns (for example the need for funds to build a church). In the Universal Church all officiants are appointed from above and there is no independent organizational structure at the level of a congregation. But the contrast can be overdone: Hoffnagel (1978: 104) also alludes to the practice in the Assemblies of sending more or less anonymous preachers to local congregations and to the dominant position of the *matriz* in the Assemblies, for whom, formally, local congregations have no independent institutional existence.

The organizational difference between this sort of Pentecostalism and the highly participatory and communal organization often assumed to prevail in evangelical Churches hardly needs to be underlined, although again closer inspection reveals a distribution on an axis rather than a polarity of types. If emphasis on the construction and preservation of a large-scale organization is taken to be one defining feature of neo-Pentecostalism, then the Universal Church and *Deus é Amor* fall at one extreme, the little Bible groups and one-man shows at the other, and the Assemblies of God in between. The Assemblies clearly operate a large-scale organization and use increasingly sophisticated methods to manage it, but on the other hand, despite formal statements which tend to minimize the independence of local congregations, field evidence shows that they build their own chapels, encourage preachers to rise 'from below', and allow closer links between officiants and their faithful, whereas the Universal Church concentrates on larger churches in or near town squares whose officiants are quite anonymous.

According to Paul Freston (1993a), the Universal Church stands out among the neo-Pentecostals on account of its leader's shrewdness in applying modern rationality to organization, for example choosing professionals to staff the top reaches of the organization, in contrast to the 'familism' of David Miranda, the leader of *Deus é Amor* and the 'personalism' of Manoel de Mello, the founder of *Brasil para Cristo*. Other features which are particularly characteristic of, but by no means exclusive to neo-Pentecostalism are: (a) the absence of any electoral or consultative procedures, either between functionaries and the faithful, or between functionaries at different levels; (b) the monopoly of external relations and provision of information to outsiders, by named highly placed individuals; (c) the demarcation, already mentioned, between a core of 'cadres' and a mass of followers – whose loose, uninstitutionalized, identification with the organization would make any sort of established procedure for consultative decision-making, especially on appointments, impossible; (d) the discouraging of horizontal consultation between congregations; and (e) the promotion of a highly standardized discourse, not only for ritual and liturgy, which is central to any religious undertaking, but also for use in the everyday business of proselytization. These are organizational, rather than religious, features which respond to the particular requirements of a Church consisting largely of converts, and they stand at an extreme end of Pentecostal variation rather than constituting something qualitatively and definitely new; for these reasons it is possible that as Churches mature and as the routinization of charisma moves on to the agenda, neo-Pentecostalism will come increasingly to resemble the more established features of Pentecostalism worldwide, represented in Brazil and in the rest of Latin America principally by the Assemblies of God.

Education and training

There are numerous indications that the Pentecostal Churches place strong emphasis on training their personnel, both paid and unpaid. The similitude of styles of speaking, of rhetorical and theatrical devices as between different preachers; the uniformity of dress (which is indeed a uniform in the Universal Church and in *Deus é Amor*), the variety of training methods ranging from straightforward drilling to an education in theology and Bible Studies, all bear witness to this concern. The Assemblies of God and the Four-Square Church both cooperate with the 'historical' Protestant Churches (Methodist, Lutheran, Baptist) in maintaining, or recognizing, a seminary in the Northeast of the country (*Seminario Pentecostal do Nordeste*) in Recife. A young pastor I met who had started a chapel of the Four-Square Church in the Liberdade area of Salvador was following, and no doubt paying for, a correspondence course at this seminary, having previously done a basic training plus three and a half years in a boarding establishment from which he received a 'Minister's Diploma'. He hoped to go on to university eventually.

The Assemblies of God run primary and secondary level (*primeiro grau* and *segundo grau*) theology courses in Salvador, secondary school level evening classes in Recife, and three university-level theology courses in Brazil as a whole. For university level courses leading to *bacharelado* – a full university-level qualification – the students are sent to one of several other seminaries belonging to 'historic' Protestant Churches. In Recife in the late 1980s pastors who had had no formal training were 'going back to school' by doing evening courses (Vasconcelos, 1986). Subjects of study include some standard secular subjects (Portuguese, Geography, English – supported occasionally by a scholarship from the British Council) but consist mostly of religious subjects clearly designed as a pastoral training programme: the Christian family, the 'doctrine of sin', 'heresiology', Bible Studies, Hermeneutics, Doctrine of 'The Final Things' (eschatology), even Hebrew and Greek. In 1991 there were 67 students in the First Year at the Assemblies' seminary, and the Congregational Seminary had room for 60 boarders following officially recognized University courses (established by a Federal Decree-Law of 1969) with standard university-level entrance requirements. The Baptist Church also offers post-graduate courses to Masters and Doctoral level. It is unclear whether the Assemblies encourage, or even allow, their future preachers or pastors, to pursue these university-level courses. The Rector of the Congregational Seminary of Recife spoke of the Assemblies' 'missionaries' as ill-educated and anti-intellectual. These are paying institutions and most students appear to be supported by their congregations – which in practice means that they are paying out of the donations and tithes. But the level of fees quoted is not high, implying that the institutions are heavily subsidized by their respective Churches, at state or even national level.

The Head Pastor of the Universal Church in Bahia stated that his Church has 800 people in Brazil training to be pastors. In Bahia itself they have a seminary which runs parallel morning, afternoon and evening courses and receives students selected by pastors on the basis of their record. But like other Pentecostal Churches the Universal Church sends people to seminaries belonging to the historical Protestant churches for higher level training – for example to train as teachers in its own institutions. If this is occurring on a significant scale it is a forerunner of the institutionalization to come, as the control over the spiritual activities of the newer Churches becomes more professionalized and independent of the charismatic leader.[11]

Women and men in the organization

The occasion of the third anniversary celebration of the Youth Prayer Group in Nova Sussuarana illustrated how the Assemblies develop institutional and representational mechanisms of including people and incorporating them into the organization. Several young women, some representing virtues and others angels, ascended and descended a ladder in a variation on Jacob's dream in Genesis 28:12, while another sang her heart out into a microphone to the accompaniment of an electric guitar and drums. The singer's demeanour and the accompaniment were straight from the television, but the words were pure evangelical. A four-part choir, which regularly met for rehearsals, encouraged both sexes and different age-groups to enact harmonious and active participation. Elsewhere, women find a role as *obreiras*, as 'missionaries' and in choirs, and in the more established Churches, such as the Assemblies or the Four-Square Gospel Church the pastor's wife is a person of prestige who participates actively in her husband's ministry – like the vicar's wife in the old-style Church of England. But in the newer churches the pastors and preachers figure as men with no attachments save to the organization; if they are married that fact is immaterial to their role. Likewise the *obreiras* appear as single persons: dressed in their uniforms, they patrol the Church

[11] There are other sources of recruitment which may be extremely important but difficult to document except on the basis of media reports. The Assemblies and also the Universal Church make much of their work in prisons and, in the case of the Universal Church, with drug addicts, and in my experience their preachers make much of their dissolute past in the world of crime, drink and drugs. So it is quite possible that the Churches use their access to these total institutions – where proselytizing is reported to be enormously successful – to recruit not only members but also new cadres.

during services, expelling demons instantly and with an almost routine gesture, and officiating in a subordinate role to the preacher, who is invariably a man. The *obreiras* in the *Deus é Amor* Church wear a simple standard overall and their hair pinned tightly back; in the Universal Church missionaries and *obreiras* each wear different colours. Such uniforms are not found in the Assemblies or the Four-Square Gospel Church.

Although the newer Churches pay particular attention to providing an individualized role for women, it is without doubt a subordinate one: they do not rise within the organization, and if they perform publicly and symbolically they do so in a subordinate capacity to male officiants who are unlikely to be more educated or more skilled than they are.

When I raised this subject with qualified persons of the Assemblies and the Universal Church the replies were different, but revealed hardly any sensitivity at all, let alone defensiveness, on the question of women's equality. They certainly would give pause for thought to those who think that the exclusion of women from the priesthood is responsible for the Catholic Church's loss of hegemony!

A pastor of the Assemblies spoke as follows: '*Elas trabalham mas do que os homens . . . só que não tem a mesma liderança religiosa*' — they work (in the affairs of the Church) as hard as men do but they do not have the same religious leadership. This, he said, was an influence of Brazilian culture, not of doctrine – but then he went on to say: '*Deus deu a liderança ão homen*' (God gave the leading role to men), so a man must open the service even if he then passes the leading role to a woman.

Pastor Rodrigues of the Universal Church said that his Church had no rules against women pastors, though he had to make an effort even to recall one single case. If these words reflected a modest awareness of contemporary sensitivities, a 17-year-old female member of his Church indicated that this was an issue and one which had led the organization to produce a 'party line' on the subject:

> No, there are no women pastors; there used to be but they found that it is difficult for a woman who is married with children to be out a lot, late at night, early in the morning, preaching. When a woman marries a man she knows what to expect and can cope with his absences, but it does not work the other way round.

The overall picture is counter-intuitive. Like all Christian churches, the Pentecostals attract more women than men; like the official-minded factions of the Catholic Church they preach sexual modesty and prudishness, and, at least in Bahia, the Assemblies even forbid the use of artificial methods of birth control; like the Catholic Church the Pentecostals in effect exclude women from positions of authority. When compared with the practices characteristic of the *basista* movement, the Pentecostals are much more repressive of women, giving them far fewer responsible or decision-making roles, and interfering far, far more with their personal and sexual lives.

On the face of it, then, from a 'naive sociological' point of view, women would seem to have little reason to be more attracted to Pentecostal Churches than to the Catholic Church. So what is the distinctive 'product' that the Pentecostal Churches might be offering, if that is the right question to ask? It is certainly the right metaphor.

One theme is that of women as mothers, rather than as wives, let alone as job-seekers or professionals. The message of the Churches may be untroubled by the subordination of women to men – with repeated recourse to St Paul in support – and the obsessive concern of some Churches with sexual propriety doubtless enhances or legitimates female subordination in the public sphere, but at the same time the detailed attention paid to the family, especially the nuclear family, has the effect of enhancing women's self-image as mothers, since so many of them are alone as heads of their households.

Beyond the private sphere, we have already seen that pains are taken to open up roles for church members and followers of both sexes, and maybe particularly for women, who are prominent among *obreiros*, in choirs, in theatrical representations, in prayer groups, in proselytizing campaigns and so on. We shall also see later how when describing their conversion and the changes it has brought about in their lives, women use the language of empowerment, in relation not to society or politics, let alone the Church apparatus, but in relation to their families and their men. The women's lives are severely circumscribed, and they have few roles if any outside the house; the means of resistance or retaliation against extreme poverty and social disorganization – the lack of a regular income or regular employment, drugs, gang warfare and the routine violence which threatens their children – are not available to them. In this light, even if the attraction of the Churches lies only in the chance of 'being somebody' outside the narrow confines of the household, it is a powerful one. It would be surprising if women then embarked on protests against discrimination in Churches which they regard, literally, as having come to their rescue.

Conclusion

In opening the discussion of Pentecostal Churches by analysing their organizational methods, this chapter has revealed the stark contrast with *basismo*, has placed in doubt some commonly held views about their organization, and has shown how if there is a new wave of neo-Pentecostalism its novelty is as much in organization as in the beliefs it promotes or the rituals it practises. This organization is characterized by personalism and centralization and also by the use of modern methods of financial and personnel management and to training. The discussion of the place of women shows that the Churches seem to have lost little ground by ignoring a feminist agenda, emphasizing instead the maternal role which is of greater immediate perceived relevance to the self-image of women in the *favelas*, and concentrating on providing a role for them in the Church, outside the home, in the public sphere.

Is this merely an organizational weapon? This ability to create large-scale organizations staffed largely by enthusiastic unpaid followers, while at the same time remaining attuned and responsive to the immediate needs and desires of the poor stands in contrast with *basismo*'s emphasis on small scale and its gingerly veneration of popular culture. The ability to raise large amounts of money from followers and then to manage it stands in contrast to *basismo*'s financial dependence on international charities. The next chapter analyses the religious dimension so as to discover whether, apart from the organizational weapon, the Pentecostal Churches have developed an armoury of particular use to them in their bid to gain control of the battlefield of culture – and also so as to discover whether this language of competition, almost of war, is appropriate to an understanding of their success.

8

The Religious Dimension

Ritual and liturgy

Pentecostal churches can be noisy places when a service is in progress, or even when a study group is gathered: the preacher's voice, often amplified by a loudspeaker, becomes barely comprehensible as it reverberates about a low-ceilinged, bare-walled room. When the faithful join in, with their own imploring prayers and Hallelujahs, the noise can beat down on a person like a train approaching through a tunnel. The preacher is often accompanied by a small band, even a one-man band, and with the help of microphone, volume control, and *bateria* (percussion) deftly manages the intensity − or at least the loudness − of prayer. Sometimes the faithful sing or chant in unison, but at other times a cacophony rises as the congregation all shout their own prayers until the preacher reduces the volume and brings them back under his guidance, cutting off even the most intense enthusiasm at its peak, rather than allowing it to die away gradually.[1]

In old Churches and long-established religions ritual is an almost subconscious affair, learnt in childhood and sanctified by an aura of timelessness; it consists of 'nonrational or nonlogical symbols', which 'arise out of the basic individual and cultural assumptions, more often unconscious than not, from which most social action springs' (Warner, 1959, quoted in Turner, 1967: 108). In contrast, the faithful in Pentecostal services are often, even in their majority, converts who have not imbibed religious practices in their childhood, and so they await instruction from

---

[1] This is not as unfamiliar as might at first appear. The noise levels and the emotionalism can for example be compared with Chassidic and other forms of ultra-orthodox Judaism.

the preacher: 'say Hallelujah!', 'stand up!', 'stamp on the piece of paper which represents your sins!', 'say Amen!', and so on.

The preacher leads the service on his own initiative: if there is a liturgical sequence it is certainly not as precisely codified as that of the Catholic Mass or an Anglican service. Pereira (1993) offers a list of the main elements, but with little indication that they really constitute a liturgy as opposed to a set of elements which usually appear, but not in a fixed sequence. It is not written down at all in public form: there are innumerable Pentecostal publications, guides, books of advice and guidance, but no prayer book with which to follow the service. The preacher can threaten and implore; he will alternately turn to the congregation and berate them, then collapse on his knees and implore God to respond to his prayers or to forgive his misdeeds or those of his congregation. The changes of mood seem to be a matter for him alone. In Wilson Gomes' study of the Universal Church in Bahia, the section entitled '*O ministerio litúrgico*' contains an account not of liturgy proper, but rather of the role of the officiants, of the pastoral corps, as controllers of the members' or followers' relationships with the divine (Gomes, 1991). Authority is conferred not so much, if at all, by the command of esoteric knowledge or procedures, but by the Church; as Edir Macedo, the leader of the Universal Church, states in his book *Orixas, caboclos e guias*, this consists of an authority to expel devils; in other Churches it is expressed in a command of a repertoire of Biblical quotations, or in the power of oratory, but once again it is derived from the institution.

The Universal Church seems to invent ritual 'on-the-hop'. Wilson Gomes (1991: 51), writing of the 'large number of symbols appearing in rituals', says that 'in this connection creativity seems to be limitless, and may be the invention of the Universal Church's Bahia leadership as much as of local congregations.' He enumerates instances of the use of *galhos de arruda* (lucky charms) to sprinkle over the congregation during a weekly service devoted to health, while on another, similar occasion, they had to drink a mixture of water, salt and oil to 'purify themselves within'. Oil — often 'brought from Israel' — seems to be frequently used in a purifying ritual procedure. During an exorcism the congregation stood barefoot on sand sprinkled in front of the podium: this sand was meant to 'burn' and torture the devils possessing them — and at the end of the service was gathered up in handfuls so that during the week they could throw it at objects they wished to acquire. Once a bag of sand, an envelope for handing in one's tithe, a plastic bag of oil, has been sanctified through its incorporation in a ritual procedure it can be used in effect as a lucky charm, especially in pursuit of economic satisfaction. I observed people taking home 'water from the River Jordan' to purify their homes, or being told to 'burn their sins' in their homes and bring the ashes to church. Water, fire and oil are the recurrent elements in this symbolic repertoire, and biblical references, with their infinitely malleable interpretations, can be adduced to justify a practice where the collective memory is short and practises going back 'to time immemorial' are unavailable: thus gold-painted decorative containers arranged at the front of a church were explained by reference to the woman who was told 'you will never lack oil'.[2]

Although these rituals can hardly be said to be part of a system, the Universal Church seems to engage in systematic borrowing of ritual elements and procedures, gestures and symbols, from popular and official Catholicism, most notoriously from the possession cults (Boyer-Araujo, 1996b), but even from children's games (cf. Gomes, ibid.). That in itself is nothing strange: the ritual practices which religious systems have borrowed from each other since time immemorial eventually come to be thought of as unsullied expressions of their own theology and identity, and the importance of metaphorical and metonymic associations in the ritual process is well known. Although brought together by these Churches in unaccustomed contexts, the purity symbolized by water, the purification and anointment by heat, fire, or oil are as ancient as the Judaeo-Christian tradition itself.

Here we observe that 'early' moment when the organization, its theology and its identity are barely formed, and the charismatic founding leader is – very much – alive. The rituals have not become incorporated into the subconscious of the organization or into the religious culture; people are still being taken by the hand and instructed what to do, trying to get it right. So the organization reaches out for suitable elements with appropriate resonances in other religious organizations and in the culture more generally: palm oil as a purifying and anointing agent evokes Christianity as well as its use in offerings to the spirits of *candomblé*; a table or container at the front of the hall receives *pedidos de oração* (prayer requests) which recall the Catholic practice of petitioning of saints and of the Virgin. Some of these elements also appear in the *Deus é Amor* Church, and the Pentecostal communion, or *santa ceia* (literally 'holy banquet') which takes place on the first Sunday of each month is common to all

[2] Possibly a reference to the woman who sought advice from the prophet Elisha: her husband had died, and she was obliged to sell her two sons into slavery to pay off his debts. The Prophet told her to get as many jars as she could, and she miraculously filled them all with her one jar, using what remained to redeem her sons (2 Kings 4:1–7).

Pentecostal Churches. As if aware of the difficulties brought about by these echoes and interchanges, at a service in a small chapel of the Four-Square Church, the pastor took care to explain that (in implicit contrast with the doctrine of transubstantiation) the bread and 'wine' were 'purely symbolic' of the blood and body of Christ.

It would be difficult to imagine anything which better fits Lévi-Strauss's interpretation of ritual as fragmentation and repetition, and just as Lévi-Strauss states that ritual harks back to myth, that its words, gestures and object manipulations only have a meaning in relation to an 'implicit mythology' (1971:600), so here the rituals hark back to the Bible, and perhaps distantly to Yoruba mythology – of which more later. But the meaning of the ritual gestures and words exists only in the context of the Church's implicit authority over the individual and its monopoly of legitimate interpretation, while a function of the rituals as they affect everyday life is that of liminarity, not in Turner's (1967) sense of marking divisions in time between one stage of the life cycle and the next, but in the sense of marking divisions in social space: ritual marks out the social boundaries of the group and restructures the lives of its members and their relationship to the rest of society, thus consolidating their exclusivity and identity as a people apart. Repetition and regularity are translated into the rhythms of the day, the month, the year and the life-cycle, and the uniformity imposed on members' dress and sexual behaviour is translated into boundaries between themselves and the rest of society.

In seeking out ritual in the sense of a liturgical sequence we found an ill-defined collage of practices, but Pentecostal Churches do develop weekly and monthly sequences of services, as well as punctuating the year with anniversaries of all kinds, mostly related to the development of the Churches themselves. The Universal Church has a weekly sequence of *correntes* or circles, devoted variously and regularly to youth, to the family, to health, to young couples, to the expulsion of evil spirits (*libertação*) and so on, and tries to persuade people to commit themselves, as in the Catholic *novena*, to attending once a week for a period – say seven weeks – to fulfil an obligation, to achieve a goal or obtain a desired possession, or simply to make a commitment to their own salvation. The Assemblies do not offer the same instrumental rationale, but they too have regular study as well as prayer sessions and their practice of dressing 'in their Sunday best' for Sunday services operates as a marker of identity. Pereira (1993) insists, in his study of the Universal Church, on the importance of the monthly *santa ceia*, which, though a replica of the standard Catholic or Anglican communion ritual, does not have the same symbolic significance. In some churches participation in the *santa ceia* is a necessary condition for remaining a fully fledged member: in the *Deus é 'Amor* Church members must even show their tithe records to be up to date as a condition for taking part.[3]

Libertação – the collective expulsion of devils

The conversion experience is the vault-key from which all Pentecostal existence flows and towards which its entire meaning tends; it combines healing and the descent of the Holy Spirit with the expulsion of devils. The Devil is a ubiquitous presence in Pentecostal and in particular neo-Pentecostal doctrine and practice: *o maligno, o malo*, or simply *o diabo* appears in ritual, in preaching, in conversation, in the musical effects accompanying the celebration of a service. All three existing studies of the Universal Church (Gomes, 1991; Pereira, 1993; Freston, 1993a, 1993b) emphasize this point, though the broader literature (Wilson, 1961; Martin, 1990; Stoll, 1990) does not.

The Devil's presence is doctrinal, practical and ritual. Doctrinal because the Pentecostal and neo-Pentecostal Churches – the former more discretely, the latter more aggressively – proclaim the power of Jesus (through the intermediation of the Church) to liberate individuals from the powers of the Devil, and from possession by the Devil, as an article of faith; practical because the permanent presence or threat of the Devil in individuals' lives and indeed in their bodies puts them on their guard and leads them to seek release with the help of their Church; and ritual because, at least in the Universal Church, the *corrente da libertação* is a weekly service on the theme of expulsion of devils, taking place every Friday. The word *libertação* has a dual meaning: 'liberation' of individuals from the devils possessing them but also liberation of the evil spirit within the individual from the body which in some sense imprisons it.

Although the Assemblies, for their part, do not use the *corrente* format of theme-based weekly cycles, or give the Devil quite such prominence, there can be little doubt that the Devil forms part of an *Assembleista's* understanding of human relationships. When, at the start of a study session in the *favela* of Sussuarana, I was welcomed by an Assembly

---

[3] In its vast hangar-like São Paulo headquarters on a Sunday there are two services, one for those taking part in the *santa ceia*, and one for those not taking part. The long queue of elderly and evidently very poor people waiting to have their credentials examined is a telling illustration of the discipline prevailing in that organization.

preacher, he told the congregation specifically how good it was that I had come to Brazil to study 'the work of God' since most foreigners come to study 'the work of the Devil' – that is, *candomblé* and the like. In another impoverished *invasão* a woman preacher/activist of the Assemblies told me in detail of her dreams of the Devil: how he appeared on the radio, and on a park bench, and so on, and told her of his plans to dominate the world. On another occasion, in Belem, I questioned a more senior pastor at the *Assembleia*'s well appointed *matriz* on the subject, and he was quite circumspect – but he too told a story of an apparent *libertação* which he either did not dare or did not want to call by its name. Reference to the Devil, which can be quite casual in an impoverished *favela* on the periphery of a city, seems to sit uneasily with the social respectability of a flagship church, and the pastor may have been wary of talking too much about the Devil with a visitor to whom he wanted to present a face of respectability.

On a Friday in December 1993 I attended one of these *correntes* in the Universal Church's large building at Dos Leões in Salvador. It lasted about 90 minutes, and began with a song, after which the congregation were invited to crowd together at the front of the hall. The preacher began by telling us how Jesus wants to hear not about our complaints and problems, only about our faith, and then embarked on an account of the miracle of Jairus's daughter (Matthew 9:18–25, Mark 5:21–43, Luke 8:40–56), but with a difference: as Jesus told Jairus he was going to cure his daughter, the evil one – *o maligno* – came and told him she was dead already, but Jairus stood fast and Jesus raised her from the dead. This is the explosive entry point for the theme of the Devil. As he recounts the story the preacher throws questions at the audience. Using a device frequently observed in these churches, some of the answers are counter-intuitive,[4] evoking a silent response, while those that are not evoke a resounding 'YES!' or 'NO!', followed by 'Amen'. Often he demands that the congregation answer, crying '*Amén gente!*' (Say Amen!) and receiving the loud response '*Amén!*' We all join hands and close our eyes, following his instructions, and the attack on the Devil begins in earnest. It is littered with evocations of deities and spirits from *candomblé* like

---

[4] Pepper (1991: 266ff.) gives a fascinating account of the resemblance between this technique and that practised by the *cordel* poets in public, off-the-cuff competitions, 'baiting his hearers into adopting a defensive stance . . . A good preacher will enthrall his audience with his ability to play the role of devil's advocate, goading his hearers into responsiveness, testing the catechism of their faith' (p. 267). In this way she illustrates how 'pentecostalism has refrained from attempting to eradicate old speech patterns', resisting the replacement of street terminologies with what she calls 'Church-speak', and retaining 'unsanctified' speech forms in the service (p. 262).

Pomba-gira, and interspersed with references to social evils: vice, misery, unemployment, corruption, 'the crises of Brazil', inflation, violence. Particular emphasis is placed on the plight of women: abandoned, betrayed, beaten, overwhelmed. 'That other woman' is threateningly pictured: 'she is tempting your husband, she is burning now a red candle, now a yellow one, putting a spell on him'. All the while, the sound is turned up to a deafening volume and pitch, evoking images of hell; unknown to the congregation (or at least to me) a new preacher takes over, and the tension is sustained for perhaps 15 or 20 minutes. It becomes ever more intense, and the wait for 'those two words' ever more unbearable until eventually they are uttered: *'em nome de JESÚS'* (in the name of Jesus) − *'SAI!'* − (OUT!). Those are the very words used by Christianity since time immemorial to exorcise the devil − an exorcism which was standard practice in the medieval Church, was condemned by the Protestants for the most part (Thomas, 1973), and has now been brought back with a vengeance by putative successors of the Reformation.

The words produce a palpable physical and emotional release among the congregation. But all is not over yet. An *obreira* has spent 20 minutes attending to a woman in front of me, her shouting inaudible in the hubbub, blowing the Devil away; the woman is crying, she resists as the *obreira* presses down on her head and neck, fastens her arm behind her back as if to force her into submission. Eventually she submits, and returns to her seat, joining as if nothing had happened in the march-like songs which express the collective sense of release and relief.

Then comes the *ofertorio* − the call for donations, described with the same traditional Catholic term. Five *obreiros* stand in line at the front, ordered symmetrically by height and sex, some holding blue collection bags, and one holding a bowl of water in which we wash our hands after making our offerings. The singing goes on, people are told when to stand and sit, when to raise one hand, then the other, the left arm on the side of the heart, while the electronic keyboard guides us with happy rhythms as the congregation swing their hips and clap their hands, ending each stanza with *'Sai, sai, sai'* (out, out, out), those same words which a few minutes before had been yelled so discordantly, and are now sung merrily and harmoniously. There are smiles on faces, and finally we turn round and on the instructions of the preacher we *chutar* the Devil out of the door of the church, just as a footballer 'shoots' at goal.

The introduction of the Jairus story illustrates the use of the biblical text in this neo-Pentecostal context. The story appears in Matthew 9:18– 25, and Mark 5:21–43 and Luke 8:40–56, though in the Matthew version the name Jairus is not mentioned. In all three Gospels it is hidden away in a cascade of miracles which are, as always, themselves miracles of condensed story-telling. But the difference for the Universal Church is that this one tells of people laughing, and therein lies the opportunity for introducing the Devil. Jesus, told by Jairus that his daughter is dying goes with two disciples to the man's house and hears 'loud crying and wailing. So he went in and said: "Why this crying and commotion? The child is not dead: she is asleep"; and they only laughed at him' (Mark 5:39). At this point the preacher brought the whole proceedings to life, as if administering a shock to the congregation, with a much elaborated version of the Gospels' brief verses. The method of making the biblical personages into real-life human beings and dramatizing every detail enabled the congregation to identify with them rather than accentuating the distance and projecting biblical personages as larger-than-life, immune to the temptations of everyday existence.

Two features stand out: the link between witchcraft, marital infidelity and practices drawn from the cults (the coloured candles) and the process of submission. The former fits with the Universal Church's general strategy, which is to emphasize the needs and aspirations of women as mothers, wives and lovers, and to denounce violently the practices of *candomblé* and *umbanda* as the work of the Devil. But the context in which it is introduced in the service is particularly violent, with the music of hell reverberating around the room and the preacher shrieking at the top of his voice. It is also significant that its mode of introduction confuses, if only for a moment, the ritual of exorcism and that of bewitchment; after all, the preacher is recognizing the efficacy of the witchcraft and his message is that only faith in Jesus will counter it.

To many the sequence just described may seem outlandish and occasionally frightening, but most surprising is the alternation of the congregation's mood from extreme tension to merriment and release, to the point where at the end they appear for all the world to regard the entire proceeding as routine. And the preachers certainly regard it as routine. Yet both the moments of intensity and the *obreiros'* routine use of that familiar gesture of exorcism on unsuspecting members of the congregation as they patrol the service, carry strong connotations of submission. Indeed, the ritual of exorcism, like the ritual – for ritual it is despite the theatre of spontaneity – of conversion has submission to the preacher, and by extension to the organization, at its heart. At conversion the new believer is asked to kneel and 'accept Jesus' in a manifest display of submission, while in exorcism the Devil within is commanded to abandon the body, and, in the face of true faith, submits.

Pentecostalism and 'Afro-Brazilian' beliefs and practices[5]

It is quite common to hear the opinion expressed in Brazil that these *evangélicos* are 'merely' another version of 'Afro-Brazilian' religion, also known simply as 'possession cults' – a term which avoids prejudging the degree of African 'authenticity' in the cults. The issue is not a simple one because whereas the possession cults are characterized by extreme localism, particularism and, perhaps above all, mysteriousness, Pentecostalism is a patterned codified set of beliefs and practices which, despite much variation and occasional tentativeness, do nevertheless share common origins and above all a sense of doctrinal coherence and textual legitimation in the Bible. This point may seem odd when set against the endless hair-splitting arguments about doctrine and the enormous variation in belief about intermediation, textual interpretation, divine healing and many other issues which have separated different groups, organizations and Churches, especially in the United States (Anderson, 1979), but when set against Afro-Brazilian belief and ritual, especially *candomblé*,[6] the contrast is surely clear. The cults are organized on a particularistic basis with named individual officiants, priestesses or, as they are known, *mães de santo* (less frequently *pais de santo*). The authoritative or representative bodies of *umbanda* exist only for corporate purposes, to defend their members in the face of the outside world, and, despite occasional attempts, find it impossible to regulate or constrain individual *centros* or *terreiros* (Boyer-Araujo, 1993a; Brown, 1986). While the Pentecostals' ideology claims that, without any prior training or initiation, an individual may by pure faith alone gain the gift of the Holy Spirit, the accent of the possession cults is, with varying emphases, on mystery, lengthy initiation procedures which vary from one ritual space to

[5] I use this term with some reservations, because the cults referred to are not purely African in origin, having also undergone influence from Indian culture among many other sources (Boyer-Araujo, 1993a). Indeed, *umbanda* was invented in the early twentieth century as a *Brazilian* religion to exclude African elements, though that turned out to be a fruitless attempt (Brown, 1986). The more technical term 'possession cults' is preferable.

[6] *Candomblé* is the Bahian elaboration of Yoruba religion whereas *umbanda* originates in a Rio-based amalgam which draws on the Afro-Brazilian pantheon and on the spiritism associated with the name of Alain Kardec. They are similar, but by no means the same, though *umbanda* draws elements from *candomblé*, and has *centros* which vary from the 'pure' to the 'African'. The best account of *umbanda*, which dispels many mistaken notions about it, especially about its relation to African beliefs and practices, is Brown (1986). Ortiz (1978) has a strong thesis but is less useful as a source of information for the 'uninitiated'. The best recent account of possession cults is Boyer-Araujo (1993a).

another, and particularistic local practices passed on secretly from one expert to her protegée or successor.[7]

Thus whereas one can grasp Pentecostalism in a universalistic sort of way, by observing many Churches operating within a common frame-work, the only way to penetrate *candomblé* ritual and belief is to spend very long periods of time over years frequenting the same place, learning the language and procedures, and gaining the confidence of practitioners. Although new chapels and prayer groups, led by preachers enjoying varying degrees of autonomy from larger centralized bodies, grow up almost daily, their independence is not founded on a claim to originality or virtuosity or obscurity, or even on the spiritual gifts or repertoires of their leaders, but rather on leadership and marketing skills allied to an apparently uniform set of core beliefs and practices. It is, after all, a central belief of Pentecostalism that anybody, literally anybody, can receive the gift of the Spirit, and that the power of healing belongs to the Holy Spirit being transmitted through, but not precisely exercised by, a preacher or a church. In contrast a *terreiro* will lay claim precisely to distinctive healing powers arrived at on the basis of secret formulae and imprecations exclusive to the officiant and pronounced in a language unknown to the client.[8]

The point in common is the element of mysteriousness, and its use in spirit possession by the cults and expulsion of evil spirits in the Churches: hidden knowledge is paradoxically transmuted, so that the ritual mysteriousness of possession cults is mirrored in neo-Pentecostalism, not in esoteric procedures but in the administrative and financial mysteriousness of Pentecostalism, especially of its neo-Pentecostal variant, in the uniforms of the officers of these Churches, the unwillingness of officials to divulge the mechanisms of appointment and succession in office, and the personality cult surrounding their leaders. The use of uniforms is a feature common to possession cults and neo-Pentecostal Churches, though the exuberance of the former and the sobriety of the latter do make a contrast.[9] In comparing the ritual procedures of possession and expulsion themselves, we see that the esoteric

---

[7] It is not surprising that some of the most authoritative anthropological experts on *candomblé* are themselves practitioners thereof – such as Pierre Verger (1982) and Joana Elbein dos Santos (1986).

[8] Not for nothing does *umbanda* include a small Jewish contingent who profess an affinity with the Kabbala, (Brown, 1986: 135).

[9] In more traditional Pentecostalism there is an additional esotericism of biblical decoding (not really interpretation in a modern sense), for example in attempts to date the Second Coming and the like on the basis of hidden correspondences in sacred texts, and the discovery of correspondences between contemporary events and biblical prophecies or the visions of the Book of the Revelation.

practices associated with mediumship in the cults are diametrically opposed to the shrill and artless imprecations of Pentecostal preachers and their followers.

The two areas where the apparent resemblance between the cults and Pentecostal Churches is most striking are healing and the expulsion of devils. The motivation for initial attendance at and involvement in cults usually arises from illness or continuing, long-term personal troubles (Brown, 1986; Boyer-Araujo, 1993a), problems in family life, sex life and so on. Likewise, as we shall later see in more detail, for Pentecostal Churches and their members the healing experience is indissolubly linked to their conversion, which in its turn is the core religious experience. Brandão (1980) even goes so far as to describe the cults as a 'service religion', a phrase which emphasizes the expert–client relation and minimizes long-term commitment, while I would add that one aspect of Pentecostalism is well captured by the phrase 'personal service Church'. The Pentecostal Churches sometimes publicize the *curas divinas* they offer, and their preachers expel those same devils which possession cults and their mediums describe as spirits and even deities.

The healing experienced by Pentecostal Church followers is, as we shall see when we come to discuss the conversion experience as a whole, described by them as a single event, a crisis in a person's life. In contrast possession cults have clients (not faithful followers) who either receive periodic cures, or else are drawn into careers as mediums so that they can hold spirits at bay or bring them under their control over the long run, and so that the *centros* and *terreiros* themselves can expand and the reputations of their leaders grow. The sicknesses thereby treated are more like long-term existential troubles than sicknesses in the usual sense, and the 'system' creates long-term dependence between an individual and his or her medium, or between the medium and the *mael pai de santo*.

The expulsion of devils raises more finely balanced issues, because of the Devil's affinity with possessing spirits, and because of the well-known and aggressively publicized hostility of Pentecostal preachers to the cults' practices and beliefs and the frequent confessions to be heard in Pentecostal Churches of all sorts from people who describe their abandonment of *candomblé* or *umbanda* and concomitant conversion to Christ in dramatic and wrenching terms. The question thus returns even more insistently: are they merely competing on a shared terrain of belief or is there true incompatibility? Both recognize the power of the practitioners of *candomblé* and *umbanda* – even though one regards it as malign and the others as beneficial. Would it not therefore be naive to suppose that the millions of followers of Pentecostalism have made a clean break, especially in a society where dual allegiance – to possession cults and Catholicism – passes without comment?

The mere knowledge that, unlike a follower of Catholicism or *umbanda* or *candomblé*, a Pentecostal would find a question about dual adherence acutely embarrassing is enough to tell us that conversion to Pentecostalism does represent a real rupture. Nonetheless there is a deeper level of inquiry, which concerns the structure of belief. On this subject we can turn to the extremely useful monograph by John Peel (1968) on the development of Aladura churches in Nigeria during the colonial period. Aladura is an umbrella term referring to a complex of Churches, some more Pentecostal, some less, some more purist, some less, in opposition to traditional Yoruba religion, and its relevance to the present discussion is obviously enhanced by the kinship between Yoruba religion and its Brazilian cousin *candomblé*, which dominates the non-Christian religious field in Bahia.[10] In a chapter on 'Beliefs and doctrine', Peel describes a range of pathways between practices based on traditional belief and others arising from the Protestant faith: in one example prayers to God are prescribed to be used in a repetitive and ritualistic manner like 'following a recipe or operating a machine', as in Yoruba ritual; dreams or visions, which most Yorubas at that time viewed as 'an attempt of the numinous world to get in touch with the dreamer' are reinterpreted in a Christian framework, as signs from God. Disease was interpreted variously in naturalistic terms, and thus to be cured by either traditional or modern medicine or a combination of the two, or, especially at times of epidemics and natural disasters, as a punishment by God – and this last lent force to those among the Christians who opposed both traditional and modern medicine and advocated the exclusive recourse to prayer and penitence as a cure. The Churches which pursued this last course are described by Peel as engaged in 'radical rationalization', even though they advocated anti-technological, or anti-'scientific' reasoning – such as the flat denial of the efficacy of anything but prayer in curing disease. By this Peel means a 'moral universe in which rational steps are taken to cover the distance between the individual and God, but where God's ultimate intentions are inscrutable, and relatively arbitrary' (p. 124). At another point he makes

---

[10] By now *candomblé* really merits an independent identity as a Brazilian cultural form. Although it harks back to Yorubaland it has tried so hard to be original and authentic that it has less and less in common with the actually existing forms persisting in Nigeria, which themselves have had a separate evolution. In addition, whereas *candomblé* has grown in the number of its adherents over the centuries and today 'its appeal and influence are probably greater than ever', its Yoruba cousin has fallen to the status of a diversion and a relic, perceived by the majority as 'little more than a form of entertainment' (Clarke, 1993: 96, 107).

it fairly clear that by rationalization he means the introduction of explanations relying on the moral quality of a person's actions: thus a text which describes the many virtues of prayer ('a power-house built by God and the saints in heaven . . . a great light to reveal all devilish acts . . .') does not fail to end without stressing 'the need for self-examination beforehand, with sixteen questions to be asked of one's moral condition' (p. 122). Finally, in the concluding chapter Peel writes: 'To rationalize is to reorder one's religious belief in a new and more coherent way to be more in line with what one knows and experiences. The distinctive Aladura characteristics represent such a solution or a reordering' (p. 294).

Yet at the same time Peel describes the absolute faith in the healing powers of prayer, to the exclusion of traditional or modern medicine, as rationalization, which could in this context be interpreted as following consistently, or clinging tenaciously to, the consequences of a core assumption – even if the assumption is wrong, for it stands in stark opposition to the mysteriousness and empiricism of traditional practices or the eclecticism tolerated by some Churches, and it also makes moral sense. Thus the epidemics and natural disasters whose consequences defeated the healing powers of both traditional and modern medicine were attributed to the moral failings of the people, but thus also 'churches mighty in prayer but weak in Scripture' might stray from reasonableness, good sense, consistency in the context of a system of thought, and above all actions consistent with the moral code they were preaching. The twin requirements of consistency with core assumptions and moral reasonableness lead eventually to the creation of mechanisms for controlling prophets or rather for controlling the interpretation of their visions, for checking on the authenticity of healing or indeed on the true faith of healers (who might even be wicked men, p. 138).

The interest of Peel's account is that it shows that even with ample negotiation between traditional and Christian religion, replete with apparent eclecticism, mechanisms of differentiation develop, defined by Peel, following Weber, as rationalization. It is a gradual process, hastened only by the periodic epidemics and natural disasters which, in Peel's interpretation, accentuate the rationalization because they render traditional explanations and cures less 'reasonable' – a word he uses quite frequently. It is also an eirenic process, in which traditional religion is the object of doubt and refutation, but not of confrontation and concerted propagand-istic offensive as is observed in Brazil, especially on the part of the neo-Pentecostal churches. The distancing of Aladura preachers and Church leaders from traditional Yoruba 'magic' had more to do with its practical ineffectiveness and with the positive attractions – spiritual and social – of

Christianity. The point about 'practical ineffectiveness' is an ambiguous but instructive one: the distinctive feature of both *candomblé* and its Yoruba cousin is that explanations are more or less infinitely malleable: if one cure or imprecation does not work, or if it is 'unreasonable' in Peel's words, the medium tries another tack, or the client has recourse to another medium; if, in the Aladura churches a person known as a 'prophet' – a status of course conferred by popular consensus and not by an institutional procedure, as would be the case with a pastor – receives disruptive instructions from her visions, there are procedures to circumvent them, but they are clearly different from, and indeed more 'rational' than, those available in traditional religion, since they involve the application of abstract norms, and the intervention of persons occupying positions of consecrated authority in an organization. The rise of Aladura appears as a gradual process, but one marked by a fundamental change in religious conceptions.

In Brazil possession cults and Pentecostal Churches all face the problem of what to do when cures 'fail', or when individuals behave in ways incompatible with their status as mediums, as officials or as baptized members. *Centros de umbanda* in Rio have recourse to a variety of instruments, ranging from practical medicine and counselling to the diagnosis of possession and the appeasement of spirits (Brown, 1986: 54ff.) In Belém possession cults allow for all sorts of doubt, challenge and response (Boyer-Araujo, 1993a): doubt by onlookers and fellow mediums, challenge by allusive gestures as if possessed by another spirit (or indeed by the same one as that purportedly called up in the trance) and so on. Mediums are expected to learn to 'manage' a trance, to avoid inappropriate, uncontrolled behaviour which brings discredit upon them and their *terreiro*. One response to these problems of authentication is the establishment of Federations, which exist in Rio and in Belém, but it is not surprising that this attempt to apply impersonal forms of association and legitimation to this deeply personal set of relationships is doomed, giving rise, at least in Belém, to a 'meta-*terreiro*' subject to the same intrigues and clientelisms as the individual *terreiro*. There is therefore no 'system' of authentication other than the success of a medium in attracting clients.

The contrast with Pentecostalism emerges from an incident described by Burdick (1993) in which a member of the Assemblies of God is successfully accused of faking receipt of the Holy Spirit: the accusation arose because he had been passed over for appointment to a position of responsibility in favour of the pastor's son, but for this same reason it was felt imprudent to discipline him. The principle of authority – constantly and structurally under threat in the cults — is preserved because the pastor's authority is not his personal property but conferred by the organization which, unlike the *umbanda* Federation mentioned above, exercises real — though not absolute — power in an impersonal fashion. The same principle of rationality applies to the authentication of expulsions and cures: the transformation is said to depend on the faith of the individual, so that failure is explained by the individual's lack of faith, while the same dissonance in the cults is overcome by a multiplication of charms and imprecations.

If there is contrast, that of course does not mean that Pentecostalism and possession cults are utterly watertight compartments. There is much migration between them and although Pentecostals talk as if migration back into the cults was unthinkable to them, it is equally unthinkable to the observer that it does not exist or that people who frequent Pentecostal churches do not occasionally, or perhaps even regularly, also visit a *terreiro*. There is also a shared belief in the efficacy of supernatural entities — in one case the various types of spirit, in the other demonic forces — and their rituals of possession/expulsion clearly raise the issue of influence and borrowing of rituals and techniques between them. In the observations of Boyer-Araujo in Belém (1996b), pastors of the Universal Church are not mere fakes — their practice of expulsions shows that they have excellent knowledge of the spirit life of *terreiros*. A gesture used to expel demons — one hand on the back of a person's neck and the other on her forehead — is habitually used 'by spirits on mediums'; clapping is a common feature, welcoming the mastery of a spirit in one case and mastery of a devil in the other; reference to the suffering incurred by a medium on account of her devotion to her spirit, and by a pastor on account of his devotion to God, is in both cases balanced by the idea of eventual reward many times greater than the sacrifice; the interrogation of the possessed person by the pastor echoes the questioning of new potential mediums by the *mae* or *pai de santo* in search of the correct *caboclo* or spirit which is possessing her, as well as the quasi-judicial procedure of traditional Catholic exorcisms. In short, in detaching herself from a possession cult and joining a church a person would encounter much that is familiar, many symbols and procedures having similar meanings, and it is therefore not surprising that not all people who join the Pentecostal Churches undergo a traumatic life crisis, or that many later drop out.

But these elements of similarity do not of themselves undermine the claim that Protestantism projects quite new elements in the culture, at the most diverse of levels — ranging from the urban design of *favelas*, where once there were no chapels and now they proliferate, to television and politics, nor should it lead us to trivialize the pervasive and standardized discourse of the Pentecostals themselves which insists on the watershed which conversion and subsequent 'change of life' (*mudança de vida*) represented for them. The evidence of continuity in symbolic language must be set beside the evidence of change not just in the meaning of symbols but also in their structure: examples include the introduction of free will in the relationship with spirits (transmuted into demons); the replacement of a relationship with spirits mediated by a clientelistic relationship with a medium by an impersonal relationship with the Church and through the Church with the realm of the sacred, as opposed to the taming, mastery and capriciousness which pervade possession cults. And the same applies to continuities with Catholicism: the monthly ritual of the *santa ceia*, reminiscent though it may be of the Eucharist, clearly acquires a quite different meaning in the hands of the *evangélicos*.

Likewise the resemblance between the way in which mediums speak of the troubles caused them by undiagnosed, unpropitiated or unpacified spirits and the retrospective description offered by converts of the illnesses and troubles which had plagued them before their conversion can be misleading: whereas the former trace their lifelong troubles, expressed in strange dreams and feelings, in incomprehensible behaviour and uncontrollable fits, to childhood and ultimately to birth, attributable to a supernatural force or entity, the latter focus on mundane problems such as illness and psychological troubles as well as family problems, alcoholism and disorderly living (in the case of men), and attribute them to their own moral failings and lack of faith. To them, the phrase 'Jesus saved me' or 'Jesus rescued me' is not equivalent to 'the *mae de santo* cured me' because it also means 'I saved myself', on account of the effort, and in a sense the sacrifice, of conversion.

Where the cults will describe life's troubles and their transcendence in terms of the relationship between an individual and his or her spirits (*caboclos* and *guías* (guides) in some cases, *orixás* in others), the Pentecostals introduce a third element, in the form of the Holy Spirit. Raboteau (1978: 63) insists on the difference between a demonic force which 'rides' a person (pervasively rendered in Brazil by the word *cavalgar* – to ride a horse)[11] and the receipt of the Holy Spirit as a gift. The possessed is 'invaded by a supernatural body' and is thus temporarily beyond self-control, his ego being subordinated to that of the intruder, whereas a

---

[11] The horse is also a pervasive symbol of uncontrollable erotic power in the European middle ages and Baroque.

'shaker' is 'drawn inward to his interaction with the spirit'.[12] The Pentecostal Churches deal with both: they expel the uncontrollable through exorcism and counter the possession and expulsion with a separate enactment of baptism by the Spirit, expressed in glossolalia and accompanied by a discourse of empowerment as opposed to one of possession. Like the healing which occurs at the time of conversion, this is a sudden, once-and-for-all experience, very different from the literally endless haggling and cajoling which characterizes spirit possession.

The word exorcism has historical Catholic connotations and denotes a set of procedures and incantations – and interrogations – which are effective by virtue of the authority vested in a hierarchy and therefore in the priest conducting the exorcism. *Libertação* avoids these connotations and means freeing the individual from possession by the devil through the invocation of Jesus.[13] However, since the Devil can hide behind all sorts of deceptive appearances, including that of the person conducting the expulsion or a person who appears to have received the Holy Spirit, a crucial issue of authority arises similar to that arising in cults – who decides whether a person is possessed or not? For in both cases the client/ believer places power in the hands of the officiant, medium or priestess and does not ask how the diagnosis is reached: the diagnosis and cure having no established ritual procedure, the way is open to the circular reasoning so prominent in the world of the occult and the esoteric. At numerous points in the book *Orixás, caboclos e guias – deuses ou demonios?* authored by Edir Macedo, and probably widely used by his organization's personnel, the answer is given in terms of the church's own authority. When Macedo says 'I have power over all demons, and over the devil himself, because Jesus gave it to me' (p. 140) he is not talking of himself personally, but in the third person, reported speech, sense. Officiants are impersonal representatives of the Church who do not claim any recondite knowledge, but rather a power to bring about *libertação* because they, or rather their Church, has received it from God. The discourse of *libertaçao* is marked by an insistence on abstract relationships very different from the personal, clientelistic relationship to be had with a medium. In the place of submission to the Devil, the individual signals submission to the Church itself when, after a summary, almost violent procedure with a minimum of ritual the 'freed' individual is physically subdued by the

---

[12] These 'shakers' are Spiritual Baptists on the island of St Vincent in the late eighteenth and early nineteenth century – not the white 'Shakers' famous for their furniture.

[13] The fact that liberation theology is known as *Teologia da Libertação* creates an irrelevant analogy. When the leader of the Universal Church, Edir Macedo, speaks ironically of *libertação da teologiã*, he is simply engaging in wordplay for the benefit of the few who know what *teologia da libertação* is.

officiant, or several officiants, and prostrate or kneeling, 'accepts Jesus'. Although this scenario is most frequently observed in the newer Churches with their particular emphasis on the Devil, in the Assemblies too without the accompanying theatre of exorcism, the person who 'accepts Jesus' signifies that acceptance and submission to the Church by kneeling in front of the congregation facing the podium. The symbolic structure, again, is transformed: where once there were many – innumerable – spirits, now they are shown to be multiple disguises of a single demonic force. Furthermore, there is a fundamental break when the Pentecostals summon the sufferer to take her own fate in her own hands, to regain control over her own life – a phrase which repeatedly figures in their preaching: '*você pode tomar conta da sua vida*' (you really can get hold over your own life).

The rationalizing process develops over time as Churches adopt procedures to bring spontaneous manifestations under control. Just as the Aladura Churches had to develop mechanisms to tame inconvenient prophecy, or the Catholic Church itself has an elaborate bureaucratic procedure which can take centuries to 'recognize' a miracle, so the Pentecostal Churches gradually institute courses to prepare people wanting to be baptized in the Holy Spirit. In contrast, the cults retain over time their reliance on relationships of personal dependence between medium and client, and between the heads of *centros* and *terreiros* and the mediums who operate under their aegis.

In the case of the Universal Church the theme of continuity can also be analysed in relation to its distinctive concept of salvation and to the very prominent role played by money both in that concept and in mediating the Church's relationship with its followers. In his account of the Universal Church in Bahia, Wilson Gomes (1994) emphasizes three elements: the Devil, or rather devils, and thus evil, expressed in mockery and temptation; prosperity, or well-being; and the wager, in Portuguese *arriscar-se* (literally 'taking a risk'). In contrast to established Pentecostal and Protestant doctrine, the Universal Church, and the *Deus é Amor* church, offer this-worldly salvation. The faithful – or simply people walking in off the street – are incited to solve their material and emotional problems through two wagers: by submitting to an expulsion of all the devils which wreck their lives, and by making a donation – on the basis of the Church's famous formula 'you only receive by giving' – which will enable them to require (not merely petition or implore) of Jesus that he provide them with the worldly goods or emotional satisfaction which, more than their desire or even their need, constitute their rightful expectation. The donation is less a sacrifice than part of a 'cosmic bargain'; suffering as an assuaging of guilt has no place in this scheme of things.

The elements which the Universal Church has drawn from popular Catholic culture and from *umbanda*, in particular the Devil, and the resemblance of the mocking devil to certain figures in the cults (*Pombagira*, the trickster, but also the wily temptress in its female guise), do not therefore mean they are 'the same thing'. The gifts which in the cults are demanded by a spirit become, in the Churches, a token of an individual's determination to change his or her life and of his or her membership of an institution. Members of the *Deus é Amor* keep a record of their contributions, duly countersigned by a church officer in a *Caderneta da Prosperidade* (Prosperity notebook). Universal Church members quote the words *é só dando que se recebe* ('only by giving can one receive'); they are not in principle propitiating Jesus − such a relationship would be more appropriate to the cults or to the offerings and petitions made to saints in Catholic churches all over the Latin world − rather they intend that the gift form part of a commitment of their own to change their lives. Hence the concomitant phrase from a teenage woman: *'Jesús da um jeito na vida gente mas a gente também tem que fazer um esforço'* (Jesus gives a hand in life, but one also has to make an effort of one's own). The individual is led to believe that he has a chance to influence the outcome of his wager. To quote Macedo again:

> Devils bring about tragedies in the lives of people who go near them, but they do not have the power to override a person's will. No one can ever say: 'Ah! I cannot become free, I haven't the strength, I can't fight back . . .' God gave us free will, he granted us willpower and that the Devil can never take away because it is God's gift. Be it only in a tiny corner of your soul, there is a way out which enables you to put your free will in motion. Place it in God's service and you will see how He will free you. (Macedo, 1982; quoted in Soares, 1990: 81)[14]

The Universal Church has captured the attention and even the imagination of social scientists, journalists and mere onlookers, because of a variety of features, many of which must surely be the result of a deliberate policy to shock and scandalize, and others, equally theatrical, which arise from the symbolic-ideological complex described by Gomes. Unlike other Pentecostal organizations it is quite consciously putting on a show.[15] Whereas other Churches are embarrassed by appearances of devils

---

[14] A book with the same title has appeared in new editions several times since 1982, but my own 1988 (11th) edition seems in fact to have a different text in which this passage does not appear.

[15] In Portuguese the English word *show* is commonly used, often to refer to a show in the theatre or a night club, but also to refer to something which is 'no more than show' with little substance behind it.

during a service, this Church focuses entire occasions on his appearance (the Devil being always described in the masculine, though sometimes disguised as a woman). But these differences must not be exaggerated: fear and hate of the diabolic power of *umbanda* and *candomblé* was fomented over many decades by the Catholic hierarchy and is not new in this *evangélico* family of religious organizations. Rather than a fundamental innovation in Pentecostalism, the neo-Pentecostal Churches should be regarded as a vanguard, like the pastors of the Assemblies of God who, as if heralding their own rise towards the ranks of the learned, described it to me as offering something a little more simple for simple people. Brazilian *evangélicos* regard themselves as a family of *crentes* (literally 'believers' – a label coined probably by the Assemblies but which has come into general usage, and which the Universal Church rejects with some disdain).[16] As a vanguard, the Universal Church represents in an acute, 'scandalous' form, with abundance of symbolic and theatrical accoutrements, the 'sharp end' of a broader process involving the Pentecostal movement as a whole.

Pentecostals trade in absolutes. They develop very clear lines of demarcation among themselves through membership systems and complex bureaucratic organization, and between themselves as a group and other religious organizations through rituals of daily life, such as uniforms, austerity of dress and the prohibition on alcohol, tobacco, and marital infidelity.[17] In the possession cults the opposite holds: uncertain boundaries, a clientelistic rather than membership relationship with non-experts, and a complete absence of impersonal organization. Where within and even among Pentecostal Churches the tendency is toward uniformity and conformity of language, gesture, ritual and doctrine, the *terreiros* are characterized by variety and by an apparently permanent reconstruction of orthodoxy through pervasive mutual interchange of rituals, 'entities', and organizational forms, to the point where the common assumption that there are a fixed number of more or less homogeneous cults with a minimum set of features in common and demarcating features is probably mistaken. The notion that *umbanda* and *candomblé* are separate and internally uniform is a construction jointly produced by the practitioners

---

[16] The reason is, I think, that the word *crente* has come to have a connotation of humble people, defiantly humble, but humble nevertheless and hungry for social respectability – an image the Universal Church avoids.

[17] Strictly speaking, the Universal Church does not prohibit alcohol or tobacco. In the words of Pastor Rodrigues it merely points outs to people that they should not destroy their bodies. Yet I have never seen a cigarette or a glass of beer any where near a member of the Church, so that in practice it seems to me that the conventional prohibition operates as in the other Churches. It is, however, clear that the Universal Church, perhaps in fulfilment of an evident policy to attract young people, does not take an active or even passive repressive line on women's make-up and dress.

themselves and the intellectuals and anthropologists who write about them (Dantas, 1988). To the established categories *candomblé* and *umbanda* must be added at least *nagô* (Recife), and *mina* (Belém). The multiple and iterative transfers and transmutations of crucial terms, beliefs and practices among *terreiros* and mediums make it clear that the names of these cults reflect little in the way of ritual or practical uniformity (Boyer-Araujo, 1993a). This is a world of uncertainty and doubt, in which no threshold is ever definitively passed, no evil spirit ever definitively dispelled, no method, trick or device ever guaranteed to be effective; the status of medium or *mãe de santo* itself can slip away if a person is careless or unlucky. The endless journey of the term *exu*, influenced by Catholic concepts of the Devil as well as ideas of both Yoruba and spiritist origin, shows both the porousness of the boundaries between established categories and also the inappropriateness of interpreting the language of the cults in either 'theological' terms or in the discourse of the established anthropology of the subject – which in Bahia in particular means a discourse of authenticity and faithfulness to African origins (Boyer-Araujo, 1993a, 1993b).

In raising the question of authenticity, we return to the theme of the projection of the popular, for anthropologists and intellectuals – especially Bastide and Verger – have encouraged the cults to project themselves in terms of authenticity and tradition; for some this is African tradition, for others it is an amalgam of traditions, but *umbanda* and *candomblé* in particular have in common this Brazilian trait of looking to the past and to the 'roots' for a legitimation of the present, and of making this search a basis for exchanges between learned and popular culture. Pentecostals reject the search itself, and also have no intellectual elite to refer – or defer – to in their pursuit of legitimation, but the prominent presence of black people in their Churches – and their studied avoidance of the issue of race in their discourse – compel us to ask whether racial identity affects their success.

Pentecostalism and race

Discussion of Afro-Brazilian belief leads to the theme of race, and thereby to a subject which, transported from the Anglo-Saxon world to Brazil, becomes infused with ambiguity. And Bahia, with a majority of 'black' population, and its status as the 'African Rome', the capital of African culture in the country, again presents characteristics all of its own. To be sure, colour (as tabulated in censuses, and therefore defined with little attention to the ambiguities of everyday life) is closely correlated to socio-economic status in Brazil (Wood and Magno de Carvalho, 1988). Indeed, it may be that, in purely income terms, and riding roughshod over the ambiguities, the races are more polarized in Brazil than in the USA, approaching even South Africa. There is no doubt that racial discrimination is rife and rarely challenged socially, let alone legally. Yet there continues to be good reason to state that the society is not polarized in a binary fashion along racial lines.[18] Political expression of 'black against white' as in the USA or South Africa is almost unheard of, and public expressions of black identity occur less through dissent or protest than in the cultural fields of religion, carnival (Rio more than Bahia, at least until recently), dance and music. Recently there has arisen a 'Movimento Negro' (Mattoso, 1994; Clarke, 1993) in which, like in many new or renovated indigenisms in the Americas,[19] the discourse of authenticity and autochthony is joined to that of protest against economic inequality and political exclusion, as in the recovery of 'traditions' like capóeira. In this field distinctiveness is not synonymous with separateness, nor is the search for authenticity restricted to those groups and individuals who might be thought to be the 'true' heirs of the authentic – especially since in the final analysis there is no way of knowing what is authentic nor who are the true heirs, and so 'identity' becomes indistinguishable from its own representation.

It is then not entirely surprising that even sectors of the Catholic Church, as if apologizing for a history of severe hostility to what they regarded as pagan rites, have recently been trying to incorporate black culture into occasional Church rituals, as during the apparently ill-fated Campanha da Fraternidade, or 'Brotherhood Campaign' which in 1988 tried somewhat awkwardly to draw attention to the race question by bringing African instruments and rituals (or versions thereof) into church (Burdick, 1991; 1993: 157–60). One of the many ironic aspects of this elaborate and selfconscious courtship of which the campaign was not an isolated instance (see Clarke, 1993) lay in the juxtaposition of an innovation at the erudite level trailing behind the popular level where Catholic and 'African' rites have been intermingled for generations: every manual of umbanda and candomblé takes great pains to explain the 'correspondences' between the Yoruba pantheon and spirits and both the Trinity and various popular Catholic saints, though quite what is meant

[18] A view which had much influence in US race relations writing and even social policy in the 1960s (see Moynihan 1969; Degler, 1971).

[19] cf. the reinvention of the indios not as an ethnic group but rather as a nation in Ecuador (Taylor, 1991; Zamosc, 1994).

by 'correspondence' in this connexion is extremely hazy.[20] Black churchgoers in particular were disconcerted and offended by the drums and cymbals introduced into church services, because they simply could not understand this *volte-face* on the part of a Church which for generations had denounced *umbanda* as the work of the Devil: were they being mocked, or condemned to eternal damnation (Burdick, 1993: 159)? The reactions to this apparently sudden change in Church policy were not a denial of the dual allegiances and ritual or even doctrinal borrowings, but rather an expression of surprise, even a defensive reaction. These 'ritual' aspects of the *campanha* broke with all the ambiguities and subtleties of the popular–erudite dialectic, which relies so heavily on the implicit and the allusive, and is threatened by attempts such as these to bring these semi-clandestine correspondences out into the open. The *campanha* resembled an attempt to rationalize, to place the popular and the erudite on the same plane, and thus to suppress the popular.

Whatever the successes or failures of that effort on the part of the Catholic hierarchy (which called forth some severe comments from Burdick), it did illustrate their acceptance of the widespread view in erudite culture that African culture in Brazil is a heritage of the entire country, not only of the black population – if they could be set apart from the rest, which they cannot.[21] This conception has not held sway in all quarters since time immemorial: the founders of *umbanda* at the turn of the century were exalting the country's *indio* heritage at the expense of an African past they despised and sought to deny or erase (Brown, 1986). *Umbanda* was to be a Brazilian religion for Brazil, with additional contributions from Oriental religions and European spiritism, but without the African element. Until the *Semana de Arte Moderna* (literally Modern Art Week) of 1929 and its explosive literary and artistic aftermath, racial mixture was considered by prominent and influential writers, in Brazil as in Europe and in other countries of the Americas, to be the path to degeneration. After the *Semana* Oswald de Andrade's image of an

[20] In my limited experience this explanation sounds like a way *mães* or *paes de santo* have found of fobbing off questions which practitioners find meaningless, unanswerable – because of their derivation from a European or Anglo-Saxon concept of religion – or just irritating.

[21] The *'Campanha da Fraternidade'* is an annual event sponsored by the Bishop's Conference – hence my use of the word hierarchy, though doubtless there was still some dissidence over this theme and the way it was presented in television advertisements and in parish churches. Priests and religious activists in the TL or People's Church movements have also taken up the theme, perhaps with more emphasis on 'modern' themes of empowerment and social injustice. For example the priest of Periperi in Salvador talked of introducing samba drums and *candomblé* apparatus into Church. Although the officially sponsored *Campanha* took a less contestatory approach, there is no indication that either approach from within the Church has made a deep impression among the faithful, let alone among the non-participant but nominal Catholics whom they are attempting to attract.

'anthropophagous' Brazil – a culture avid to absorb (or 'devour') other cultures – gained currency among the intellectual and artistic elite. Much as the racial democracy it proclaimed may eventually have cemented a conservative mind-set, Gilberto Freyre's The *Masters and the Slaves* (1933) was a revolutionary contribution in its time, which laid the basis for the establishment of the African heritage at the centre of the erudite idea of the country's culture.

Today, in the words of the *doyenne* of Brazilian sociology, Maria Isaura Pereira de Queiroz, the African 'stamp' has climbed the social scale to the point where its imprint can be seen in all social strata, up to the very top: 'Brazilians of ancient lineage, children of immigrants, newly-arrived immigrants' all share an adherence to African music, dance and song, to the point where cultural mixture has been recognized by the elite as the distinctive feature of 'being Brazilian' (Pereira de Queiroz, 1988: 72, 78).[22] Pereira de Queiroz elaborates the counterpoint further by showing how the process has also operated in the opposite direction: carnival, originally a Portuguese Catholic and indeed pre-Christian festival, a celebration of disorder,[23] has during this century been appropriated by the poor. It has become an elaborately choreographed and officially sponsored festival in which the black population predominate, even while representing European kings and queens dressed in eighteenth century dress and so on, side by side of course, with an exhibition of mulatto sexuality perhaps designed to embody the fantasies of the lighter-skinned onlookers paying stratospheric prices to view the samba school parades from the banked seats of the *sambódromo* (Pereira de Queiroz, 1992).[24]

The implication of this discussion is that although no one could conduct research on Brazilian Pentecostal Churches (or for that matter on the country's penitentiaries) without noticing the predominance of black people in them, it would still be wrong to describe them as 'Black Churches'. This is an image drawn from the North American churches which have gone by that name for generations. The striking statistic quoted by Baer and Singer (1992), to the effect that 90 per cent of church-going black Americans belong to black-controlled religious organizations,

---

[22] It must be also said that this may fit a pattern found throughout the corner Portuguese empire. Peter Fry has explained to me that Angola and Mozambique also exhibit radically different patterns of race relations from those found in the neighbouring former British colonies and of course South Africa. This is clearly a fertile subject for future research.

[23] Recall the 'lord of misrule' of early modern European carnivals. see Burke, 1978.

[24] Note that despite its title – *Carnaval Brésilien* – Pereira de Queiroz is writing exclusively about the Rio carnival: carnival in Salvador is a very different affair, above all on account of multi-racial participation and of the absence of the separation between performers and onlookers. For a judicious and lively journalist's account of the Rio carnaval see Guillermoprieto (1990).

with its assumption that blackness is a ready-made clear-cut category and that black-controlled organizations are synonymous with 'Black Churches' would be simply meaningless in a Brazilian context. In both countries the explanation for the racial composition of both Pentecostal and evangelical/mainstream Churches lies more in the difference between mechanisms of discrimination and exclusion in the wider society, and in the white-dominated churches, than in a link between religious affiliation and socio-political struggle. The evidence for the discrimination in the wider society need hardly be adduced, and that for the sense of exclusion of blacks in US churches, especially after the Civil War, is also clear enough, but Burdick's account of Church life in the working-class suburbs of Rio de Janeiro also reveals undercurrents of tetchiness, reflecting pervasive racial sensitivity and insensitivity in church life across the religious field – among 'progressive' Catholics, Protestants and practitioners of *umbanda* (Burdick, 1993: chap. 6). It is therefore quite possible that the darker racial complexion of Pentecostal Churches in Brazil, as compared with 'historic' Protestant Churches and with the Catholic Church, is due to a social dynamic not dissimilar from that of the United States whereby people experiencing discrimination, exclusion, disrespect, or lack of opportunity in one Church migrate to another when eventually the opportunity arises.

But although the Pentecostal Churches of Brazil, like the Black Churches (Pentecostal and mainstream) of the USA, reflect the country's distinctive pattern of discrimination, in neither country are they involved, as Churches, in political or social struggle over racial issues.[25] Black Church leaders have participated in the US civil rights movement as prominent citizens whose ecclesiastical status has lent legitimacy to the cause; the black struggle itself, however, has not been the basis of their Churches' foundation or continued existence. Although nothing of the sort has been observed in Brazil as far as the issue of race is concerned, as we shall come to see, the Pentecostal Churches there can be highly political, more so than the Black Pentecostal Churches in the USA, and once again the characteristics of their political involvements correspond to the wider political culture of the country, as does the political involvement of 'white' North American evangelicalism, of which the Christian Coalition and earlier the Moral Majority are recent examples.

Most disconcerting is the parallel with the Nation of Islam, which has

[25] This absence of an organic relationship between religious belief and political liberation was a source of great disappointment to believing writers committed to the cause of black liberation, such as Joseph Washington (1972), whose approach has something in common with that of liberation theology, though at least in the early 1970s he seemed unaware of its existence.

in common with the neo-Pentecostal Churches I have described, especially the Universal Church, the cult of the personality of its leader, its encouragement of and involvement in business enterprise, its severe condemnation of alcohol and drug consumption and engagement in anti-drugs campaigns in the ghettoes, its advocacy of orthodox modern family values – all characteristics which seem to have been accentuated by Louis Farrakhan, who in the 1970s reconstituted the Nation of Islam against the more orthodox Islam and more accommodating political posture of Elijah Muhammed's son and successor (Baer and Singer, 1992; Kepel, 1994).[26] These comparisons show that a holistic approach to classification tends to obscure the extent to which religious organizations treat the available array of symbolic, ideological and organizational resources as a divisible repertoire. If similar social needs facilitate the creation of such diverse religious organizations, the space for innovation and 'spiritual entrepreneurship' comes clearly into view.

It is therefore not surprising to recall that the missionaries whose work lies at the origin of Pentecostal Churches in Central and South America came from overwhelmingly 'white' North American Churches, who themselves had lost vast contingents of black members in the separation of Black Churches (Anderson, 1979). When they set out to convert the countries to the south, those self-same Churches were to have enormous success among the poor, who in Brazil include a high proportion of blacks, especially in the Northeast, as well as among indigenous peoples in Central America and the Andes (Rostas and Droogers, 1993).[27] In my research I have seen no indication of any awareness among Pentecostal preachers and pastors of the existence of either Black Pentecostal or Black 'mainstream' Churches in the United States (Baer and Singer, 1992: chap. 5), even though many of those preachers are themselves black and even though their congregants are – in the city of Salvador at least – overwhelmingly non-white. Conversely, preachers and congregants alike explain at length that the United States is a rich country because its

[26] Farrakhan is of course notorious for his own and his organization's 'war' with the Jewish community, but his organization is also known for the primacy it has given to the moral regeneration of urban black communities.

[27] I am not counting here the well-known aggressive proselytizing campaigns of the Wycliffe Bible Society and the Summer Institute of Linguistics among lowland indigenous peoples. For an anthropological account see the relevant passages in Philippe Descola (1993) which cast some interesting light on these situations, such as the reaction of a society riddled with feuding to the invitation of the preacher to forgive one's enemies; or the possibility of an affinity between Jesus, when walking on the waters of Lake Galilee, and the spirit of the waters; not to speak of the confusion when Lazarus is raised from the dead on the part of people who live in perpetual fear of the returning spirits of the dead . . .

people are Christian – by which is meant Protestant, not Catholic.[28] Clearly these observations muddy the waters of much discussion about the ideological and political implications of Pentecostalism; they also show how the meaning of apparently similar practices and doctrines shifts as they move between different cultures.[29]

The latest of a long line of 'theorists of Brazil', Roberto DaMatta, has linked a discussion of race with the issue of Protestantism, comparing Brazil with the USA during the period from Abolition to the Civil Rights movement, not in relation to Brazilian Protestantism, but in relation to the egalitarian ethos of the United States and its origins in the Reformation and the Industrial Revolution. In an argument reminiscent of that advanced by Louis Dumont (Dumont, 1960), he compares the situation in the United States before and after the Civil War and the victory of the North. After the War, the capitalist and individualist ethos dominated and individuals were able to dispose at will of their persons in a competitive market, so that racism had to take legal and exclusionary forms, since the 'relational' (i.e. clientelistic or paternalistic) ethos, which had prevailed in the Southern states, was not available to encompass these new relations of profound inequality. Brazil, in contrast, is still a relational society, in which according to DaMatta the whole encompasses the individual, in which the identity of a person comes from his or her family and social circle. The result is that racial discrimination and inequality 'Brazilian style' do not require racist institutions because Brazilians 'know their place', while in the United States the culture invites them to create and achieve it, and so in Brazil race becomes one of a long and for ever incomplete list of criteria of inequality which govern a profoundly hierarchical society (DaMatta, 1986).

Yet that incompleteness is double-edged: it opens the way to ever-renewed fields of discrimination, as well as ever-renewed fields of contestation, observable not only in hierachy but also in style, difference, distinction. Thus, writing about Bahia, Sansone (1994) distinguishes 'hard' and 'soft' fields of race: the hard ones are the labour market and the workplace, marriage and courtship, and relations with the police. The rest is 'soft': people can use a wide variety of terms in the same conversation, in

---

[28] On one occasion I raised the subject with the leader of a small chapel of the Four-Square Church (*Igreja Quadrangular* – a large-scale organization similar in style and doctrine to the Assemblies with a presence in the South and Northeast of Brazil) and he did then talk about the discrimination people faced; but this was after I had raised the subject and I did not have the impression that it was a major issue for him in the context of his Church life.

[29] The case of South Africa further supports my point for there the 'Zion' churches developed in a quite independent and apolitical manner, while keeping the name Zion (Sundkler, 1961).

describing themselves and others, and the new culture of youth and globalization offers a myriad of ways in which a person can handle his or her colour. The popularity of contemporary Bahian pop music, incorporating and transforming elements from a variety of other cultures and countries, enables people to think of themselves regionally or culturally as *bahianos* rather than in terms of colour; the intermediate term *moreno* (literally 'brown') is being used more and more by people who in other times might have been constrained to describe themselves as *negro* or *branco*. The *Movimento Negro*, theoretically committed to a version of black power, has infused 'black pride' through a repackaged *capóeira* or the drums of the samba, and also by producing symbolic alternatives to the marks of behaviour, dress and self-presentation which tradition has associated negatively with race – symbols associated with other, newly discovered traditions, more distant in time and in space, yet strongly charged with the theme of cultural authenticity, such as dreadlocks and similar Afro-Caribbean accoutrements.

This schematic discussion is sufficient, in combination with the earlier account of Afro-Brazilian culture, to cast doubt on the usage of the term 'black' as if it were an unambiguous category in Brazil, and although there is no reason to cast doubt on the reality of discrimination and social distance in the country, we can also see how, although Pentecostalism and colour-related identities seem largely independent of one another, they offer parallel pathways to participation in a global culture and thus an escape from the ever-incomplete list of criteria of inequality which DaMatta attributes to Brazilian social hierarchies.

It is thus not entirely surprising that Burdick found *negros* felt more discrimination in CEBs (Christian base communities) than in Pentecostal Churches. For CEBs cannot escape their identification and continuity with the cultural hegemony of Catholicism, and thus with the dominant culture: the social composition of participants is much the same as it would have been in the pre-conciliar Church. The Pentecostals, in contrast, offer new social ties and a clean slate uncontaminated by either the *negros'* past or the past of popular religion. They do not consider the racial problem in the context of Church activities, and so they offer an escape – but no remedy.

It will by now be apparent that whereas certain general observations can be made about the relationships between Pentecostals and *umbanda* and *candomblé*, the place of race in Pentecostalism, or indeed of Pentecostalism in changing (or preserving) the pattern of race relations in the country, is a matter of some doubt and controversy: even the superficially 'obvious' observation that Pentecostal Churches have 'more than their share' of blacks is fraught with confusion with respect both to its meaning and to its implications. However, the broader question of domination, of which this question of race forms a part, will not go away: religious involvement and commitment is also about the power of the word, and about the words of power, and if we approach the question of domination from another angle by reflecting again, as we did in the context of *basista* Catholicism, on how, in their discourses and their symbolic practices, the different Churches have dealt with the dialectic of erudite and popular culture outlined in the Introduction, we may make some progress toward understanding the extent and character of the fractures brought about by the Pentecostal Churches.

Religious culture and taste, high and low: changing the rules of engagement

In September 1982 a well-known French sociologist visited the church of Santa Maria Novella in Florence. The church stands in an unalluring location, facing one of Mussolini's many railway stations to the east, surrounded by sidewalks littered with the detritus of drug abuse, while the square to the west provides a meeting place, even a market place, for Florence's Somali community, but it is one of the city's most cherished treasures. In publishing some reflections arising out of that visit 12 years later under the title 'Pieté religieuse et dévotion artistique', Pierre Bourdieu (1994b) was not intending to compete with tourist guides or art historians, nor was he limiting himself to a play on words, juxtaposing two forms of reverence – those expressed by the actions and expectations of the tourists or art lovers and those of the faithful. Rather he wanted to draw attention to the different form and function of works of art at different times and in the eyes of different onlookers and worshippers, 'users' and visitors, and also to external differences in the artistic quality of objects appealing to different tastes: in this case to the contrast between . artistic forms characteristic of objects of magical devotion, on the part of 'popular religion', and those of objects of artistic devotion by practitioners of the cult of the higher, more lettered, aesthetic, of the form. (It is important to notice Bourdieu's insistence on the objective quality of differences in taste, for he resists strongly their reduction to mere differences of subjective disposition, and in his accounts of the objects themselves, shows that there are clear differences in the objects appreciated by different 'aesthetic dispositions'.) Thus the epithet 'popular' applies both to the religious and to the aesthetic, and refers to objects or practices which attract the disapproval of the 'clerks of the Church' and the educated classes (*les lettrés*), as well as to the 'reality' of the object represented in works – no longer properly 'of art' – which attract magical devotion.[30] These would in consequence be described more appropriately as effigies instead of sculptures, as images instead of paintings.[31] Later in the paper Bourdieu enters further into the particular features of objects of 'popular' adoration, noting, so as not to utter the words 'bad taste', the 'sort of contempt' (*sorte de discrédit*) in which they are held as works which have the function of representing their referent in the clearest possible fashion, as opposed to works of art which refer only to themselves and are revered for their formal qualities.[32] Such, in his view, is the depth of the chasm between effigies and works of art, that the Ghirlandaio frescoes and other masterpieces in Santa Maria Novella, by virtue of their status as objects[33] of artistic admiration, need to be complemented (*pour doubler*)[33] by works of purely religious devotion, and these, in the place of aesthetic veneration, are the object of 'Hollywood-like idealization associated with items of "popular" consumption such as large circulation women's

---

[30] Although several authors already quoted in this work – Brandão, Droogers, for example – have mentioned Bourdieu in their writing, I resisted using his work because it has suffered so much from precisely the sort of reverence which he refers to as that of popular religion in this very paper. His name is invoked, in the way that one might summon a guardian spirit, and as a decoration to the argument (like the garish reliquaries in which a thorn from the crown of thorns or a relic of a martyred saint, might, for example, be exhibited), and rarely is anything more than a vague relationship established between the actual content of the work referred to and the content of the author's own argument. In addition, Bourdieu currently suffers from being in fashion among Brazilian social scientists, and the irremediable *vedettismo* of Brazilian academia, as indeed of sociology in general, has a similarly inoculating effect on me. However, the accidental discovery of this paper in a bookshop has led me to revise my own prejudice, as the text will show, though with the reservation that Bourdieu's work is not easy to understand; it certainly cannot be read as a sequential construction of a theory, being rather an archipelago of reflections and observations written in a style heavily and transparently influenced by Proust especially in the multiplication of adjectives which often are constructed in such a way as to avoid the 'obvious' usage and to provide a 'layered' rather than a precise interpretation of the processes or phenomena under discussion. The text itself is often interspersed with inserts of an empirical kind, containing quotations from interviews or statistical details. The translations are mine.

[31] In this respect Bourdieu quotes an ancient paper by Panofsky in which an elaborate distinction is drawn between three types of image: a 'devotional image', a 'historical scenic image' and a 'hieratic or cultural representation' (1994b: 71). The discussion is reminiscent of the difficulties experienced by Franciscan friars in sixteenth-century Mexico when they tried to persuade the newly 'converted' Indians that the image of the Virgin they placed before them was not to be object of their adoration, but merely an image thereof.

[32] As he remarks, someone who was to kneel down in front of a Pietá in a museum would be taken for a lunatic.

[33] A word which means both dubbed (as in films) and, figuratively, 'repeating'.

magazines, photographic cartoon strips . . . soap operas[34] . . . tourist souvenirs etc.' (p. 73). Thus the popular and the erudite are divided both intrinsically and also in the type of appreciation they receive.

Bourdieu dislikes the term 'popular culture', largely because he understands it to refer precisely to a counter-culture of resistance or dissent. He seems prepared to admit that 'the people' have a culture, but rejects the description of it as 'popular'. He describes the term dismissively in *La Distinction*, as an oxymoron (*alliance de mots*) 'through which an attempt is made to impose, willingly or unwillingly, the dominant definition of culture' and which on closer inspection will only consist of 'dispersed fragments of a more or less age-old erudite culture (such as "medical knowledge") selected and refashioned in accordance with the class habitus and integrated in a unified world view it engenders, and by no means the so-called counter-culture which some conceive as a culture developed in opposition to the dominant culture' (1979: 459).[35]

Whereas Bourdieu refers to high culture with a vast artillery of terms such as 'legitimate', 'official', 'lettered', 'dominant', 'learned' – though never 'elite' for example – when writing of 'low' culture he rarely uses an epithet or adjective at all, preferring to use a noun – the bearers themselves, the 'working class' or the 'popular classes'. Though polarized and dualistic, his is still a unitary conception of culture. He does not hold the view that the culture of the lettered and popular classes have nothing to do with each other. In his conception the poles are united, by social conflict of an ill-defined sort and by their inter-dependent definition:

> the legitimacy of a pure disposition [for which read 'high', 'lettered', or 'erudite' taste] receives such universal recognition that no source comes forward to remind us that the definition of art, and through it of the art of living, is an object of struggle between classes. The dominated arts of living *which have almost never been expressed in a systematic way*, are almost always perceived by the very people who speak up in their defence, from a destructive or reductionist point of view, to the point that all that remains for them is degradation or a self-destructive rehabilitation ('popular culture', as it is called). (Bourdieu, 1979: 50; emphasis in the original).

Or again, apropos now not of the paraphernalia of everyday life but of 'ways of seeing' works of art (*le regard*): '. . . it is not so easy to describe that "pure" way of seeing without at the same time describing its

---

[34] The words, 'soap operas' are in English in the original text.

[35] Interestingly, this resembles the description of Latin American Pentecostalism by Jean-Pierre Bastian (1994) as a *bricolage* of popular culture, a word Bastian himself clarifies in his text as 'patchwork'.

untutored counterpart against which it is defined, and vice versa' (1979: 33). Later, in a lengthy parenthesis he makes an unusually clear statement in which the subordinate, dependent character of popular taste is underlined: the impossibility of a neutral, impartial description 'of these antagonic visions' does not mean that one should 'subscribe to an aesthetic relativism, for it is quite evident that a "popular aesthetic" defines itself in relation to the various learned aesthetics and that the popular experience of beauty is forever haunted by a reference to legitimate art and its negative evaluation of "popular" taste' (ibid.). No one could possibly complain that Bourdieu idealizes popular culture – on the contrary as our quotations show, his text is littered with contemptuous references to the illusion of the autonomy of the culture of the dominated.

Bourdieu wants us to think about the multi-layered ways whereby taste and the paraphernalia of everyday life divide societies into what he calls classes, even though he avoids claims about the possible ways in which the resulting division might be perpetuated by the polarization of taste. Indeed, in a recent book of lectures and essays (1994a) which seems designed to provide a summary of his thought in a manner radically different from the discursive, multi-layered style of *La Distinction* and similar works, it is striking to note the unelaborated and dualistic approach to the notion of class (and thus by implication, but only and significantly by implication, of inequality) and also the physical and analytical separation between discussion of the subjects of class and of power.[36]

Nonetheless, the remarks about Santa Maria Novella, like so much of his work, illustrate his assumption of a radical break between the culture of the lettered and educated and that of the 'popular' classes, a term possibly better rendered in English as 'the masses'. In Santa Maria Novella the gap between official and popular religion and aesthetics is so wide that it even finds expression in the form of the objects themselves and in the daily rounds of church officials, and Bourdieu notes ironically how Church personnel (the 'clerks'), supposedly disdainful of popular forms of worship, cater to the needs of the art-lovers who have no religious motivation or even interest, yet also move discreetly around the place of worship ensuring that the odd votive candle is burning and that the objects of adoration remain lit.[37]

This unmediated binary opposition needs modification. Bourdieu does not take account of the exchanges or transfers between the erudite and the

---

[36] That is, on pages 25–27, '*La logique des classes*', and 53–57, '*Espace social et champ du pouvoir*'; as opposed to pp. 19–25 where differences of *dispositions* (interchangeable with his widely quoted usage 'habitus') are discussed. The link is not made, and I am sure that is not by accident.

[37] This involves, for example, popping the odd coin into the time switches put out for tourists or worshippers to light up objects of particular interest or devotion.

popular, as embodied, among innumerable examples, in cultural tourism itself.[38] Yet this is curious, for his remark, already quoted in the Introduction, describing 'popular culture' as 'dispersed fragments of a more or less age-old erudite culture . . . selected and refashioned in accordance with the class habitus . . . ' contains within it an unconscious awareness precisely of the exchanges involved in these gradations.

Bourdieu's literary and artistic sensibility, and indeed erudition, allied with a rare sociological insight, and his undoubted Proustian inspiration, provide a description, in endless captivating detail, of the forms which the polarization, often more accurately differences, of taste, may take, and we shall see how his work can contribute to an analysis which gives real body to the claim in this book that Pentecostalism is operating a cultural revolution. This is surprising because Bourdieu's work has – after his early studies in Algeria – concentrated almost obsessively on a country where the state has devoted more resources than any other over a prolonged period of time to the construction and perpetuation of a legitimate, official culture, and he would have difficulty even in imagining an official culture contaminated by the popular, let alone a revolution in culture.[39]

I have already mentioned the gradations and dialectical relationship between erudite and popular religion, and culture more generally, which seem to me to stand in contrast to a polarized conception of that relationship. As an illustration we might ask what Bourdieu would say of the multiple divisions which radically separate Pentecostals from the complex of relationships contained in Brazil's shakily dominant Catholic culture: separation is so radical, in the fields stretching from artistic representation and decoration, to the routines of everyday life, such as dress and even comportment, and much else besides, that it transcends the category of hostility and is better described as a relationship of disdainful and supreme indifference. It operates at several levels: one is the studied avoidance of a wide range of official and 'highbrow' cultural

---

[38] Well illustrated by the fable of the American couple who, having frittered away their time in Paris in shops and cafés, suddenly realize they have only half an hour to 'do' Notre-Dame and agree that 'I will do the outside while you do the inside'.

[39] Except in the obligatory vein of moralizing sociology in the very last sentence, for example, of the Santa Maria Novella paper where he writes that the universalization of the requirements of a society without superstitious practices and cultural lags could only come about if everything is done to universalize the means of fulfilling the requirements of enlightened or high culture ('*On n'est en droit d'universaliser les exigences qu'à condition de mettre tout en oeuvre pour universaliser l'accès aux moyens de les remplir*'). The confrontation of the religious world of Brazil with Bourdieu's work might indeed double up as a confrontation between Brazilian and French culture, and would be all the more interesting for the enormous influence of French culture on the Brazilian intelligentsia, from Auguste Comte through Lévi-Strauss and on to Jacques Lacan and Bourdieu himself, not to speak of the influences through the Catholic Church mentioned elsewhere in this book.

forms, such as the elaborate choreography of the Eucharist – replaced by the *Santa Ceia* in which the faithful queue for plastic cups of grape juice on a tray. Another level is to be seen in the avoidance of a set of practices and an aesthetic which have become so routine as to form part of secular popular culture, yet which are regarded by all *evangélicos* as idolatrous, such as church decorations and images of any kind. These decorations and images are hybrids in Bourdieu's approach: they fit his notion of that (aesthetically legitimate) art which is its own referent, since, as if in a parody of Bourdieu's definition of legitimate, respected culture, the evangelicals regard them as 'useless'. Yet at the same time the images obviously also conform to his description of devotional art, associated with a popular, as opposed to a learned, aesthetic (Bourdieu, 1979: 33). In short, the *evangélicos* are hostile at once both to the established erudite forms of religious representation, not to speak of established learning and expertise, and also to obviously 'popular' practices such as devotions to saints, or simply the presence of effigies in church.

The binary (or, in Peter Brown's words, 'two-tier') model is further unsettled by the complex relationship within Catholicism itself between the erudite 'clerks of the Church' and the popular devotions and superstitions they oppose either openly by banning or attempting to ban them, or implicitly, by seeking to control them. This tension has been continuous in Spanish America but in recent times, as described in the chapters on *basista* Catholicism, the relationship has been transformed once again in some quarters. Priests and religious and lay activists have attempted to construct an alliance, even a synthesis, between post-conciliar theology and ritual practice and the popular religion which their modernist education ought to have taught them to be wary of, either because of its irrationality or because of the conformist social attitudes it might breed.

While these modernized 'clerks of the Church' go out in search of popular culture and religion, to rescue and somehow incorporate it into the mainstream, the *evangélicos* adopt an attitude of utter indifference to established forms of popular Catholicism. They turn their backs on the rootedness and historicism of a popular culture projected by the intelligentsia time and time again, in the dialectic relationship described in the Introduction. Even their extreme hostility towards the possession cults, to the point occasionally of physical aggression, reflects their non-participation in that tradition because it takes the cults at their face value, without any of the ambiguities and uncertainties which, as explained above, are central to 'Afro-Brazilian' ritual. Where popular religion is a way of life, the *evangélicos* turn their backs on it as a system of belief; where the cults are an endless weaving of relationships, the *evangélicos* attack them as subject–object relationships – not as devilish tricks, but as, literally, the work of the devil. The *evangélico* disposition towards the world replaces ambiguity, irony, uncertainty, groping for truth or hope with literal meanings, sarcasm, certainty and sudden flashes of truth and faith.[40] Through their indifference to popular culture, and in particular to the dialectic of the erudite and the popular which shapes it, the *evangélicos* transcend the underlying structures of popular religion which I derived from Brandão in the Introduction. They are playing according to quite different rules.

We can begin to approach an understanding of this change in culture via Roberto DaMatta's (1979) account of carnival. DaMatta describes carnival as an inversion of hierarchy, and indeed of many other features of everyday life – modesty, respect – and samba as music 'from below', from the periphery of society, invented in the *favelas* and the slave quarters, and utterly disconnected from the comforting schmaltz of everyday popular rhythms and harmonies.[41] Samba would have itself be subversive, especially in the eyes of its fans from the Zona Sur, Rio's chic southern neighbourhood, yet it is nothing of the sort:

> both samba and the carnival organizations (especially the samba schools)[42] look upwards, in search of conversion, approval and legitimation by the upper strata of society. Thus again at this level the system is integrated . . . because, divided as it is into clearly visible social groups, it recovers its own integration by adopting as generalizable and universal everything which comes from below. (DaMatta, 1979: 112)[43]

[40] In the middle of the night, late in October 1995, a preacher of the Universal Church of the Kingdom of God brought an effigy of the patron saint of Brazil – the Virgin of Aparecida – onto his television session on the day of the saint's festival and attacked it with an axe, to prove it had no miraculous powers, that it was just a 'graven image'. It was an exceptional incident, provoking a national scandal, and processions to restore the Virgin's honour in many cities, and bringing apologies from Edir Macedo. It was also a curious and perhaps exceptional incident because my experience is that these Churches reserve their bitter public hostility more for the possession cults than for the Catholic Church (*Journal de Genève*, 26/10/95).

[41] cf. '*Choroes e chorinhos*' ('Laments and tearlets'), the jauntified rhythms of the *sertão* as interpreted by Luis Gonzaga and his accordion, or, on a different track, straight North American and European-based rock.

[42] Samba schools are the core of carnival organization: they take part in the parade and compete for the prizes for the best floats. They are not really schools at all, but large co-operative undertakings led by the kings and princes of the underworld (Pereira de Queiroz, 1992)

[43] My translation. Parts of the sentence are no less obscure in the original: '*Tanto samba quanto os grupos do Carnaval (sobretudo as escolas de samba) estão voltados para cima, na busca da conversão, aprobação dos segmentos {seguimentos in the original must be a misprint} superiores da sociedade. Assim, o sistema se integra também nesse nível quando a sociedade se individualiza. Pois agora, dividida em grupos bem visíveis, ela se integra novamente adotando como forma generalizável e universal tudo que nasceu embaixo.*' The second sentence is to me incomprehensible in this context.

This is very suggestive, but the big picture, like that presented by Bourdieu, is too unitary, the word integration is used in too facile a dialectic with the repeated reference to hierarchy and polarization: the culture ought instead to be thought of as constantly in flux, and unified only by the endless exchanges of symbols, rituals and practices and the transformations of their meaning.[44]

Irremediable as these polarizations and hierarchies are, how can one fail to notice the proliferation in Brazilian culture – and perhaps in other cultures or even in all cultures – of self-aware borrowings and appropriations across the divisions of class and race which are not confined to the ritualized temporal and spatial boundaries of carnival, or similar rituals of social inversion,[45] and therefore (on account of the strong implicit function of such rituals as 'safety-valves') cannot be absorbed into a self-reproducing model of integrated hierarchy? *Umbanda* exhibits a wide range of borrowings and imitations, of enactments and representations, in which individuals and groups represent each other and, beyond that, try to rework their own and each others' identities as black, whites, spiritists and intermediaries of African deities. *Candomblé*, as we have seen (Clarke, 1993; Agier, 1994) is subject to multiple tensions as its rituals, practices and symbols are appropriated by different groups for their own purposes, some trying to make it more African, others trying to make it more Catholic, and so on. Where contemporary social science constantly harps on the theme of drawing boundaries between self and the ever-present 'other', the practitioners of these cults, like the samba schools in Rio, are under pressure not perhaps precisely to 'be' or 'become' the other, or even to absorb the other, but to enact each other. The theatrical quality of these representations cannot be overlooked. In the Ilê-Ayê carnival association (*bloco*) in Salvador (Agier, 1994),[46] whose membership is exclusively confined to blacks (though Agier does not explain in this short piece how this exclusivity is enforced), we are shown how the affirmation of the bonhomie and family outing feeling of their carnival processions enable the participants to affirm black respectability, to act as if they were members of a black elite, which is the *bloco*'s cultivated image, but

---

[44] This too, it should be said, was a motive for some dissent from Brandão's account in the Introduction, marred as it is by an elision of popular culture and popular dissent which borrows Bourdieu's social projection of polarization but adopts, of course, a radically different, less sceptical concept of popular culture than that of Bourdieu.

[45] Notably the urban *jacqueries* known as *quebra-quebra* (literally 'break-break') which can occasionally evolve into a carnivalesque celebration (Moisés and Martinez-Alier, 1977.

[46] Carnival in Salvador is a very different affair from Rio: there is no distinction between spectator and participants because everyone is a participant, there is nothing resembling a *sambódromo*, nor is there the corporatism of the samba schools of Rio.

thereby also to enhance their respectability in the eyes of the city's popular classes. In this case they are not enacting a white élite, but they are enacting, and they do so not only at carnival, for the *bloco* functions all year round, as do the samba schools in Rio.

If members of the black population, in trying to affirm themselves as blacks, find themselves at the same time affirming themselves as respectable members of society, likewise the white people who attend *candomblé* do not 'become' black, or African, but they must surely thereby be enacting those personages. *Umbanda centros* may conduct charitable works in their tens of thousands, thus enacting a patronizing 'white' role, yet their mediums are in touch with an African pantheon and with emblematic figures from the black past, like Preto Velho (the 'old black man' – a sorrowful, philosophical, but controversial figure representing an aged slave.) These are instances in which there is theatre to be sure, but the spectators are invited, tempted, sometimes almost forced, to themselves become actors and participants, and even in the samba schools of Rio one finds innumerable middle-class people from the Zona Sur banging on the doors and hoping to take part in training sessions: if they pay enough they are allowed in (Guillermoprieto, 1990).

The best documented of all these dialectical co-existences is that of the relationship in *candomblé* and *umbanda* between the writings of anthropologists and those of practitioners and the evolution of the practice of the cults themselves (Dantas, 1988; Boyer-Araujo, 1996a). Since the first Afro-Brazilian Congress, in Recife in 1934, the anthropological community, Brazilian and foreign, has provided practitioners with a rationale for what they are doing in terms of authenticity and has moved them to reject the 'syncretism' of which they had previously been utterly unaware in favour of authenticity and fidelity to African traditions. This has brought about a 'folklorization' of the entire enterprise, and of course further 'syncretisms' as the cult of authenticity and of the African element – at the expense of the Indian element – to the point where to 'Africanise' is to intellectualize and where, at least in São Paulo, ethnographic literature has to some extent taken the place of oral transmission of the rite (Prandi, 1993, quoted in Boyer-Araujo 1996a). In their pursuit of respectability the practitioners[47] invoke the learned culture and in pursuit of a mirage of authenticity the representatives of learned culture contribute to the production of a patchwork of the authenticities they are looking for.

[47] Roger Bastide was the pre-eminent influence in the development of this current. Boyer also describes the proliferating esoteric literature written by non-anthropologist practitioners in which legitimation via scientific anthropological analysis is replaced by the multiple registers of spirit possession, rendered in the text by italics, capital letters and decorations.

These are instances drawn from Brazilian life of the ways in which members of social groups separated by hierarchies of wealth and status and respectability imitate each other, try to join themselves to each other, enact scenes from each others' lives. Whether or not these exchanges merit the label 'peculiarly Brazilian', it is hard to imagine a similar engagement, involving not just intimate contact and sexual transgression, but the celebration thereof, between *mestizo* and *indio* culture in the Andean countries, for example, or in Mexico or Guatemala, let alone between white and black in the USA.[48] It is in the light of this comparison that I also have my doubts about linking these exchanges directly with domination and power in the way that DaMatta does and Bourdieu would no doubt have us do.

Pentecostals turn their backs — almost literally — on this pattern of exchanges as much as they do on the exchanges and dialectic observed between 'traditional' erudite and popular Catholicism and also on the self-conscious exchanges of *basista* Catholicism. To be sure they do away with the apparatus of popular Catholicism: local saintly cults, faith in the curative powers of particular effigies, the proliferation of saintly intermediaries who pass on the prayers of the faithful, brotherhoods perpetuating long-standing fiestas in the face of priestly opposition (Ireland, 1992; de Theije, 1990). But the difference goes deeper, for in Pentecostalism there is also no ritual developed from below, no un-authorized borrowing from other cultures, of the sort which for centuries has alternately met with grudging tolerance, co-optation or repression from the Catholic hierarchy. The dialectic between the erudite and the popular which lies at the heart of religious culture in almost the entire Latin Catholic world simply does not exist in Pentecostalism.

This one-dimensional character can be seen at various levels: the profound anti-intellectualism of Pentecostalism, its distrust of theological learning and its advocacy of the doctrine of biblical inerrancy; the absence of a ritual separation between officiant and congregation; the pedagogic rather than ritual character of the celebration of religious services; the discouragement of religious — as opposed to social — rituals in general; the lack of programmed formalized ritual in practices such as healing, exorcism, giving money; all this closes off the opportunity of initiative

---

[48] Despite the extremely theatrical reenactments of Ancient Mexico by the *concheros*, an association of groups professing various degrees of pre-Columbian and mixed belief and ethnicity, who perform ancient ceremonial dances in public places. This is not enactment, but straightforwardly performance of dances rescued from a distant past, with a strong pedagogic content and none of the projection and transgression observed in Brazil (Rostas, 1993).

from below. Pentecostalism's transcendence – or maybe self-conscious unawareness – of the popular-erudite dialectic can be seen in the realms of architecture and music, even of dress – taste in short. In the following pages these elements are described in more detail.

'Fundamentalism', biblical inerrancy and anti-intellectualism

The term fundamentalism was originally coined in North America with the publication in 1910 of *The Fundamentals*, a text written to counter the influence of 'New Christianity', especially the 'social' reading of the Gospel, and to defend 'conservative' theology (Hunter, 1987). In its contemporary ideological usage, the word has come to combine a reference to intolerance – *intégrisme* in the apt French term[49] – biblical inerrancy, and the attempt to subordinate political systems to the dictates of biblical texts as interpreted by a 'lay priesthood of inerrancy', both in Islamic countries and also in the USA. While the concluding chapter will explore common themes in fundamentalist religious movements, this section concentrates on the manifestation among Brazilian Pentecostals of one of those themes, namely a belief in biblical inerrancy and its corollary, the direct access of the formally untutored faithful to the meaning of the biblical text.

The hand-held Bible, bound in a zipped leather case, is a badge of participation in most Pentecostal Churches, except the Universal Church which steers its followers away from that austere style of religious identity. The phrase '*A Biblia diz . . .*' (the Bible says . . .) is constantly used as an introduction to an observation on all sorts of matters. In response to a question, about their dress regulations, for example, an Assembly leader in Nova Sussuarana referred to a passage in the book of Jeremiah, quoting the precise chapter and verse; questions about the authority of men over women, at home and in the Church, are invariably answered with reference to a famous passage in St Paul's Epistle to the Ephesians 5:21–4. A standard phrase to defend or condemn a practice is to say that it is *bíblico* or *anti-bíblico*. An extreme example of what might be called the tokenism of biblical quotation can be found in publications of the *Deus é Amor* church, whose booklet entitled *Doutrina Biblica para os*

---

[49] The word was originally used to refer to the advocacy of a Catholic theocracy associated with the name of Charles Maurras, but today is used almost exclusively with reference to the most extreme forms of Islamism, as for example in Iran, Egypt and Algeria.

dias de hoje[50] (biblical doctrine today) contains statements on 137 items ranging from the correct formula for the invocation at the time of baptism in water to punishments for marital misconduct or procedures for the management of Church funds, each accompanied by several abbreviated biblical references, mostly to St Paul's Epistles. This is an extreme example: the use and discussion of the Bible in published texts of Pentecostal Churches varies from very few in texts by the leader of the Universal Church through to quite complex discussions in publications of the Assemblies, and the multiplication of references in the *Deus é Amor* text referred to.

The Churches' pedagogic publications exhibit differences in the degree of elaboration on the text – and thus the degree of expert, or theological interpretation – which is encouraged or brought to the attention of the reader. Compare a quarterly publication from the Assemblies of God – designed principally for the use of preachers and officers – with a Sunday School manual of Church management issued by *Deus é Amor*.[51] In both texts passages of roughly 10 verses are transcribed. In the Assemblies text each is followed by a commentary which brings out the lessons to be learnt for personal behaviour. In an account of the death of Absalom, son of David, the emphasis is placed on his ambition, his usurpation of his father's role, his demagogy, his conspiratorial activities, his arrogance. His death at the hands of a servant of his father David, who thought he was doing the King a service, came 'as if by divine judgement', and was a consequence of his disobedience, arrogance, rebellion and violence. In another commentary, this time on the mission of Abraham's servant Eliezer, to find a wife for Isaac, the servant's excellent moral qualities are stressed, but in addition, his mission is likened to one inspired by the Holy Spirit which does not reveal itself, but rather reveals Christ; the bride is likened to the Church which is the bride of Christ; Isaac's house is likened to heaven, and this is related to the fact that the meeting of Isaac and Rebecca did not take place in the house of either of them because Rebecca's house (which she is leaving) symbolizes the earth which we shall leave, and Isaac's house (where she will go) symbolizes heaven where we will go, after appearing before Christ on Judgement Day. We see here how, in contrast to the radical 'historicization' we found in the *basista*

---

[50] *Doutrina* here refers to prescription concerning everyday life rather than doctrine in the theological sense of the word. As is explained further on the word is often used by Church members and followers to refer to rules about austerity of dress and behaviour.

[51] The texts are as follows: *Deus é Amor*: *Manual bíblico para escola dominical (jovens e adultos)* (Biblical manual for Sunday School – young people and adults), January–March 1991 (this is also a periodic publication); Assemblies of God: *Lições bíblicas Maturidade Cristã* (Bible lessons for adults – literally 'Christian maturity'), 3rd quarter, 1991.

commentaries, here biblical texts are placed outside time, having no temporal sequence or even insertion. We observe a similar process in the Pentecostal treatment of the Jewish people: the time separating modern Brazilian followers of Pentecostalism from the biblical Children of Israel is placed on the same plane as the space separating them from the modern State of Israel. In Pentecostal discourse, biblical texts are a combination of cautionary tales, moral fables and prescriptive pronouncements.

The *Deus é Amor* manual is simpler, since it presents the text and then follows it only with a learning aid – a series of questions about the story itself, not about its implications, while the Assemblies manual ends its textual commentaries with slightly more complex learning aids. Both therefore have this element of providing a tool for the autodidact, the self-improving person. Both also draw exclusively on the Old Testament, and the Assemblies manual centres each extract on a strong individual or collective figure, making it an exemplary story. This fits in with a pattern found in much Pentecostal preaching, namely the emphasis on prophetic or epic figures and an identification of the listeners with them. The figure is described as facing similar trials and tribulations and temptations to those faced by the faithful in their daily moral or religious life, as in the case of Absalom.

The Bible is a source of exemplary stories about exemplary individuals and peoples, and it is a source of moral precepts. There is scarcely a hint of higher or theological learning or of the existence of any expertise other than knowledge of the text. The expertise in the Assemblies' texts consists almost exclusively of cross-references to biblical texts, but this merely reflects the knowledge of people who have spent a lot of time reading the Bible, rather like a musical virtuoso who might play Bach backwards or upside down, and at top speed, but cannot tell these versions from the original. The texts of the Bible are all taken to be on a level with each other, constituting an indivisible whole. Once again, though, we need to pay attention to differences between Churches: those observed as between the Assemblies and *Deus é Amor* may reflect the higher degree of institutional development in the Assemblies which would in the end lead to the full emergence of theological expertise, for as the material they produce becomes more elaborate, and perhaps as they develop a corps of experts to produce the texts, so they will be under pressure from the experts and from outside to compete also in the theological market, if only to gain in respectability – something which the Assemblies in particular emphasize heavily in the social sphere and may come to pursue in the theological sphere as well. These pressures tend to produce a process of professionalization of biblical commentary, and therefore a reduction of literal interpretations of the Bible, which may occur first in the Assemblies, and then in other churches as well.[52]

The above account applies particularly to the two Churches mentioned, and to others like the Four Square Gospel Church. But once again the Universal Church reminds us both of the variations within Pentecostalism and also of its own very distinctive and innovative methods, for its members do not carry the Bible like an emblem or token, and neither they nor their preachers seem to feel compelled to quote chapter and verse at every turn.[53] The Bible is used in a casual, almost incidental, way, as a point of departure or inspiration, but without the veneration accorded to its text by *Assembleistas* and even by members of the *Deus é Amor* Church – for whose followers there is no greater anathema than the epithet *anti-bíblico*. The account of a *corrente da libertação* service given previously confirms Gomes' view that it is hard to describe the interpretation offered of the Bible by preachers in the Universal Church as exegetic, and most quotations are approximate versions spoken from memory. The treatment of the text by the preachers, in his view, does not reflect extensive familiarity with the Scriptures, nor do they add supplementary quotations from memory with chapter and verse, as one hears in other evangelical Churches (Gomes, 1991: 57). Gomes asks whether the Bible is not used as a talisman, to ward off evil forces, but one would need to have heard preachers make some reference to its use in this regard to support that view – which, if accurate would have far-reaching implications in Churches which scarcely even use the cross. What is evident is that members of all Pentecostal Churches, even those who cannot read, carry their Bible as a mark of their identity as believers and members (*crentes*) just as the peppering of preaching and conversation with chapter-and-verse quotation is an emblematic guarantee of the truth of what is being said.

If Pentecostals resist scholarly interpretation of the Bible, they are avid practitioners of its esoteric decoding – that is of discovering hidden

---

[52] No mention has been made of the possible 'improving' role these Churches might play in teaching people to read as part of their emphasis on direct access to the Word. Although the Assemblies in particular do set up educational activities in relation to their chapels, both for children and for adults, I think this is quite a separate activity, that is a type of social work, which is only incidentally related to the religious experience of their members. The religious appeal of Pentecostal Churches and the speed of their expansion, cannot be explained by reference to the literacy training they might provide in the course of preaching the Bible and of bringing the faithful into contact with biblical texts. Such a reductionism approach impoverishes the phenomenon.

[53] Pereira (1993) writes that about a fifth of people attending a Universal Chariot service would have a Bible with them.

messages for example among numbers or letters in the Bible. This is observed in their fascination with the apocalyptic vision of the Book of the Revelation, with announcements of the end of the world, with their belief in the literal truth – though not necessarily the imminence – of the Second Coming, with the division between those who will be saved on account of their conversion and baptism in life, and those who might be saved on account of their works. The expertise required to pronounce on these matters has not given rise to an expert corps, though there may exist 'full-time' or professional adepts, but there are indications of quite an elaborate, less public, world of biblical decoding in pursuit, for example, of foreknowledge of the Second Coming.[54] This activity remains discreet: there has been no high profile propagation of creationism in Brazil as occurs in the United States, nor any of the accompanying wide-ranging attack on scientific scholarship as a whole and the human sciences in particular, not to speak of the artistic expressions of high culture.[55]

Esoteric knowledge favours the formation of a closed circle of experts, but its irrational basis – that is, the lack of any basis other than authority on which it will allow its claims to be tested – confers a particular, arbitrary character on admission to the circle, and thus stands in contrast to the power exercised by, or legitimated by, theological elites (the 'clerks of the Church'). It is not intellectual knowledge in the usual sense, because it is not professionalized or bureaucratized. In 'mainstream' Christian religions theological elites rarely exercise power themselves in the ecclesiastical structure, being cast rather in the role of specialized, advisory, experts, and applying their expertise in universities or similar institutions which embody their independence,[56] but which are precisely the object of derision by the defenders of biblical inerrancy. The defenders of inerrancy decry the pretensions of theologians to interpret the

---

[54] It is certainly tempting to think of Brazilian culture as peculiarly receptive to esoteric learning of the most varied kinds. Lacanian psychoanalysis 'Brazilian style', spiritualism, astrology, numerology, Tarot cards and more seem to enjoy a rare level of legitimacy and credence among all social classes, so that there are indeed full-time professionals who make a living from these and many other beliefs and practices. I have resisted the temptation to interpret Pentecostalism as simply another reflection of this 'hierarchy of Brazilian cures' because, although such a version might be superficially persuasive, it would also be seriously incomplete, and would also infringe the delicate separation between sociological analysis and cultural exoticism.

[55] Note the prominent presence in Islamicist movements of engineering and electronics students (Kepel, 1991) and of course the fondness of evangelicals for modern means of communication, which they handle much more adeptly than the Catholic Church: the attack is on the academic rather than the applied branches of modern knowledge.

[56] The degree of independence has varied over the centuries and recently there have been some celebrated cases of hierarchical interference in Catholic theological institutions; but the basic principle remains – otherwise the cases mentioned would not be regarded as 'interference'.

Scriptures on the basis of science – an issue which goes back a long way and blew up early in the twentieth century over what came to be called the 'higher criticism'. Similarly contemporary Islamists in North Africa are ferociously opposed to the learning of the ancient Al-Azhar university in Cairo which they regard as corrupted by power and academic pretensions detached from the faith of the masses.[57]

Biblical inerrancy claims to place the individual member or worshipper in direct relation to the Word, in stark contrast to the elaborate expert theological intermediation which has been a hallmark of Catholicism for centuries, exemplified by the exclusion of the laity from access to sacred texts. But the Pentecostal preacher's freedom of action in choosing a text and commenting upon it, does embody a process of interpretation, and the difference between Pentecostal and Catholic uses of the Bible lies in the absence, in the latter case, of a professional corps of interpreters, rather than in the absence of any intervening interpretation at all, while a crucial difference in their power structures lies in the unity in Pentecostal Churches of administrative power and the authority to produce the correct interpretation of the Bible.

To discover how Pentecostals do use the Bible, and how their selection of quotations and their retelling of biblical stories with abundance of metaphorical and allegorical devices constitutes an interpretation, we can turn to examples from television and from church services in Salvador.

We begin with a television programme broadcast every Saturday morning in 1991 on the Manchete network by a woman preacher, Walnicy, from São Paulo.[58] She strides up and down her podium in an attitude of complete command, her mouth fixed in a smile revealing a perfect set of teeth, brandishing her microphone. Her diction is perfectly honed, her analysis of biblical texts admirably clear, accompanied by sub-titles, and sequenced from one week to the next. In this didactic performance, the metaphors are elaborately developed, for example that of the *aliança* – the covenant, but also the wedding ring – between God and the Children of Israel, embodied in the ark – a word which in Portuguese can also mean a chest, as in treasure chest. The metaphors are exploited to the full:

[57] Hostility to Al-Azhar goes back a long way and there is as much politics to it as there is religion. The history of Arab nationalism – not just Islamic revival – is marked from the outset in the inter-war period by attacks on it as a body protected, co-opted and corrupted by the state for its own political purposes and by the search to ally a renewal of Islam with an Arab political project in the wake of the collapse of the Ottoman empire (Enayat, 1982).

[58] To judge by the advertisements at the end of the programme, she is inspired by Jimmy Swaggart.

'*Nesta hora Jesus se torna o que eu sou . . .*' (In this hour Jesus becomes what I am . . .)

'*Ele entra em mim e eu entro nele.*' (He enters in me and I in him.)

'*A união, a aliança! Jesus vai plantar a sua semente no coraċao do homen . . .*' (Union! The Covenant! Jesus will sow his seed in the heart of man.)

'*Não há aliança com Jesus sem morrer.*' (The covenant/marriage with Jesus is not possible without dying.)

'*Adão planta sua semente no útero da mulher . . .*' ('Adam sows his seed in the woman's uterus' . . . but Jesus generates spiritual children.)

'*Eu estou nele e ele esta em mim.*' (I am in Him and He in me).

'*retire o sangue contaminado do meu espirito*' (remove the infested blood from my spirit)

'*Jesus entrou em mim . . . em 1963 . . . são 28 anos que andamos juntos com esse sentimento gostoso . . . que ele me possui e eu o possuo . . . na aliança . . . até as arvores sorriam . . . ele dá tudo e voce recebe . . .*' (Jesus entered into me . . . in 1963 . . . it is now 28 years since the two of us began to march together with that delicious feeling . . . that he possesses me and I possess him . . . in the covenant/marriage . . . even the trees are smiling . . . He gives everything and you just receive . . .)

The text is a point of departure whose relationship to the message as a whole is metaphorical and even metonymic: the avenue through which she passes side by side with Jesus is bordered by trees — which smile upon her. The seed planted by Adam in Eve's body becomes the seed of faith planted by Christ in man's heart. Having no erudition, no context, recognizing no authoritative method or school of interpretation, the imagination is allowed to wander freely, sprinkled with references to a *bricolage* of sacred allusions (blood, the marriage with Christ, the seed).

The performance of Walnicy must be carefully rehearsed: it has coherence and unity in the development of the themes and the integration of the metaphors in the exposition. In these respects it differs from what one might hear in church or chapel. But it has in common with other Pentecostal preaching the immediacy of the link between the listener and the personages in the text: they are exemplary personages (in this case Moses and the Children of Israel) whose histories are worthy of imitation, not saints to whom votive offerings or petitions are made. The personages may be heroic, or virtuous, but they are not super-human: on the contrary, their humanity is emphasized so that the listener can identify with them, and the moral has to be explicated every time the story is told. More than anything the Bible is used as a source of cautionary tales.

In another example, a preacher from the Assemblies of God sent by the *matriz* to the outlying chapel of Nova Sussuarana, takes two texts, first the Prodigal Son (Luke 15:11–31), then Jacob's Struggle (Genesis, 32:22–29). The Prodigal Son is presented by Luke in the context of a rebuke to the Pharisees and others who 'began grumbling among themselves: "This fellow", they said, "welcomes sinners and eats with them" ', and under the moral 'there will be greater joy in heaven over one sinner who repents than over ninety-nine righteous people who do not need to repent'. The preacher's interpretation was as follows: 'and when his money had run out he said to himself "my father's workers are eating better than I am so I will return home".' Moral: if you leave your father's house – which also means the house of God the Father – then you will lose everything. The preacher then gave a dramatic account of Jacob's struggle with the angel and concluded – in an allusion to the procedure whereby devils are expelled by forcing them to pronounce their name – that 'just as Jacob had a struggle to say his name, so if you say your name to Jesus he will save you'. Jacob's name change (from Jacob to Israel) led him to speak of the Jews and the State of Israel – 'the People of God' – and of the Gulf War, praising Israel's forbearance, and saying God extended his hand to Israel.[59] Returning to Jacob he evoked with impressive eloquence the rivalry between Jacob and Esau and, as in the case of the Prodigal Son, related the biblical story to the everyday family life of the congregation: the rivalry was like that which occurs every day in families where one child will complain that 'Daddy gives him more clothes than me'. Isaac's blessing to his son was described as a gift from God, not just from Isaac himself, and the explanation as to why it was given to Jacob, the younger son, was that Esau had not appreciated his father's blessing. Conclusion: if God's blessing is upon us then we will overcome, as did Jacob, as Joseph did when accused of seducing Potiphar's wife (Genesis 39:7–23) and so on. And he concluded saying that the chapel where the congregation was meeting was like the place where Jacob dreamed of angels going up and down a ladder to heaven, Beth-El, the House of God: it still had to be completed, so it was uncomfortable 'but we can feel God among us'. The summary shows the 'gobbet' approach to the biblical texts: for an untutored congregation, the Bible is portrayed as a vast compendium of practical moral tales. Distinctions of status, period, or authorship, between Prophets and Gospel, or between the Old and the New Testament, or between the children of Israel and the Prodigal Son,

---

[59] A reference to the 'arm outstretched' with which God promises to redeem his people enslaved in Egypt cf. Exodus 6:6 and many other instances thereafter.

disappear.[60] The text is not surrounded with the ritual of veneration one finds in Catholic (or Anglican) churches or in synagogues: no ceremonial surrounds its treatment, and there are no procedures or programmes governing the appropriate text for particular occasions.

Moving now from a preacher's peroration to everyday conversation we find routine invocation of stories from the Bible, again in a manner which suggests that the teaching received by the faithful connects certain passages to certain moral issues, but also that the connection is somewhat arbitrary, and often the relation established is, to say the least, obscure, implying again that the approach is not to read the Bible but rather to extract opportune quotations from it. Asked to describe their own role in the Church, women refer to Mary Magdalene: she was the first at the tomb of Christ – or to Mary who brought him down from the Cross; they were the first *missionarias* and they are invoked to show that women have a special disposition towards the sacred – '*tem mais autoridade de falar de Cristo*' (they may speak of Christ with greater authority).[61] The obligation to give money to the Church is illustrated with reference to Job: 'Jesus said: look at Job, how rich he was – but he gave it all to God'.[62] Or again, the parable of the talents (Matthew 25:14–30) is introduced to show we must not put money above everything else: Jesus upbraided the '*servo mau e negligente*' (the bad and negligent servant) who buried his talents. Finally, the passage about marriage in St Paul's Letter to the Ephesians 5:22–4, is very frequently quoted in justification of the need to obey one's husband and also of the predominant role of men in senior positions in most Churches. (The subsequent verses which call on husbands to love and respect their wives are less often quoted.)

These quotations illustrate what biblical inerrancy implies in the everyday life of the faithful. For the Pentecostals the mere existence of a verse in the biblical text confers upon it a validity in itself with direct

[60] Later in the day the congregation reassembled to watch a performance put on by the Youth Group (*Círculo da Oração da Mocidade*) celebrating its third anniversary. The theme was Jacob's dream, again, and a ladder at the front of the chapel had seven steps, representing Faith, Humility, Self-sacrifice, Repentance, Obedience, Purity and Love. The young people preached, alluded to biblical stories such as that of the rebel leaders in the desert who were devoured by the earth which opened up beneath them (Numbers 26:10). Seven speeches elaborated on each of the seven virtues depicted on the ladder: among them, humility – Jesus raised the humble and attacked the Pharisees – and repentance – the door to grace which opens the gateway to heaven. The mention of the raising of the humble would have warmed the heart of a *basista*, but more important is once again the 'gobbet' approach, mixing angels on the ladder with the seven virtues.

[61] The term *missionaria* has particular significance because it is in the feminine and also because in some churches it is a title conferred on members, especially women who go out to proselytize, often dressed in uniform.

[62] The reference is incomprehensible in the context of the Book of Job, but that is what the preacher said.

relevance for their everyday life. In the place of an elaborate, learned apparatus brought to bear on the text and its context, we find an open-ended set of moral prescriptions bolstered by a repertoire of ready-made decontextualized quotations. The result is not in the least an absence of interpretation: there is no less interpretation and no less imposition of an interpretation than we find in Catholicism. The power of the word replaces the power of the saints and their intermediation.

'Le choix du necessaire': church architecture and music

One of the disappointing features of the sociological literature on both Catholicism and Protestantism is that it is aesthetically unmusical. Apart from David Martin's remarks about music as an expression of community sentiment (1990: 175), and those of Raboteau, observers concentrate on the conscious and the purposive dimensions of experience, unmindful of the fundamental role played by music and architecture in the formation of a religious identity. It is impossible to imagine Western Christianity without the architecture and the music which are indissolubly associated with the unconscious substratum of religious experience.

The 'choice of the necessary' which appears in the heading of this section is also the title of a chapter in Bourdieu's *La Distinction* where it is defined as a principle of *les pratiques populaires* (p. 441). The *pratiques populaires* limit themselves to choosing that which will serve its purpose within the minimum standards of propriety for 'les gens "simples" et "modestes" ' (' "simple", "humble" people') and they stand in contrast to 'art for art's sake' ('l'art pour l'art'), to the bourgeois taste for form,[63] and to the ways of living propagated by fashion magazines, home decoration magazines, child-rearing manuals and the like, all of which represent the way of life of those who know how to 'spend uselessly'. This does not mean that *la distinction* is always an ostentatious taste; on the contrary one of the effects it seeks is 'to suggest with the smallest possible number of objects the greatest possible expenditure of time, money and ingenuity' (p. 442). Although Bourdieu's elaborate account of taste in its innumerable forms sits uneasily with his simplistic usage of the term 'popular classes', placed in neat opposition to those variously described as 'bourgeois', 'learned', 'educated', wealthier and so on, it remains extremely suggestive. It opposes — not without nuances and gradations, to

[63] The French word *'bourgeois'* as used here has precisely the opposite connotation to that it would have in English: whereas in English it would mean conformist and 'middle-class' it is clear that Bourdieu means to refer to the 'good taste' of those educated to 'high culture'.

be sure — the taste for which austerity is a choice to that for which it is a way of showing 'a sense of one's place' (p. 544 — in English in the original), and those who would see in a photograph of a pair of elderly, wrinkled, weathered hands the mere depiction of a case of rheumatism or deformity to those who take it for a work of art calling for aesthetic comment (p. 47) on poverty, old age, beauty. It would be unthinkable, in this context, for such a photograph to be described as 'beautiful' in the language of the taste for the necessary.

This sort of approach fits remarkably well with the language used by Pentecostals who make much of the austerity of their churches — often referred to in Old Testament vein as *templos* — which they contrast with the *fasto* (luxury) and *feitiço* (embellishment) of Catholic churches. In their words — '*naquelas tudo e obra do homen e nos so fazemos a obra de Deus*' (everything in Catholic churches is the work of man, whereas we only do the work of God). In a city like Bahia whose central districts are enveloped in a Baroque Church architecture intertwined with the city's very identity, the contrast is indeed striking, but it is equally so even when the more austere modern Catholic churches (Plate 1) are compared with Pentecostal ones — for theirs is an austerity of choice which reflects precisely the expenditure of time and money in the production of the effect of austerity.

This does not mean to say that the design of Pentecostal chapels and churches is without interest or significance; the *choix du necessaire* itself is, precisely, a choice. The choice of the necessary in this context can be thought of as the choice of designs which say something about the people who use the buildings rather than about pure form itself or indeed about their beliefs or their God. On two occasions in Bahia I saw preachers working with great care on building or reconstructing their small chapels. These may have been functional, but they were designed as spaces apart with uniform benches and whitewashed walls. The Universal Church in 1991 had numerous hangar-like rented buildings in outlying and poor neighbourhoods, but by 1993 its services seemed to be concentrated in grandiose constructions built in central locations where once cinemas or suchlike had stood.

Among more established Pentecostal Churches, such as the Assemblies, the variation, according to the money available, the neighbourhood and the length of time during which a community has been established, reflected an aspiration to social mobility and respectability. The little chapels are aggressively functional, displaying nothing but a podium and not even always that. Larger ones are reverberating, cavernous meeting-halls whose aggressively angular lines and bare walls offer no rest to the eye or the ear. The extreme case is *Deus é Amor*: even its headquarters church, whose São Paulo address is advertised outside each one of its places of worship, is simply a large-scale version of the hangar design. The furniture in all these cases is highly uniform, consisting of benches and nothing more: no choir stalls or preacher's seat, just more benches placed slightly apart. Much emphasis is placed on standards of cleanliness and tidiness, discreetly maintained by the uniformed *obreiras*.

In Belém, where they were founded in 1911, the Assemblies' vast building can hold 8,000 people. It contains offices, a large banqueting area, and a pool for baptism by full immersion. The church hall itself has generously spaced benches made of high quality wood and rises to two vast balconies overlooking a wide podium behind which a further imposing area is reserved for a choir. The whole could be described as functional, yet redolent of the self-satisfaction of a community which has 'arrived', has established itself, and has attained unabashed bourgeois solidity. In Salvador, in the well-established district of Liberdade, which could be described as 'respectable working-class and lower middle-class', a similar, though smaller, structure has been built by the Assemblies with the same functions. Looking to move to a more stately location, in 1991 plans were afoot for a bigger, prouder, headquarters in a location away from the hurly-burly of Liberdade. At all levels there is no fixed decoration at all — in the Assemblies not even a cross. The Universal Church, which for a time exhibited a cross modified in such a way that it resembled a trade mark more than an object of religious devotion, has discarded it in favour of a white dove in a red heart. Decoration takes the form of flowers placed around the pulpit or podium.

The design of the two *matriz* churches mentioned does not fit Bourdieu's schema in one crucial respect, namely the pride and self-satisfaction they express. Here there is no sense of a dominated or subordinate culture, but rather a statement that whatever others may think of their taste, the people who attend these churches are proud of it. Like the care with which *crentes* dress for Sunday service, the men in their suits, ties and even frilled white shirts, the women in their Sunday best picking their way between the *favela*'s heaps of discarded rubbish, it is also a statement of separateness from the mass, from the 'darkness', from 'this-worldliness' (*as trevas, as coisas do mundo*). It is also not necessarily austere: the *Deus é Amor* case apart, designs do become bigger and more comfortable, though continuing to embody the most vigorous possible denial of *l'art pour l'art*.

If the *Deus é Amor* Church holds fast to the extreme of dislocated space, and the Assemblies combine hostility to artistic form with a Brazilian answer to middle-European *burgerlichkeit*, the Universal Church had apparently adopted a new policy between 1991 and 1993. In 1993 in the town centre of the suburb of Periperi, an old cinema was replaced by a spacious new building with gleaming whitewashed walls, arched doorways with heavy wood panelled doors and marble flooring (Plate 4). Smaller chapels dotted around the neighbourhoods of the suburb had been closed down and their congregations now attended this single venue. The Church seemed to have decided to establish something like a parish church, set firmly in the centre of the municipality as an institution, not just a place of prayer. In its design, this building, which resembles others belonging to the same Church, borrowed more from the Catholic tradition than from the style of other Pentecostal Churches. This is hardly surprising, since the Universal Church wants to set itself up as an institution, looking out towards society, and its leaders have the ambition to influence, even exercise, political power, as evidenced by their promotion of 'their' candidates to elected office, and by their purchase of a nationwide TV network – TV Record.

While these large-scale constructions built by the Universal Church are designed to present an image of prestige to the world beyond, and to be welcoming to outsiders, the large-scale *matrizes* belonging to the Assemblies look imposing but undistinguished and uninviting from without, like office blocks, and from within resemble meeting halls to concentrate the attention of the faithful on themselves as a fellowship of the elect. Assembly churches and chapels are locked when not in use, whereas the Universal Church keeps its doors open all day. The design of these new churches it is building is not that of an organization which is concerned (like the Assemblies) with tight membership lists or calibrated induction procedures, but rather presents an image of confident expansion towards society as a whole.

In contrast, recently built Catholic churches in poor neighbourhoods[64] are 'designed to be simple', placing them in the realm of erudite, legitimate culture. Their lines contain a reference to traditional forms of ecclesiastical architecture: a whitewashed façade with arches, at least a hint of a bell tower and sometimes more, making of them a local landmark. They contain a simple altar and the sparsely and symmetrically arranged images of a Virgin or a saint, together with the curved lines of arches and windows make for a fundamental and doctrinal difference. The design guides the eye along certain lines towards an altar or an image of the cross: the lines converge and usually in a curved pattern. In the traditional Pentecostal church the effect is that of a banqueting hall or a

---

[64] Examples include those in Sussuarana, Jardim Cruzeiro, Periperi, and a *favela* behind the bus station. See Plate 2.

1   Modern chapel built to commemorate the place where the Pope celebrated Mass on his visit to Salvador in 1991. Note the austere curves of the chapel, in contrast to the Portuguese colonial Baroque which characterizes most traditional Catholic churches in the city.

2   The parish church of São Jorge (1991). Note the discreteness of the building and the care taken to preserve the surrounding vegetation. The painted sign 'Igreja de São Jorge' implies that but for the sign people might mistake the church for a secular community centre, for example.

3 and 4　Two churches of the Universal Church of the Kingdom of God, both post 1991, both in Salvador: no. 3 in Ribeira and no. 4 in Periperi. The juxtaposition illustrates (a) the use of a more or less standardized model by the Universal Church and (b) that Church's aspiration, through the design and location of its buildings, to represent itself as an institution which takes the place once occupied by imposing Catholic edifices. It is unlikely to be accidental that the design is reminiscent of the representation of the Jerusalem Temple in popular editions of the Bible.

grandiose club, rather than a symbol of a neighbourhood, community or parish. The object is to glorify the congregation – their prosperity and respectability, their 'arrival', the sacrifices endured to build their place of worship. These modern, Catholic churches on the other hand, in their contrived austerity, are designed to be 'uplifting': having an arch, or a gable above the doorway, and windows which let in light, like the great cathedrals whose architecture in some way they echo, they draw the eye and the thoughts of the faithful upwards towards heaven. And they too are institutions, set in a precinct, however small, serving as community centres and meeting places for local organizations.

Like architecture, so also music contributes to the ritual atmosphere. Apart from supporting the preacher's management of emotional expression, music also provides a vehicle for the expression of collective unity: the songs in Pentecostal churches are usually in a march-like four-beat rhythm and in a major key. They bear no relation to any Brazilian musical tradition, though occasionally in the Universal Church a tune seems to have been borrowed from a current hit: no syncopation, no rising seventh, not a hint of *saudade*. The songs are relentlessly optimistic and cheerful and the audience sing them from memory. The congregation in the Universal Church, in keeping with that organization's orientation towards modern youth culture, enjoy clapping and swaying their hips in tune with the rhythm, especially at the end of a service when the tension is relaxed. In *basista* meetings and churches, in contrast, one hears more syncopated rhythms, more minor keys, more *saudade*, and more reference to samba or samba-like rhythms, as well as tunes reminiscent of the Southern United States 'spiritual', accompanied by a guitar on its own rather than by an electric guitar with wind and drums and sound synthesizer. The grander Pentecostal Churches have an electric organ.

A more technical account of music and architecture would be more illuminating, but these few remarks are inserted to illustrate the potential richness of a full analysis of music and Church architecture or design. They also offer further illustration of the Pentecostals' resolute indifference to both the exigencies of sophisticated modern taste and to the taste for authenticity which is itself a sub-product of that taste as it projects popular culture onto itself and itself onto popular culture. And within that opposition, we once again find the Universal Church, representative of both the most modern and the most charismatic wing of Pentecostalism, doing something different.

9

The Experience of Pentecostals: Exaltation, Loyalty and Liminality

The relation between officiant and congregation

In the sub-culture of *basismo*, as observed in Salvador, priests are shy about leadership, preferring to exercise it through the popular organizations they set up rather than from the altar or the pulpit. In church they lead gently: taking their cue from the post-conciliar reaction against the social, spatial and ritual distance which in Catholic worship separated them from the faithful, priests now invite their congregations to participate, rather than instructing them; they speak to them in a familiar, non-deprecating and non-didactic, language, placing the liturgical sequence in a context which they hope will clarify its meaning; they make liberal use of colloquialisms and of references to the daily life of the neighbourhood. A reduction of mysteriousness is at work, and the priest is departing from the role of ritual leader and guardian of moral authority acquired over a long period in Latin countries, even though Catholic priests are highly educated. Even the increasing number of Brazilian priests who are of relatively humble social origin have, through their lengthy and rigorous education, become members of the 'learned' classes.

The use both of social and ritual space and of language is utterly different in Pentecostal Churches. In local chapels in the *favelas* the preachers are much closer in social status to their congregations than a priest can ever be, and we have seen that the Churches have a graded system of offices to enable people to emerge from the ranks and acquire a formal status and in their different ways to encourage people who show a 'gift of speaking' or of praying.

Despite the closeness in social status between preacher and congregation, the style of speech in Pentecostal services and study sessions emphasizes distance and the tone of familiarity adopted by the *basista* priest is absent. The authority of the preacher is established in a variety of ways depending on the setting and other factors. In a tiny chapel of the Assemblies of God one finds a woman leading a prayer group on a weekday morning. They meet every day. She has no recognized status in the Church except informal recognition of her rhetorical talent. She yells at them, she exhorts them to shout 'Hallelujah', she calls on them to respond 'Amen' or *Louvado seja Deus* (God be praised) at very frequent intervals; she expounds a miracle of Jesus and leads them in Psalms interspersed with spontaneous outcries and much speaking in tongues. If we now shift to the Assemblies' *matriz* in Liberdade, the preacher is a man, and an established figure, less hectoring, confident in his status as a fully fledged pastor which enables him to keep his distance. If we move across to the Universal Church we find that even in one of that organization's large churches the preacher's social status, observed on the basis of his colour, his accent, the turns of phrase he uses, is close to that of his congregants, but the distance between preacher and congregants is expressed and reinforced by his tone of authority: he tells them he does not like people who neglect to make donations they have promised, he summons them to shout 'Amen' and 'Hallelujah!'.

The *basista* priest adopts forms of popular parlance which do not come to him entirely naturally, and in doing so expresses a reverential respect for popular culture, whereas Pentecostal pastors and preachers use the popular language which comes to them naturally in order to denounce popular culture. Preachers and pastors whose social and educational status is similar to that of their congregations keep control of the liturgical sequence (such as it is), while in Catholic Churches, priests who are far more educated than their congregations and, merely by virtue of their priesthood, of far higher social status, give up some of that control. Although the social status of preachers rises in accordance with their rank in the Church this does not cause them any discomfiture in addressing people who are poorer or less educated than they are.

The Assemblies allow and encourage people with the *Dom da palavra* — the gift of speaking in public, but also the gift of speaking the word of God — to 'emerge' and to exercise responsibilities of a spiritual and administrative kind much more independently than the Universal Church (Hoffnagel, 1978). In the *invasão* of Nova Constituinte a woman recounted the innumerable personal problems which had prevented her from making a career in the Assemblies, but she still was often invited to preach, and to take part in dramatic representations because her inspirational gifts were recognized.[1]

These vignettes show us that the Pentecostal recruitment policy, combined with the availability of numerous positions between the 'grass roots' faithful and fully-fledged pastors, minimizes the social distance between the congregation and the officiant, but it does not necessarily minimize ritual distance: the officiant, whatever his social origin, still finds a basis within the Church for exercising effective authority and monopolizing it within his authorized sphere, and this stands in contrast to a post-conciliar Catholic Church in which the priest not infrequently lacks the confidence or even the conviction of the rightness of the hierarchical monopoly, to impose himself on a congregation.

The personal service Church

Church attendance is one of the salient marks of belonging to a Pentecostal Church – far more salient than it is for Catholics, Anglicans or Jews, for example, who have built up multiple marks of belonging over centuries of existence in civil society. The more institutionalized or prominent Assembly churches are open only for services and principally on Sundays, but many chapels evidently are open several times every day. In Recife in the 1970s, according to Hoffnagel's survey, one third of *Assambleistas* attended a church function every day, and 58 per cent four times every week (1978: chap. 5). The Assemblies promote activities which create and cement social networks among the membership, such as youth groups, drama groups, and choirs who rehearse and meet regularly.

The Universal Church and *Deus é Amor* keep their doors open permanently, as if to welcome casual passers-by, have services as often as four times a day, and have a weekly rota of themes for the service which serve as a device to commit individuals to come back on a regular basis. Whereas the Assemblies pay attention to bringing their members' children into the life of the church, in the Universal Church participation is on a much more individual basis, emphasizing members' opportunities

---

[1] She was an itinerant preacher outside the formal organization, recognized for her spiritual gifts, and it was particularly interesting to note that she had none of the hesitations observed among pastors and preachers of the Assemblies to speak of the presence of the Devil, of her dreams of the Devil, and of the Devil's presence in possession cults. The visit of a pastor from the *matriz* while I was talking to her confirmed that such a person can feel herself valued in the organization even without exercising any power in it.

to aspire to new roles outside the family context. Although this pattern reflects the difference between Church as organization and Church as community, it may also reflect the difference between a well-established Church and a newcomer: in the long run, if the Universal Church is to establish itself, it will have to pay attention to mechanisms for family participation so as to attract its members' children.

The rituals of the Assemblies tend to reaffirm the community of believers while those of the Universal Church emphasize the relationship between individuals and the organization. The *Assambleistas* take part in choirs and dramatic representations, adopt a common austere style of dress (but not a uniform), and an austere lifestyle, and attend church with their family. Members of the Universal Church wear a uniform (if they are *obreiros*), queue for counselling, deposit *pedidos de oraçao* (written petitions for solutions to their personal problems) on a table at the front of the hall, and attend church on their own. Also, the rituals of expulsion of devils and healing emphasize the relationship between the individual and the organization. In the Universal Church people can enter at any time and find an authorized person – a preacher or *obreira* – on hand to offer counselling, and it will be a person of the same social class as the membership. At a well-attended service the officiants take up position both before and after the formal proceedings and queues of members form to talk individually to them. Even the Head Pastor of the Universal Church in Bahia takes part, despite his high status and heavy workload.

For those who see the neo-Pentecostal churches as a radically new phenomenon (or 'third wave' as Freston calls it) this attention to the provision of personal attention is one feature of a new approach adapted for new times, but these are differences of emphasis rather than of kind, and it remains to be seen whether over the longer run the older and newer Churches will not come to resemble each other more.

Restructuring the calendar

I have spoken of the expansion of Pentecostalism as an onslaught on the traditions of popular culture evolved in dialectic interaction with the hegemonic culture of Catholicism, and one facet of this is the way in which the lives of Pentecostal Church members and churchgoers take on a quite different rhythm from that of the Brazil of popular Catholicism – as expressed in *festas* and carnival, in anniversaries of saints and communal commemorations linked to local patron saints. Pentecostals regard all that goes on at carnival or in the raucous celebrations of São João (St John) as the work of the Devil: one person spoke of carnival as a *festa triste* (a sad festival). The leader of the prayer group in Nova Constituinte (mentioned above) tells her listeners that the New Year — a time for resolutions, for personal renewal — is more important than Christmas and they should not worry if they have no money to buy presents for their children.[2] Easter is even less important to them in the annual cycle. Hoffnagel (1978) states quite categorically that neither of these festivals was celebrated by the Assemblies of God in Recife in the 1970s, and that 'internal' commemorations were the salient markers of the annual cycle. According to Gomes (1991) in the last week of December 1989, instead of commemorating the birth of Jesus Christ, the Universal Church centred its weekly cycle of services/*correntes* on the solution of members' emotional problems.

Moving to the weekly cycle we have seen the intense churchgoing of some Pentecostals, and the neo-Pentecostals' use of weekly or daily themes and of vows to commit people to regular attendance. In the Universal Church the daily themes are: Monday — Prosperity; Tuesday — Health; Wednesday — 'Children of God'; Thursday — Family; Friday — Expulsion of demons; Saturday — Glory of God (which in fact means financial problems, Freston explains); Sunday morning — the Holy Spirit, and Sunday afternoon — emotional (in Portuguese 'sentimental') problems (Freston, 1993a: 100; Pereira, 1993; Gomes, 1991). *Correntes* aim to create commitment, but they also have the effect of undermining Sunday as a pre-eminent day of worship. Beyond the weekly cycle, the *Santa Ceia* is a monthly occasion. Just as in theory Holy Communion, on which it is modelled, was traditionally a ritual open only to those who had confessed their sins, and been absolved of them, so the *Santa Ceia* is open only to those who are in good standing with their church — that is, who have not incurred suspension or sanction on account of violation of the rules, and who are up to date with their contributions.

Finally, the Pentecostal rules about baptism, which they only perform once a person has reached maturity, mark a restructuring of the life cycle as a whole. Unable to baptize their children in the traditional way in the early days of their life, some Church members even make arrangements to have them baptized as Catholics because if they die early they will risk suffering like lost souls. Baptism by total immersion provides a rite of

---

[2] Christmas does not in any case have the place in the life of the popular sectors in Latin America which it has acquired in Anglo-Saxon culture, but the atmosphere of present-giving is nonetheless palpable: in the *favelas* of Salvador Santa sweats absurdly in the afternoon December heat and throws cheap rubber balls from a municipal pick-up truck.

passage both for the younger generation emerging into adulthood and for converts new to the community of believers.

Conversion: sex, empowerment and the family

In giving an account of their lives, Church members quickly come to the point of their conversion, an experience which is much more important to them than baptism. It is so central that Pepper (1991) writes of a 'ritual of backsliding' whereby the children of Pentecostals adopt non-conforming behaviour patterns which enable them later to return to the fold through a conversion experience. Technically, Pentecostals regard conversion as only a stage in a series of events marking the receipt of spiritual gifts: thereafter a person will aspire to baptism by immersion and baptism 'by fire', that is by the Holy Spirit, as signified by glossolalia, but these events figure much less prominently in the autobiographies offered by Church followers and members, for whom conversion, whether sudden or not, is one single experience. In the neo-Pentecostal Churches we observe a twofold evolution: baptism receives less attention than it does in the Assemblies; it happens, but is not spoken of as a salient ritual, while baptism 'by fire' is not distinguished from the conversion experience itself. But as if to compensate for this loss of ritual control, the conversion experience itself begins to take on the characteristics of ritual, conducted in church with all the endlessly repeated and highly stylized paraphernalia of wrestling with the possessed and expulsion of devils. The baptisms in established Pentecostal Churches are better regarded as rites of passage than life-crises, especially since the baptism by fire, theoretically a spontaneous event, is ritually brought under control through induction procedures and courses of study.

The conversion is almost invariably described by women, not men, in terms of illness and cure, physical and psychological, and even social.

Eu era derrotada, endemoninhada, a minha vida era um desgosto. (I was defeated, possessed, my life was all bitterness).

Another word frequently used in this context is '*acabada*' (I was at the end of my tether). In the words of a 50-year old woman, with 12 children and a wayward husband, an *obreira* of the Universal Church:

Cheguei na Igreja arrasada, cheia de problemas, doente, e triste, oprimida e sobrecarregada, e Jesus me abençoou a minha vida, mudou o marido . . . (I came to the

Church defeated, full of problems, sick and sad, oppressed and over-burdened, and Jesus blessed my life and changed my husband).

The account, which is absolutely standard and yet could not be said to sound hollow or rehearsed, is dominated by a detailed description of illnesses and often repellent symptoms suffered prior to conversion. Unlike adepts of possession cults who may undergo any number of cures, the Pentecostal experience of healing is indissolubly linked to conversion. Except 'out-of-the-blue' occurrences which they attribute to Jesus, but are independent of any purposive action, healing ritual or life-crisis,[3] members describe no other cure in their lives: They do not experience healing after conversion, but the phrase *'pronto socorro espiritual na vida dos derrotados'* (a spiritual emergency service in the life of the defeated) shows how the metaphor of illness continues to apply to the place of the Church in their lives.

Conversion must be public: like speaking in tongues, like the experience of receiving the Holy Spirit, its authenticity cannot be recognized if it happens in private, and it is signified by kneeling before a podium at the front of the congregation. The gesture of submission symbolizes 'acceptance of Jesus'. Conversion in other religions may involve lengthy reflection or the maturing of an inspiration, but among Pentecostals it is very often a lightning (*fulminante*) experience intimately related – at least in the retelling – to illness and cure.

While women's conversion accounts show a strong concern with physical and psychological illness, men concentrate on social and moral failings. The Churches' awareness and exploitation of these differences is patent, as illustrated by the words of this daily early morning TV broadcast on behalf of the Universal Church: Referring to John 4 the preacher asked viewers how many had not looked in the mirror and said to themselves: *'eu não presto* – "I am useless" (literally "I am good for nothing" or worse "I am on the shelf") – but then Jesus looks into your eyes and sees potential, even when you see nothing'.[4]

---

[3] Especially cases of children whose condition, after being pronounced incurable by the doctors, undergoes an inexplicable improvement which the doctors cannot explain.

[4] Evidently the preacher was a man and was referring to women looking in the mirror. The allusion is to a Samaritan woman who is surprised when, on approaching a well, Jesus asks her for a drink. In the New English Bible the text goes on: 'The Samaritan woman said: "What! You, a Jew, ask of me, a Samaritan woman?" (Jews and Samaritans, it should be noted, do not use vessels in common).' The passage from the Gospels, in which Jesus once again flouts established rules and conventions in order to raise the poor or the victims of discrimination, is transmuted by the television preacher into a quite different framework in which the social discrimination becomes psychological depression, and the remedy is found within the victim, not in changing the attitudes or behaviour of oppressors.

In contrast, a man will be less likely to decribe his previous condition as one of depression: he will refer to women as 'the Devil' when they make themselves attractive with pretty clothes and make-up. His life of drugs, alcohol, street life and womanizing offered but temporary relief from a tormented existence. In a near-hysterical interview a lawyer from the Universal Church of the Kingdom of God repeatedly described the practitioners of *candomblé* and *umbanda* as women; he told of a girlfriend who, seeing him eye her sister or cousin, had cast a jealous spell on him so that he did not sleep with a woman for two years; the magic and incantations of *macumba* may bring pleasure, but that pleasure is poisoned – a poison symbolized in his eyes by the rituals of animal sacrifice, even human sacrifice, and the imbibing of blood which accompanies them. A *mãe de santo* could attain pleasure by incantation – but one day she would pay for it. It is not surprising that later, referring to the Catholic Church, he used the well-worn comparison with the Great Prostitute of the Apocalypse (Revelation 17).

Men tell of the ephemeral, and self-defeating, satisfactions gained from womanizing, smoking, drinking, or just hanging around with their male friends, and recount how after their conversion such pleasures lose their attraction; conversion is liberation from temptation – temptation often embodied by women, so for example Joseph's heroism and integrity (*o homen íntegro* in the words of one preacher) is illustrated by his resistance to the blandishments of Potiphar's wife (Genesis 39:7–23). Note the use of the strong word *concupiscencia* (the sin of unfettered sexual desire) in the following words of a *diâcono* of a small chapel of the Igreja Quadrangular in Liberdade: '*eu vivia na concupiscencia carnal, nas farras, nas bebedeiras, e um dia resolvi mudar*'. (I used to lead a life of indulgence of the flesh, of parties and drinking sessions until one day I decided to change.) Addiction, to drugs of all sorts, is mentioned side-by-side with sinful living and subordination to the Devil: '*Minha vida não era boa, eu era nervosa, usava tranquilizante e nao podia deixar . . .*' (My life was not good, I used to take tranquilizers and could not give them up, until . . . God entered my life and proved to be a better remedy than the pills.) (Heard in sermon at a *Deus é Amor* church.)

They also contrast their new life with their old one in terms of the opposition between *o amigo* (the friend) and *o irmão* (the brother): 'friends' are good-time friends, people who join you on the street, in the brothels, encouraging you to confuse fun with true happiness, while your brothers are brethren who protect you against temptation. When a preacher from the Assemblies says there are *amigos que são inimigos* – 'friends who are enemies' – he is playing on the double meaning of the word 'inemigo' which also refers to the Devil, and is saying that behind the laughter of fun there lurks the mocking cackle of the Devil. Pentecostal happiness is a different kind of happiness: happiness but not fun, joy but not laughter, love not desire.

Beyond conversion as a personal solution, women also describe how the benefits of Church membership extend to their whole family. A woman who had been in the Universal Church for '10 years at least' told how her daughter's sight had deteriorated over a long period to the point where her eyes were given up as lost by the doctors. Nevertheless, the girl did well in school and qualified as a bookkeeper (note the allusion to the girl's own efforts), and when at the age of 18 she came to the church her eyes improved and now she could see everything without glasses and soon would be getting married. This story about her daughter was complemented by her own story which contrasts her previous life where she worked in *other people's* homes, washing *other people's* clothes, lived in *other people's* (i.e. rented) houses, with her present life where she only has to wash *her own* clothes and owns *her own* house 'plus one on top of it and one next door'. Although her daughter's cure is linked to the time her daughter began to go to the church, the transformation in her own life is a longer term process encompassing a transformation in her material circumstances and the achievement of a degree of independence, graphically illustrated by the references to 'other people's washing'. Another Universal Church member described the material transformation more succinctly: '*tenho casa propia — não tinha; tenho TV a cores — não tinha; tudo isso e benção*' (I have my own house — I used not to; I have a colour TV — I used not to: all that is a blessing from God.) Quite apart from the content of this sentence, its syntax alone expresses eloquently the sense of a caesura in the person's life, the transformation brought about by joining the Church.

Healing the family means bringing one's husband under control. Thus the *obreira* of the Universal Church mentioned above elaborated: '. . . *meu marido tinha cuatro mulheres na rua e eu morava numa barraca*' (my husband had four women 'in the street' and I lived in a shack) — but now she had two houses. The houses were definitely described as 'mine' not 'ours' and she made a point of saying that although her husband had not joined the Church at least he no longer had other women, and he was making a lot of money (a word which prompted her to wink knowingly at me) as a *mestre de obras* (a foreman on a building site). All this she owed to the Church. This is the same theme of control as we find in the men's accounts, though whereas the men talk of achieving *self*-control or *self*-discipline, women talk of bringing their *men* under control, implying that there are demonic forces which at once control their men and put them 'out of control'.

These demonic forces putting men out of control are underlined by Pastor Rodriguez (leader of the Universal Church in Bahia), praying in front of his congregation for Jesus to: 'arranca(r) esse exu do pai que gasta seu dinheiro em cachaça e nao deixa nada para seus filhos'. (expel that exu from the father who spends his money on drink and leaves nothing for his children!)

In Periperi a woman described her search for a way of stopping her husband from drinking, first through Spiritism – which only made it worse and, she hinted, brought her under the sway of the Devil – and later through two successive churches and successive baptisms. The account culminated in a description of a fit suffered by her husband – which sounded very much like an epileptic attack. The episode ended in hospital where the pastor visited him three times, and after that the fits and the drinking stopped: 'Deus me deu vitoria – venceu a epilepsi, a bebida e o fumo' (God gave me my victory – he conquered epilepsy, drink and tobacco).[5]

In these accounts the men sustain the classic Mediterranean – and therefore Latin American – pattern in which the woman is the bearer of vulnerability and endangers family honour, but the women present an inverse model, in which their men's vulnerability to temptation turns them into the weak link endangering the well-being of entire families. The latter version is more in tune with the reality of Brazil, especially Northeast Brazil, where, as in the Caribbean, networks of women manage domestic affairs while men circulate between partners in a sequence of unstable partnerships (Boyer-Araujo, 1993a), but it also shows that the ambition among Pentecostals to reconstruct nuclear families represents a project of profound cultural change aimed at both the traditional family system and also the prevailing trend away from the nuclear household: there is an increasing prominence in low-income urban neighbourhoods in Latin America, beyond the Caribbean and Northeast Brazil, of networks of women who are the principle providers of their families and also manage community life (Boyer-Araujo, 1993a; Delano and Lehmann, 1993).

Conversion for women is represented then as a cure for their illness and depression but also by extension a cure for their entire families and an opportunity for them to reassert themselves in the household. While women speak of securing control over their men through conversion, the men speak of securing control over themselves. No man ever spoke to me about his wife having returned to the 'straight and narrow' after his conversion. The stylized accounts of conversion emphasize male weakness and female resolve and strength in the face of adversity and of temptation.

---

[5] The usage 'epilepsy' may be due to my own use of the word during the conversation to explain the fit – she for her part did not explicitly mention the Devil in the description of the attack.

There are, on the face of it, three different and not easily conciliated strands in the Pentecostal discourse on sex and family relations: the preachers exhort women to establish their control over their men and their households, at the same time as they insist on women's obligation to subordinate themselves to their husbands as 'heads' — a favourite metaphor. The words of one woman crystallize the link between a God-fearing life and marital obedience: '*As mulheres cristas são obedientes, são tementes a Deus*' (Christian women are obedient and God-fearing). The evident tension between these two elements is resolved by the emphasis — in a very 'modern' vein — on the nuclear family, which is common to Pentecostal penetration in the most varied cultural contexts[6] as well as on the psychological, even sentimental, aspects of the marital relationship. A young woman in a small Pentecostal church in Periperi, explains: '*nós cristãos temos outra visão da familia . . . entre os outros é só briga e briga . . . entre nós ha comunicação entre os casais*'. (We Christians[7] have a different vision of the family . . . among the others it's all fight, fight, fight . . . among us there is communication between couples.)

In the same vein, another young woman, from the Assemblies of God in the Nova Constituinte 'invasion', says that the Devil '*quer o matrimonio agua abaixo*' (wants marriages to go downhill). Women, she continues, can resist this, for example by staying calm and when a husband arrives home drunk, trying to '*apaciguar*' (reduce the tension), while in another conversation, also with a woman, she explains that, seeing his wife treating the children properly the husband will learn, little by little: '*O marido ve a mulher tratar bem os filhos e assim ele vai aprender*'. The discourse of authority and submission, then, placed in the flow of conversation, is far from undiluted: the woman who made this last remark about husbands learning had begun by describing husbands' drunkenness and violence as the work of the Devil and, far from justifying disobedience, called for the devil to be expelled. These examples show that in the *evangélico* discourse on marriage and masculinity, the slogans and ready-made phrases which are offensive to a liberal sensibility, and seem to legitimate oppressive male behaviour, especially within marriage, are balanced by the propagation of an idealized vision of modern middle-class marriage as 'partnership' based on dialogue and understanding.

[6] In the Andes, where the importance of the extended family and of *compadrozgo* mean that this emphasis constitutes a rupture with established social relationships and obligations, the effects can be quite conflictive, since they may cut women and the household itself off from the support network provided by extended kinship relationships, thus increasing the women's burden. On the other hand, there are also interpretations which describe women as welcoming the conversion because it reduces drunkenness and unnecessary expenditure on *fiestas* (Spier, 1993; Muratorio, 1980).

[7] As explained earlier, this refers only to *evangéicos*.

Although it is difficult to imagine that Pentecostal allegiance would bring about fundamental change in family patterns in the *favelas* of Salvador, that possibility should not be excluded. It should be recalled that it is precisely this change which, in the highland Andean communities of Peru and Ecuador, has made Pentecostalism a source of conflict, because of the cutting of the extended kinship ties and communal obligations which underpin the reproduction of households and the annual cycle of fiestas which 'reproduce' the community (Spier, 1993; Muratorio, 1980). Pepper (1991) states that the family and the household are the privileged channels of penetration for missionary activity and that women have a prominent role in facilitating it, and there is growing evidence among *evangélicos* of a break from popular Catholicism, and other aspects of family organization which have historically accommodated *machista* behaviour. This break may sometimes be dramatic, but there are evidently many instances in which it is gradual, subtle, maybe subsconscious. Whereas Catholic festivals in the Andes and Mesoamerica tend to take men away from the household, to act as *fiesta* organizers and to consume large amounts of alcohol with other members of their fraternities,[8] *evangélicos* emphasize joint family participation. Brusco (1986: 117ff.) describes a Lutheran pastor dealing with the role conflict he faced when on becoming *Presidente* of a town *fiesta* in Colombia: he called on the menfolk to celebrate the *fiesta* together with their families, rather than by drinking with their *compadres*, and he distributed milk instead of alcohol – milk being a white liquid symbolizing peace! The conciliation of a partnership ideal of family life with males' public salience is evidenced by Boyer-Araujo (1995), who observes that pastor's wives are deeply involved in their husbands' duties, and often encourage them to embark on the career, while some of the people I interviewed allowed that the only woman who could officiate at a service was the pastor's wife – and then only in clearly a temporary capacity as her husband's replacement.

Identity and liminality[9]

All Pentecostal Churches impose a complete prohibition on alcohol and tobacco, and a variety of controls on sexual behaviour. *Deus é Amor* is

---

[8] *Corfrarias* in Brazil, *cofradías* in Spanish-speaking countries: lay Catholic groups which organize *fiestas*, processions, charity and the like.

[9] I use the term with some hesitation because its usage has been enshrined in anthropology in the sense of rituals denoting liminality in time between different states, and specifically in relation to rites of passage (Turner, 1967). Nevertheless, the analysis will show that the extension of the concept to

strictest, and the Universal Church is more liberal, emphasizing the 'internal' qualities of personal responsibility and free will as against the 'externality' of dress rules, but their rules on tobacco and alcohol are the same, though less stringent in matters of dress, make-up and sex. Like conventions of dress and dietary rules in orthodox Judaism, these are constitutive elements of the liminality which demarcates the community, but *evangélicos* also see the rules as setting them apart from the world of irreligion, or simply from 'the world', drawing boundaries between the world of darkness and the domain of light, and between believers and unbelievers. [10] All these mechanisms serve to underline believers' separation from what they call *o mundo* (the world), and in the extreme example of the *Deus é Amor* Church to forbid marriage with non-members. [11] *Assembleistas* use the word *doutrina* to refer not to doctrine in the usual sense but to these rules as marks of religious orthodoxy, yet at the same time as marks of pride. When a service is about to take place in a *favela*, *Assembleistas* can be seen converging on their chapel, the men in suits and ties, the women in dresses which make of the severe austerity rules imposed by their Church an embellishment more than a constraint. When asked for an explanation, a member quoted the Book of Lamentations – 'by your appearance you shall be known'. [12]

The Universal Church does not discourage either modern or attractive dress, does not disapprove of *amigados* (unmarried couples) or discourage artificial methods of birth control: a pastor said that people must behave responsibly and not overload themselves with children. One of its members said the *Assambleistas* and *Deus é Amor* go too far, that they are 'very fanatical' (which is not to say they are 'fanatics'), and Pastor Rodrigues said they were 'irrational'. But the Universal Church also has its markers, in the uniforms of its personnel and the self-consciously scandalous violations of social, political and religious convention.

In the Assemblies television is disapproved of and contraception is also frowned upon, although such rules vary from state to state: [13] in the words

denote the place of ritual in the construction and preservation of social and spatial boundaries is extremely useful.

[10] The phrase frequently heard, complete with the archaism *trevas* (as in the French *ténèbres*) was '*as trevas não se unem com a luz*' (the forces of darkness cannot be joined with the forces of light) or '*as trevas não podem conviver com as luzes*' (darkness cannot live together with light).

[11] Again, a member used the metaphor of the cohabitation of darkness and light (*as trevas com a luz*) in defending this rule. This is the formal position: it is difficult to verify how it is applied in practice because the members of that Church are unwilling to speak to outsiders, but presumably the rule is accommodated by enabling outsiders to convert and join.

[12] Exceptionally he did not give chapter and verse, and I have been unable to find the reference.

[13] In Belem an authoritative pastor was less trenchant though also less clear on the subject: 'it is a matter we leave free with God – God will not allow us to carry too heavy a burden' (*a gente deixa livre*

of the superintendent of the Assembly congregation in Nova Sussuarana, a lot of TV programmes 'influence your spirituality and distort your conception of the world'. In the *Deus é Amor* Church women attend services with no make-up at all and their hair pinned back and held down in a self-consciously austere and uncomely fashion, as if to deny any hint of attractiveness; men and women are segregated in church and the rules contain elaborate prohibitions on sexual relations outside, before and during marriage, contraception (except on doctor's orders) and abortion.[14] Men too are prohibited from dressing in provocative ways.

The role of these rules as markers is more important than the strictness of observance. In the presentation by the Youth Group of the Assembly of God in Nova Sussuarana (already mentioned in connection with the use of biblical texts) the girls performed songs with techniques drawn straight from television, like aspiring media stars, but evidently with the full approval of the Church's leaders. The differences between the Churches' rules bear an affinity with the differences between their constituencies or 'market niches': *Deus é Amor* attracts the very poor and the elderly, as has been noted; the Assemblies attract the very poor but also hold out a prospect of social mobility and increasing respectability in the mode of 'bad taste' previously described; and the Universal Church, looking to the young, and to strata slightly above the very poor, would not wish to distance itself excessively from youth culture.

Liminality is expressed not only as markers delineating the Church from 'the world' but also as thresholds and degrees of seniority within the organization, encouraging a sense among members that there are always more barriers to overcome before they can penetrate the inner core of the elect. Those who only attend are not quite members – they are said to 'frequent' a church or chapel; members have not all been baptised; some have undergone 'spiritual baptism' while others have undergone baptism by immersion. To undergo immersion one has to follow a course of study (at least in the Assembly and in Churches of the 'renewed Baptist' tradition).[15] In the canteen at the Assembly's *matriz* in Bahia there are

---

com Dues – Deus não vai consentir que a gente carga). The repression of contraceptive practices by the Assembly in Bahia should be noted by those who would attribute to Catholic doctrine on the subject a reason for Catholicism's loss of active faithful. An Assembly member, also from Nova Sussuarana, revealed the prominence of rules governing sexual mores when he expressed disapproval of the laxity of the Universal Church but approval of the more 'rigorous' attitude of *Deus é Amor*, as did other members of the congregation.

[14] This guidance is contained in the booklet *Doutrina Bíblica para os dias de hoje* (Biblica Doctrine Today).

[15] The 'Baptista Renovada' group, which is very similar to the Assemblies, having its origin in breakaways from the historic Baptist Church, and joined in a loose Convenção Baptista Nacional. This

separate tables for '*Diretoria*', '*Visitantes*' and '*Secretaria*' ('Management', 'Visitors' and 'Secretariat'). Neo-Pentecostal Churches, as we have seen, symbolize levels of authority by differences in dress or uniform, which also represent degrees of closeness to the 'inner core' of Church members. Pentecostal identity is – among many other things – about living with thresholds, not one but many, and just as orthodoxy of dress and behaviour is never completely or exhaustively codified,[16] so also there is no limit to the number of thresholds, which is subject to arbitrary modification and adjudication from Church authorities.

Money: symbolic and material delimitations of the elect

Money is a sensitive subject in describing religious organizations, and yet it impinges at many levels: the contribution of churchgoers and church members, the representation of this contribution, the management of the church's funds and the relationship between religious adherence and material and social advancement.

The theme relates, once again, to that of taste. The neo-Pentecostal Churches in particular break noisily, even outrageously, with the customary discretion which surrounds church fund-raising – though they are even more secretive than other Churches with respect to the management of their finances. Their behaviour on this score is self-consciously scandalous, and their image in the media is without doubt associated with this.[17] In April 1991 the newspapers published photographs of sackloads of money being carried away at the Universal Church's massive meeting in the Maracaná stadium, as if to discredit the organization by implying that its only interest was raising money from its followers.

But no amount of mocking disapproval incurred in the columns of newspapers of the educated classes can undo the evident success of a strategy which is probably less reliant on foreign funding than the more nationalistic *basista* movement. The followers themselves seem utterly indifferent to this issue, expressing their pride in the churches they have set up in New York and Miami, in Portugal, Angola, Guinea-Bissau, and South Africa.

Pentecostal Churches all practise tithing – members are expected to give 10 per cent of their income on a regular basis – and call it the

is an association which provides prayer books, offers courses and the like to member churches, and in which membership provides a badge of respectability and recognition.

[16] Once again a feature of reminiscent of orthodox Judaism.

[17] On one occasion the *Jornal do Brasil* described Macedo as 'nothing more than a *caixa-niquel* (money-box)'.

dízimo.[18] In the Assemblies and similar Churches this is done discretely, but in the neo-Pentecostal Churches, as we have seen, discretion is thrown to the winds. How much people really give, whether it amounts to one tenth of their income, and whether the Church tries to 'police' this, remains a mystery. If members fall behind with their contributions someone may simply have 'a word in their ear' – at worst they will be excluded from the *santa ceia*. Sanctions for moral offences such as adultery are more severe – at least in those Churches which keep records. The Universal Church, which does not keep records of those who attend its services, presumably relies more on regular contributions from its own volunteers – the *obreiras* – and on the insistent pressure to give, and to make advance commitments to give, which features so prominently in its services.

Various rationalistic or functionalist arguments can be adduced to explain why people contribute: that the *dízimo* forces people to plan, and therefore rationalize, their finances, even – maybe especially – if they are very poor, or that it diverts expenditure from unnecessary items such as alcohol and tobacco, which Churches prohibit anyway.[19] This type of explanation, which can also be applied to the austerity rule, may or may not be valid in individual cases, but it does not shed light on the cultural significance and representation of the system of contributions: this system is radically different from the offerings or fees paid in Catholicism and possession cults, both symbolically and at the level of the relationships between contributors and church or *terreiro* or medium. When Pentecostals talk about donations and tithes they do not refer to specific benefits from specific offerings, whereas Catholics accompany theirs with an *ex-voto* or a petition to a saint's effigy, and contributions to a *terreiro* form part of a clientelistic relationship.

Contributing to a Pentecostal Church is a way of signifying membership in an organization[20] – a concept quite foreign to Catholic religious participation or to the cults – but it also possesses a more

[18] This is the precise word for tithe, but to avoid the feudal connotations, I shall henceforth use the Portuguese word.

[19] Studies conducted in the Andes have produced contradictory indications in this regard: some mention the interest of women in reducing heavy expenditures on *cargos* (obligations which rotate among community members, to pay for festivals) and the heavy drinking which goes with the 'pagan' festivals which Pentecostals identify as the work of the Devil, while others point in the opposite direction. Spier (1993) notes that the dissolution of the relationship of labour and produce exchange embedded in extended kinship networks, as a result of Petecostals' 'separation', and also of their greater focus on the nuclear family, places extra burdens on the women in Pentecostal families.

[20] It also should in principle give the member rights to elect leaders, to participate in decision-making and so on, but in the Churches under consideration this is academic since they do not have a system of internal democracy.

important abstract, symbolic significance. Wilson Gomes' interpretation in terms of a 'wager' can account for large lump-sum donations, but it does not take into consideration one crucial feature of the *dízimo*, both objectively and in the words of Church members, namely its regularity, and it is the regularity of contribution which underlies the explanations offered by followers and members and also preachers' and pastors' words on the subject. In their accounts we find reference not to specific benefits but to a generalized effect on the lives of those who give. Pastors tell the congregations that '*quem da com alegria nao vai faltar*' (those who give gladly will not experience deprivation), or that those who give 'will see how the money multiplies in their pockets'. In the Universal Church they sing a song to the refrain *Quem dá com alegria vai prosperar* (he who gives happily will prosper). This is intended in a metaphorical sense: the congregation are expected to believe not that a miracle will occur in their pockets, but rather that the element of reciprocity in the giving relationship will change their lives.

In the Universal Church pastors remind their followers that 'our Church' cannot survive without funds, but they also insist that there is 'no obligation' to give: 'you are free: if you give you do so not out of obligation to the Church, or the Pastor, or the Bishop [Macedo], but because you want to do God's will'; or again: 'Jesus will not bless you on account of your offering, but on account of your faith'. Apart from containing an undoubted tacit rebuttal of accusations in the media that they are extorting money from their naive followers, the formula also sets them apart from the dyadic clientelism embodied in gifts to saints and contributions to mediums (though we shall see that the reciprocity is merely shifted to another register): thus a preacher criticizes those who commit themselves to giving 1,000 (by taking home an envelope with that number on it) and then return with only 100. He says he will fast[21] for three days, praying that those who commit themselves will fulfil their promise. The moral he draws is not that they should have brought the 1,000; rather it is a highly rationalizing one, in the Weberian sense, that they should make a realistic commitment which is within their means.

The shift in the register of reciprocity is illustrated by the type of benefits which followers are led to expect from their contributions. A preacher warns his congregation that '*não dar dízimo é roubar a Deus*' (not giving the *dízimo* is like stealing from God); at the same time he adds '*se quer ser benҫoado tem que fazer sacrifícios*' (if you want to be blessed with gifts you must make sacrifices). The gifts sought and expected are a change in

---

[21] He does not mean he will go without eating at all, but that he will deprive himself, for example, of one of his meals.

one's way of life, a new dawn, but also support for one's own efforts to achieve that goal. Thus a young girl who had been listening to this same pastor explained to me that '*Jesus da um jeito na vida das pessoas*' (Jesus gives people a hand) . . . but she added that they must also do their bit to help themselves. Furthermore, in referring to a ritual gesture the pastor had recommended, she said 'it is no good if you are unemployed putting your *dízimo* on your social security card (*carteira de trabalho*) if you stay in bed until noon instead of getting up and going out to look for a job'. Her words were a common-sense version of standard references: the parable of the talents (Matthew 25:14–30) in which the man who buried his talent, thinking his master would be pleased by his prudence, is then chided and loses 'even that which he hath', is a favourite with preachers, illustrating the lesson that gifts from God also place upon the faithful an obligation to make an effort of their own (as well as being a nice metaphor for capital accumulation).

How can this rationalization be conciliated with the ready-made phrases which might lead one to see in the offering of money and tithing a mere magical gesture? Such an interpretation is similar in structure to that which would see in the Churches a 'mere' continuation of the possession cults, or which would explain their success by claiming that the high cost of professional medical attention leads very poor people to seek a cheaper alternative. If the former had any validity the Churches would indeed degenerate into cults (in the style of the Reverend Moon); if the latter were true they would consist of multiple individual consultation rooms. Rather, the magical expressions should be interpreted in a metaphorical way. For example, when a woman in the *favela* of Nova Sussuarana described how thanks to joining her church she had moved from 'down there' to 'up here' – from the damp and fetid lower reaches to the (slightly) more sanitary upper parts of the neighbourhood – and that she had progressed to the point where now she owned her own shop, I asked her how she could afford this when she gave so much money to the Church. Her immediate reply consisted simply of the Universal Church motto *é só dando que se recebe* (only by giving shall you receive). Other phrases echo this generalized (not dyadic) reciprocity, such as the following more complex formulation: *se recibimos de graça, de graça a gente da*. The phrase, from the lips of a rank and file churchgoer, plays on the double meaning of *graça* (grace) and *de graça* (free of charge). It means literally 'if we receive for free we also give for free' but also, and above all, 'if we receive the gift of grace for free we give for free': it is the gift of grace which is received, not a favour or wealth or power.

Beyond theological niceties, in the discourse of the faithful, the 'gift' can mean personal empowerment and the capacity, as one woman said, to grow: *'eu só comecei a crescer quando comecei a dar o dízimo . . . é dando que se recebe'* (I only started to grow when I started to give the dízimo . . . it is by giving that you receive). By giving she is entering into a set of obligations, a community of *dizimistas*, of the 'elect', symbolized by habits of dress and an aura of separateness and partaking of the *santa ceia*, who by committing themselves to the relationship, hope to create new opportunities in their lives. Some will 'fall by the wayside', temporarily or permanently, but the Church has mechanisms to bring them back into the fold — counselling, a word in the ear, and so on. The status of *dizimista* places a person in a community of the elect, and in an abstract relationship of membership of an organization.

The elect do not think of themselves as inward-looking local communities. On the contrary, by joining the *dizimistas* a person believes she is joining a larger, even world-wide community, as reflected in the following, typical, response to the question 'Why is there so much poverty?': *'Falta de Deus . . . ninguém da dízimo, então ladrão leva tudo . . . nos Estados Unidos tudos são dizimistas e o capital é mais rico'*. (It's a lack of godliness . . . no one pays their *dízimo* and so the thieves run off with everything . . . in the United States everyone pays their *dízimo* and so capital is richer there.)[22]

These are churches for very poor people, and if we have seen how the faithful give their real money to purchase the immaterial benefit of membership in the community of the elect, at the same time they make immaterial gestures to obtain real material goods and benefits. Hence phrases such as 'the McDonald's of contemporary religion' (*Folha de São Paulo*, 17 September 1995) describing pastors who incite their congregations to think of their most cherished desire in terms of consumption and material well-being: 'do you want a car? a house? a fridge? . . . then just think hard about it, have faith in Jesus and . . .'. The phrase also echoes practices such as depositing *pedidos de oração* (written requests to Jesus for help or for a benefit). When taken together with the practice of the *dízimo* and with the dreams of social mobility which the Churches undoubtedly encourage among their followers, these are crumbs of ritual, transplanted from popular and official Catholic practice, which more than anything else express desire, just as Catholic rituals express often a desire for salvation in the next world. For people living in such dire poverty, possession of a house or car is as remote as the Kingdom of God itself.

---

[22] The last phrase does not mean that capitalists are wealthier in the United States, but is simply a way of saying that the country is richer. The first phrase should be interpreted as 'godlessness' or 'an absence of the fear of God'.

The Pentecostal Churches attack the Catholic Church for its finery and show, while at the same time assuring their followers that to aspire to wealth is not at all ungodly. They place enormous importance on donations by their followers yet seem not at all ashamed to allow their pastors and preachers to lead a much more prosperous lifestyle than their congregations, and in the case of the Universal Church the top leaders' lifestyle is sumptuous even by international standards. They do not regard charity as a high priority. The words of Pastor Rodrigues of the Universal Church, accusing the elites of Brazil of creating the garbage and then calling on the Churches to clean it up, are instructive: 'I am not in the business of picking up society's garbage' (*eu não sou lixeiro para limpar lixo da sociedade*). The Churches do some educational work, through schools run by the Assemblies for instance, and some work in prisons and with drug addiction. But again these activities are marginal to their principal concerns, and the work with prisons and drug addicts seems to be geared to recruitment of personnel and proselytizing.

Conclusion

The multiple significances of money, donations, material prosperity, and their organizational and ritual importance enable us to tie together certain central features of Pentecostalism and neo-Pentecostalism. Once again, the global character of the phenomenon reappears, and the question of their purported role as entry points for the penetration of 'American' culture. Recent writing on Africa (Gifford, 1993; *Review of African Political Economy*, 1991) has noted the spread of a theology of 'prosperity' or 'health and wealth' which has some points in common with the ideas propagated by the neo-Pentecostals in Brazil. It is spread by missionaries who place exclusive emphasis on the promise of material success as a reason for conversion and faith in Jesus, mount large-scale mission campaigns accompanied by lavish publicity, and also seem to place much store by the close relations they forge with dubious political leaders. Such activities and ideas may be thought of as 'American' but they are also global, and one feature of globalism is the favourable context it provides for irony in cultural borrowings and projections. The approach to financial matters is but one of a string of areas in which we can see how, while borrowing innumerable elements from the traditions of popular culture, Pentecostal Churches at the same time turn those traditions against the institutions and social groups which have for generations or even centuries sponsored them.

Side-by-side with the 'foreign' inspirations for their doctrines, methods, symbols and rituals which one would normally expect in any Western Church or religious movement since the Reformation at least, the Pentecostal Churches are distinguished by this complex and sometimes harsh relationship to the established traditions of local popular culture. Thus the Universal Church has derived the *pedidos de oração*, from the practice of petitioning the saints, and the *santa ceia* common to all Pentecostal Churches in Brazil is evidently based on Holy Communion; yet at the same time we have seen in some detail the use of incantations and gestures borrowed from the possession cults in a war against the cults themselves, and likewise the practice of healing and exorcism. The obsession of some churches with the control of female sexual activity has evident continuities with Catholicism, but appears among the Pentecostals without any of the sensuality of Catholic art or any of the institutionalized exuberance of Catholic culture, expressed in *fiestas* and carnival. All this, combined with the turning away from the tradition of projection which has bound popular and literate culture together in the Catholic and Latin traditions, shows that, much as they may have found pathways into these cultures, as David Martin has said, they also represent a profound rupture with unforeseeable consequences for the future (Martin, 1990). Little by little, we begin to perceive here the cultural counterpart to the 'social earthquake' which has affected these societies in the past generation.

Appendix: Pentecostalism's Social Base

It is generally agreed that the Pentecostal growth in Latin America is concentrated among the poor. Available data in Brazil and elsewhere broadly confirm this. The Census of Religious Establishments in the Rio de Janeiro area carried out by the Institute Superior de Estudos da Religião (ISER) and published in 1992 shows that it is in the poorer western suburbs of Rio where the greatest number of Evangelical establishments are to be found in relation to the population (3.63 per 10,000 inhabitants, as contrasted with 1.41 in the prosperous Zona Sul). The contrast is illustrated by the estimate that in the former region only 16 per cent of persons earn more than 10 times the minimum wage, whereas in the Zona Sul the corresponding figure is 54 per cent (Fernandes, 1994). Although interesting, the unit of enumeration in this Census of Rio was the Church, not the individual. For the individual level, the ISER reports the findings of the national sample survey (PNAD) regularly conducted by the official statistical office (IBGE), which are less polarized: according to PNAD the *evangélicos* are distributed roughly in the same proportions as the overall population, except that they are seriously under-represented among those earning more than 20 times the minimum wage – and are more heavily represented among the poorest groups (those earning five times the minimum wages or less) than Catholics, more precisely practising Catholics. Unfortunately, the data are reported only at the nationwide level and are therefore of limited usefulness.

Wilson Gomes in 1990 and Cláudio Pereira in 1992 both conducted detailed studies of Pentecostal Churches in Salvador da Bahia, Gomes in the city as a whole, and Pereira in the populous working-class and lower middle-class neighbourhood of Cosmé de Farias. Gomes found 80 per cent of his sample of 271 had not completed six years of schooling – *primeiro grau* — while Pereira's corresponding figure in a sample of 123 was 65 per cent. In addition, Gomes found an illiteracy rate of 31 per cent. Hoffnagel (1978) surveyed 125 Assembly members in 1975 in Recife and also found that 31 per cent were illiterate: this compares with a 24 per cent illiteracy rate for Recife as a whole in the 1970 Census. In contrast, a few years later, in 1985, Pepper (1991) found a lower illiteracy rate among Pentecostals — especially among the men — than in the city's population: 17 per cent for men and 24 per cent for women — but her figures are too far out of line with all other findings to be credible. Using Church sources rather than her own sample, Hoffnagel found that among baptized men, if they were economically active, 43 per cent were manual unskilled workers and 18 per cent non-manual unskilled. An over-representation of persons with very little or no schooling also emerges in John Joseph Page's survey of 202 members of the *Brasil para Cristo* Church in Rio de Janeiro (1984), a nationwide and still prominent organization though somewhat eclipsed in the public eye by the rise of the Universal Church in the late 1980s and 1990s.

The predominance of women is no surprise: 64 per cent in Hoffnagel's study, 63 per cent in Pereira's survey of the Universal Church and an extraordinary 87 per cent in Gomes, which must shed doubt on his sample. Beyond Salvador, Page in Rio also found a strong over-representation of women. Age distribution complicates matters more: measured by the proportion of members over 40, Page's Rio sample from *Brasil para Cristo* were above average age, in contrast to Pereira's sample of Universal Church members in Salvador several years later, in which 70 per cent were under 40; yet in Gomes' study which was more or less contemporaneous with that of Pereira, this number is only 50 per cent. The PNAD 1988 nationwide survey found that 60 per cent of *evangélicos* were under 44, compared with 50 per cent of practising Catholics. Problems of procedure apart — which might, if we had the details, explain much — the higher figures in Pereira and Gomes may reflect the particular focus on young people on the part of the Universal Church which figured prominently in these last two studies — and that in turn takes us back to the point that explanations must be sought as much in the strategies of the organizations themselves as in the characteristics of the *evangélico* populations.

In the 1980s among his Rio sample of members of *Brasil para Cristo* Page found a high proportion of widowed and separated people, and in general of people residing in 'truncated families'; in both the later Salvador studies half the sample were unmarried, although these numbers require clarification by sex and also in the light of the wide gamut of partnerships and household types observable among the urban popular classes. In the Universal Church, though, which was the focus for these two studies, the low rate of marriage may be in part an artefact of the age structure of the samples.

Migrants are often said to contribute a large share of Pentecostals, but Pereira's sample showed that one third of the members and participants had been born outside the city of Salvador, compared with an extraordinarily high 70 per cent in Hoffnagel's study of Recife some 15 years earlier. Even taking into account problems of comparability, this difference may reflect a change in the constituency of Pentecostal Churches.

Studies comparing *evangélicos* with Catholics show even more pronounced differences than those comparing them with the average for a relevant population. David Martin quotes apparently large-scale sample surveys conducted in the late 1980s by the Centro de Estudios Públicos in Santiago de Chile, in which 'nearly half of practising evangelical Protestants were in the low categories 2 and 3' on an ascending scale of 1 to 11, in contrast to nearly half of practising Catholics who were in categories 4, 5 and 6. Even more strikingly, classes A, B, C1 and C2 accounted for only 6.8 per cent of practising evangelicals, compared with 36.4 per cent of their Catholic counterparts (Martin, 1995: 224). In the most detailed published survey on the subject thus far available, Coleman et al. (1993) show a similar pattern: in a sample of just over 1,000 people in the Central American country of El Salvador, Protestants were shown to be markedly poorer and less educated than both practising and non-practising Catholics, but also to resemble closely those counted as religiously unaffiliated. This should not necessarily lead us to believe that they were below the average for the relevant population, and the authors are careful to avoid that particular comparison.

Burdick's (1990) sample, taken in 1988, comparing Catholics and Evangelicals in the Rio de Janeiro working-class suburb of Duque de Caxias shows that the latter were older, less skilled and poorer than their Catholic counterparts. Likewise Mariz (1989: 84) states that her sample of CEB participants in Recife showed higher than average education and better economic background than the majority of Pentecostals.

As a comparison, Levine (1992: 181), though he does not present quantitative evidence, found that the urban CEB participants in his study, conducted in Venezuela and Colombia, came from 'the stable lower and lower-middle classes', with few 'migrant labourers' or 'residents of very new invasion barrios', and no one from the 'classic urban lumpen', while the rural participants were 'typically drawn from smallholding peasants and their families, with a smattering of local schoolteachers and tradespersons' — not, as he remarks, from the 'very poorest of the poor'. It is a profile which fits with my notion of a popular intelligentsia formed in the CEBs.

The coincidences between these statistics are so strong, and their coincidence also with every available qualitative observation, that there can be little doubt concerning the concentration of Pentecostal Churches on and among the poor, at least when compared with those professing a Catholic allegiance. However, the El Salvador survey in particular raises the possibility that we are really observing the relatively high status of Catholics (practising and non-practising) rather than the low status of Protestants and Evangelicals. Pentecostals and their leaders seem to see themselves as members of the poorest social groups, as witness the abundant evidence that they target the poor in their proselytizing strategy. This strategy is not one of including the poor in a multi-class organization, but rather of creating organizations adapted to their language and their needs. As Pastor Rodrigues of the Universal Church in Bahia said: 'if you fill a rich people's Church with poor people, the rich will leave'. The same conversation revealed the apparently boundless ambition of the Universal Church when he said: '*toda revolução cultural, tuda coisa que der certo, começou de baixo*' (every cultural revolution, everything which worked, has to come from below). Likewise note other remarks quoted in which pastors of the Assemblies speak of the Universal Church's emphasis on cures and possession as well adapted to the 'level' of understanding of poorer strata, and thus to proselytizing among them.

These comparisons return us once again to an issue which has already been raised several times: the contrasts observed may have more to do with the strategies and preferences of the different Churches and their personnel than one might assume, and correspondingly be less readily explained by an assumed disposition on the part of different social strata to one or another religious affiliation or practice — especially since the contrasts seem to be more marked between Evangelicals as compared with Catholics rather than with the overall population average. To be sure, in the case of the Catholic Church in particular, it is not possible to distinguish clearly between institutional strategies and social structural factors because the Church is so deeply rooted in these societies and their culture that it is itself part of the structure. Those who would reorient the Catholic Church, as has been shown in this account, face almost insuperable obstacles.

Beyond this there are many incognita and beyond the elementary sample surveys quoted there is a vast and promising field for quantitative research. Thus whereas some Churches or preachers seem eager to hold out to the poor the prospect of a relationship between religious conversion, awakening or faith, and material prosperity, others are wary of finding themselves overwhelmed, as a pastor of a small church in the Cosme de Farias neighbourhood of Salvador said to me: 'the pastors are quite frightened (*assustados*) by the waves of people pouring through the doors of their churches'; they feared that people came to the churches to solve their economic problems rather than out of faith. On another occasion a preacher at an Assemblies of God service stated clearly that people were mistaken if they thought that the Church was for improving their economic or social situation: literally, they were entering 'by the wrong door' (*pela porta errada*). On the other hand quotations given above in the analysis of the *dízimo* show that the relationship between Church participation and enrichment has penetrated the metaphors of everyday speech among Church members, and there is no shortage of preachers ready and willing to make the link:

o homen sem condições financieiras não consegue prosperar — com cachaça, cerveja ele não prospera — quando ele passa a entender as coisas espiritualmente ele passa a prosperar. Nao é pelas obras que le da salvação. (A man who has no financial means cannot find prosperity — beer and rum will lead him nowhere — but when he begins to understand things spiritually, then he begins to prosper. Salvation does not come from good works.) (Pastor's assistant in Deus é Amor church.)

Many claims are made about Pentecostals which could only be properly substantiated by carefully conducted and complex surveys and sophisticated analysis of their results — something which none of those quoted, except for Coleman et al., found it worth their while to undertake, preferring to treat their surveys, quite legitimately, as offering useful background to their main concern, namely qualitative research on the meaning of the phenomenon. Issues of social mobility, of the relationship between gender and mobility in Pentecostalism, of inter-generational shifts in class status, of family stability and instability, of the reality, or otherwise, of austerity and abstention and their effects — all these can only be explored systematically with the full armoury of modern social research.

CONCLUSION

Fundamentalism, Globalism and Politics

Politics

The short-run political implications of the Evangelical or Pentecostal upsurge are ambiguous: despite a firm doctrinal separation between the religious and political spheres, which denies that Churches may legitimately advise their followers how to vote, other than forbidding them to vote for atheistic parties (i.e. the Communists and by implication often the left in general), evangelical pastors and leaders and their followings are increasing their political prominence in Latin America. They have reached the Presidency itself twice in Guatemala,[1] and the Vice-Presidency of Peru in 1980 – though all of these cases ended in resignation or overthrow – and are becoming an established presence at the parliamentary level. But is this high political profile accompanied by a common ideological commitment – or even by any ideological commitment at all? In Brazil pastors of the Assemblies of God and the Universal Church vaunt the numbers of their colleagues who have been elected to local, state and even federal office:[2] they are consummate clientelistic operators, and seem principally concerned with the the short-run interests of their Churches with little concern for ideology apart from an aversion to socialism. In Brazil, during the 1987–91 period 14 of them changed party within 18 months of taking their seats, showing a particular attraction to 'physiological' parties – parties which have the reputation of existing exclusively as flags of convenience for free-floating politicians.

---

[1] First in the person of Riós Montt, who seized power in an internal army coup in 1982, and was overthrown a year later; and later in the person of Jorge Serrano Elias, elected in 1991 but removed after attempting to close the Congress and seize all power for himself, in 1994.

[2] 17 Federal Deputies openly identified as Protestants, mostly from Evangelical Churches, were elected in 1983, rising to 32 in 1991 but then falling to 23 in 1991 (Freston: 1993a: 191).

Most owe their positions in Congress exclusively to their Churches so the weakness of party identification is hardly surprising. The Assemblies' and the Four-Square Gospel Church's deputies are all pastors well placed in the Church organization, while the leader of the Universal Church chooses candidates who are not necessarily active in the organization, but whose success is guaranteed to the point where they barely have to campaign at all, being elected simply by virtue of the disciplined voting of the Church's followers (Freston, 1993a: chap. 12).

One rationale behind this pattern of political activity is that new organizations need to obtain the approval or support of the government for many of their activities, especially where radio and television are involved; they need respectability, and they need treatment equal to that received by the Catholic Church. Representation in Congress is one way of achieving these aims. In this respect the Evangelicals are no different from other interest groups in countries with a corporatist state and a clientelistic political culture, and they have the additional advantage of access to a very tightly knit electoral bloc, which, in a proportional voting system, is at least as important as the size of the bloc itself.[3] Political office does bring costs, though: the National Convention of the Assemblies of God decided not to officially endorse any presidential candidate in 1994, largely (according to Corten, 1995: 208) because of the controversies and scandals arising from the behaviour of Evangelical deputies in the preceding years – though it is quite likely that this official pronouncement at the level of a rather weak national body was tacitly overridden by the more powerful state-level leaders and at the local level.

Furthermore, the support of the Universal Church for Collor and Cardoso against Lula in the 1990 and 1994 Presidential elections respectively, sheds some doubt on the 'non-ideological' interpretation of the Evangelical Churches' political intervention. On the face of it, Evangelical deputies – who by the early 1990s already constituted a discernible if volatile *bancada*, or 'bloc' in the Brazilian Congress – have only voted 'ideologically' on issues of conscience, for example against the death penalty and homosexual marriage (as they call it), and in favour of religious freedom with equal treatment for all faiths, and censorship of pornography. Even an incident which would appear to be 'ideological' –

---

[3] Corten (1995:207) states understandably that 'only' 31 per cent of Pentecostals in São Paulo voted for Evangelical candidates – but this is not by any means necessarily an unfavourable statistic, especially in the light of the high turnover among Pentecostals, the shortage of candidates, and the diversity of Churches. Indeed, 31 per cent would seem to me to be rather a high figure! In this system voters can support several candidates for state or federal deputy, so the opportunity costs of following their Church's recommendations are small, especially since as a rule – though not invariably (Freston, 1993a) – Church candidates are not in direct competition with each other.

namely their vote against stringent powers for the State to implement Land Reform in the 1987 Constituent Assembly – is attributed by Freston to donations from a landowners' interest group (p. 241). But this may be deceptive: would the *bancada* have voted the other way without this additional 'encouragement'? And we observe that although the founder of the *Brasil para Cristo* Church, Manõel de Mello, adopted left-wing and anti-dictatorial positions, after his retirement in 1986 that Church rapidly changed position, and by now has fallen in with the dominant 'physiological' trend (Freston, 1993a: 91). It is very hard indeed to believe that evangelical representatives and their Churches would ever support measures departing significantly from the neo-liberalism which now reigns supreme in the entire region.

Far from drawing on Christianity's millenarian tradition of movements heralding a new world of peace and justice, with the collective or community-based solutions that would entail, Evangelical discourse and the metaphorical armoury it marshalls, place enterprise and the single-minded pursuit of consumption to the forefront, applying their quasi-magical language to such things as financial success, changing one's life, or the acquisition of consumer durables and real estate. Thus the symbols and metaphors in which they luxuriate do not easily translate into the language of political choice, and they do not advocate specific positions on issues of political debate, other than those involving personal morality in the narrow sense, preferring to couch their voting recommendations in terms of a 'worldly' adjunct to their proselytism.

It is therefore not at the level of explicit political programmes or statements that we should interpret the political impact of Pentecostalism. Rather we should observe the symbolic and imaginary world which it is projecting, and also its impact on the broader political theatre of these countries, taking into account the 'scandals' provoked by the neo-Pentecostal Churches, the media, and also the possible effects on the world-view of their followers. For despite this ease of entry on the part of Pentecostal Churchmen into politics, and their hostility to parties of the left, the Pentecostals do not enjoy uniformly peaceful relations with the political establishment. The discomfiture of established centres of power, influence and cultural prestige in the face of the Universal Church in particular, is palpable. Despite supporting the same candidates in the 1990 and 1994 Presidential elections, it has been in continuous conflict with the media giant, *Rede Globo* (the Globo Network). *Globo* may have been the force attempting to undermine the Church's purchase of the *TV Record* network with allegations of laundered money in 1991, and in 1995 *Globo* broadcast a mini-series entitled *Decadência*, about the seamy side of

Evangelical Church life, whose leading character is a thinly disguised replica of the leader of the Universal Church (*Financial Times*, 9 Sept. 1995). In response, the Universal Church has declared 'war' on *Rede Globo*.

In terms of ready-made categories of political analysis, then, the neo-Pentecostals in particular, defy classification: they support positions of the 'right' yet they offend the political establishment. To explain away this paradox simply in terms of power play, corporate interest, clientelism or even competition in the media, important as these are, is to trivialize them, while to denounce or dismiss them as an imperialist cultural offensive is to ignore their profound impact on culture and society which this book has documented. What we observe rather is that just as in popular culture they have invested techniques, rituals, gestures and locutions handed down over generations, with a completely new meaning, so in politics they have revealed a remarkable adeptness in marshalling the methods of traditional clientelism and the dreams of triumphant neo-liberalism with a powerful sense of the theatre of politics, a grasp of the power of the visual and spoken media, and above all a capacity for intervention in post-ideological political discourse. Unencumbered by party apparatuses or even the semblance of a political programme, but enjoying a bedrock of electoral support, they are practititioners of the politics of infinitely sub-divisible outcomes, in which the State is not an instrument of social transformation – left or right – but rather an arena for factional power struggles. This is not clientelism in the 'old' sense, because it is not based on networks of personal fiefdoms founded on relationships of personal dependence. These politicans enjoy the support of large-scale religious organizations which are organized on a modern, bureaucratic basis.

To be sure, there are many examples of Evangelicals operating on the 'left': as active trade unionists in Brazil (Burdick, 1993), or becoming involved in social movements and land conflicts, as in Colombia (Rappoport, 1984) and in Chiapas and even on occasions co-operating with guerrilla armies as in Guatemala (Le Bot, 1993). Indeed, Rappoport shows how an indigenous group is able to assimilate Pentecostal beliefs without necessarily following the political ideology of the North American missionaries who first introduced them. But these are individual examples, and they also do not take into account the impact of this very new phenomenon of Evangelical Churches, as Churches, intervening directly in the political arena.

The contrast with *basismo* is palpable. Despite their distrust of the State apparatus, and indeed of large-scale apparatuses generally, *basistas* do believe in political programmes, but even if they are Catholics and identified with Catholic causes, such as base communities, they present their politics in a rationalistic way with little religious reference, and they do not mobilize their followers on the basis of religious belief or belonging. Their religious beliefs may be inspired by a religious commitment, but they fight for them on a rationalistic basis, while the Evangelicals, who proclaim the radical separation of religion and politics, campaign explicitly on the basis that their followers should vote for the candidate of 'our Church'. *Basistas* feel more comfortable, however, in local level politics and in small-scale organizations such as NGOs, and their struggles in these contexts are much more apt to take the form of bringing pressure to bear on the bureaucracy rather than standing for election and taking part in party politics. Their resistance to the exercise of state power at any level makes it very difficult for them to present an alternative, while their dependence on projects requiring external finance inhibits their ability to function autonomously at the grass roots. Thus we face the paradox that a movement which proclaims the power and potential of the people at the grass roots has had its principal effect in the ways in which bureaucracies at many levels — national and international — carry out their development plans — effects which research is now beginning to reveal.[4]

It will be clear that although Evangelicals also 'go to the people', they do so in an utterly different spirit, and one that has much in common with other fundamentalisms. At the level of formal policy, indeed theology, the politics of Evangelicals and Pentecostals in Latin America have little, if anything, in common with the Islamists — the *intégristes* as they are called in French: the former declare that politics and religion are utterly separate spheres, whereas the Islamists believe the exact opposite. Yet, in stark contrast to *basista* reverence for the traditions of popular culture handed down over generations and sanctified by an ideology of rootedness in history and origins, the two have in common a project of cultural onslaught. This onslaught is conducted, in Gilles Kepel's phrase, 'from below', through the gradual penetration of the interstices of society,

---

[4] An example of how the State itself has learnt from the NGO movement is in health programmes in the state of Ceará in Northeast Brazil: using deft techniques to encourage participation and popular monitoring from below; sending professionals to villages where they had never been seen before; concentrating on preventive care and education. But since this is the government it is done with infinitely more care and education. But since this is the government it is done with infinitely more resources than NGOs could muster on their own, and since the Governor of the state in question had a clear political will, he was able to institute a clear anti-clientelistic mechanism at the core of the programme (Tendler and Freedheim, 1994). It is not insignificant that this highly laudatory paper was written with the support of the World Bank, showing how such institutions are learning from the *basistas*. It is furthermore ironic that 'movement of health professionals', operating from within the political and professional culture of *basismo*, was sadly unsuccessful in its campaign to reform the country's health system at the national level (Weyland, 1995).

especially among the poor. Likewise, in Judaism, since the 1967 Arab-Israeli Six-Day War a politicized ultra-orthodoxy, centred around the issue of Israel's territorial entitlement, has constituted an entirely new departure from the Hassidic tradition of political quietism (Don-Yehiya, 1994). This has been accompanied by a worldwide cultural offensive among Jewish communities, encouraging the adoption of a strictly orthodox lifestyle, and by a fierce sectarianism *vis-à-vis* other Jewish traditions — indeed in a sense, and like their Christian counterparts, against Jewish tradition in general.

The role of intellectuals

A central feature of all religious fundamentalisms is the belief in biblical inerrancy and its concomitant, a deep distrust of intellectuals and established theological and academic institutions. They believe that access to the sacred text and to its meaning is open to all and not just to expert mediators or theologians. The Jews draw from the doctrine of inerrancy the conclusion not that access is intuitive or innocent, but rather that everyone can study and become an expert; but the anti-intellectual attitude is still there, for Talmudic study is learning of a legalistic, esoteric, unscientific kind, sometimes not very different from the millennial calculations of certain Evangelicals (the 'dispensationalists') and not unrelated to techniques of kabbalistic decipherment. The opacity of the doctrine of biblical inerrancy arises from our puzzlement in the face of the dual claim that although the truth is there for anyone to grasp in the text, yet there is only one truth. In fundamentalist eyes that truth is not strictly an interpretation, since that phrase would imply human mediation between the text and its meaning, which they reject. Thus we find in these organizations a superimposition of organizational and theological authority, and a veritable industry producing quotations for appropriate moments and morals. In the long run, this superimposition is not sustainable and some kind of expert category must grow up which, being distinct from administrative and pastoral authority, can produce interpretations without placing that authority at risk. But this is a long run political process punctuated by numerous power struggles, splits and expulsions.[5]

[5] Although they believe that access to the sacred text and to its meaning is open to all and not just to expert mediators or theologians, the need to orient their own followers and to institutionalize their own organizations leads them to establish institutions of their own. The Islamists in Egypt regard the established institutions of higher learning as corrupt, and from Nasser's time set about infiltrating them, to the point where now they occupy positions of great influence within the Al Azhar University

The doctrine of inerrancy forms part of the broader mind-set of cultural dissidence and anti-intellectualism, of hostility towards the symbols and bearers of established intellectual and religious authority, and it is not to be underestimated merely because it is restricted to the cultural sphere and wills itself thus. Bookish learning is held in contempt; the Bible, historicized by modern learning, is converted into a series of morality tales and epic stories wrenched out of their historical context. Thus turning away from 'the world' is a turning away from those who would preach to the people from on high, from the pulpits (real and metaphorical) of the higher learning, of fancy phrases and the lessons of history. In classic Weberian mould, turning away from the world does not disqualify accumulation, but in a late twentieth century innovation, it also allows the unashamed desire of worldly goods. It advocates political passivity and discourages participation in political parties, calling on the faithful simply to vote for the candidates proposed by their religious leaders. It announces a fundamental change in the social order by foretelling, with abundant biblical quotation in support, the imminent end of the world, when those who are chosen will be saved. It is therefore not a millenarian movement, because it does not mobilize in a messianic fashion. But these changes in the political and social imaginary, in what might be termed a popular eschatology, do signify a cultural break because it is a break with the inherited and legitimating symbolic apparatus of a system of authority. The media moguls of *Globo* have understood the nature of this revolution in the imaginary better than the spokesmen of a variety of tendencies within Catholicism who focus instead on the explicit content of the Pentecostal message. To gain control of the utterance 'the people' is not a matter of markets and class relations, but it remains a very serious matter which ultimately has implications for the exercise of power in society.

Basismo could hardly be more different: where the fundamentalists take the Bible out of history, they put history back into the Bible; where the fundamentalists deny the authority of the intelligentsia, they themselves are or aspire to be intellectuals so as to better guide the people and so as to reinvent the people in all their innocence and return them to their roots — those roots which for the fundamentalists are pagan and diabolic. Somehow, the *basistas* preserve the pulpit, if not literally, then metaphorically, by using an analytical historicist language and erudite

in Cairo. The Pentecostals descend from a tradition which took a fierce line of opposition to the 'higher criticism' of German nineteenth-century scholars, and yet they also establish seminaries and theological institutions of their own, initiating a dynamic of institutionalization which eventually will produce a theological profession.

sources even while trying to popularize their message. Where the fundamentalists deny the virtues of political participation at the grass roots and insist on the gains to be made from mediated participation in the institutions of the State, *basistas* deeply distrust the State and seek endlessly for the true spirit of the people; where the fundamentalists call on the people to dig into their pockets to finance their Church, the *basistas* shrink from such exploitation and call on the people to give of their time and their labour for their projects, while going to the international charitable community to obtain the capital which will complement that labour; where fundamentalists insist on the primacy of personal conversion and its fulminating effect on people's lives, the *basistas* insist on the *caminhada* — the long journey through the wilderness of political struggle towards an unknowable destination. And where *basistas* place all their emphasis on changes in the condition of poverty afflicting the masses, fundamentalists insist on the primacy of cultural and personal change.

Modernity: cosmopolitanism and globalism

It is often thought that fundamentalism is a reaction against modernity, though stated thus the formulation is so vague as to cover almost any relationship to a vast array of institutions and practices. But if globalization, the ability to communicate across cultural boundaries, is a feature of modernity, then fundamentalists are extremely well suited to it, as David Martin (1990) and others have remarked. This globalism is not cosmopolitan in the way I have described *basismo* to be, for it does not valorize difference nor does it cultivate an ability to exchange across culture in a spirit even of curiosity, let alone of what liberals might call mutual respect and others 'political correctness'. Pentecostals do not share *basismo*'s historical view of difference being produced by processes exploding and unfolding over time, through relations of domination and exploitation. It is instead a globalism in which the world is divided into those who have seen the light and those who have not, with no hint of awareness of ethnic or national differences. Pentecostals are able to implant like practices and beliefs across a vast array of cultures, conveying in each case a sense that theirs is a worldwide movement, global in form as much as in content. Standardized methods of preaching, organization, money-raising, even church design seem to vary little across the most diverse cultures.[6] The replication is reinforced by the use of radio and television, of common devotional texts translated from English, and in some cases by participation in international revivalist roadshows led by preacher-showmen like Luis Palau (Kamsteeg, 1993).

The global form comes from common methods of organization and a common reference to the consumer society, symbolized by a utopia they call the 'United States'. To some this seems extremely ethnocentric, an imposition of American values, but that complaint is based on the assumption that it is taking place in a sense against the will of the converts (which may be true in individual cases but can hardly be generally the case), and that mass consumption is a peculiarly American habit, which it is not. The claim that this is an imposition is as ethnocentric as the imposition it seeks to criticize, being based on a romantic notion of 'untouched cultures' which 'we' are obliged to protect.

Likewise Jewish neo-orthodoxy may appear narrowly provincial and inward-looking to some, but certain aspects cast it in a different light. It appeals purposively to Jews in vastly differing cultures, Sephardi and Ashkenazi, post-Soviet as well as North American, and so on. Although all see themselves as Jewish 'by birth' they can hardly be said to participate in the same culture, especially since the targets of these campaigns of 'reconversion' are precisely people who have had little exposure to Jewish culture of any kind. The Bronx accents of spokesmen and spokeswomen for ultra-nationalist groups in Israel and the occupied territories reveal Israel as a crucible of trans-cultural encounters, as much as a coming together of people with a common heritage. The Habad Hassidim (not to be confused with ultra-orthodox *haredim*) go out to convert non-religious Jews in the same way as Pentecostals go out to convert, and set themselves deliberately and visibly apart by adopting a certain mode of dress and subordinating themselves to tight authority structures. Under the motto 'America is different', and in a marked departure from the inward-looking Hassidism of Eastern Europe before the Holocaust, they have adopted the United States – not Israel – as their headquarters, because it is the epitome of modernity and the centre of international communication, and despite their support of the continued occupation by Israel of the occupied territories, they will not regard the Israeli state as properly legitimate until the Messiah brings the

---

[6] As indeed was the case when Christianity was taken across the Atlantic in the fifteenth century and later to Asia and Africa.

redemption of the Jewish people.[7] The Habad Hassidim even resemble the Pentecostals in the organization of their missions, sending missionaries off to far-flung places where they are expected very quickly to become self-financing through the contributions of local followers, and demanding complete obedience to their leader, overriding family and community (Friedman, 1994).

Islamists also, for all that they may appear to share a single culture, have shown an ability to move across cultural divides, from the mountains of Afghanistan to the slums of Cairo and Algiers, and the second-generation immigrants in French cities, showing that theirs too is a multi-cultural movement, just as their use of modern technologies of communication and their appeal to students in science and engineering shows they are quite at home with many aspects of modern society and also that, like the Pentecostals, they find footholds in local cultures. We have observed how this occurs in Brazil and, through the work of John Peel, in Nigeria, and we may have difficulty in understanding how it is that missionaries barely able to speak Spanish, and utterly unconversant with the indigenous languages or local cultures, can make converts among lowland tribes. Yet it is nothing new: the Spaniards did it in the sixteenth century, originating violently and painfully a 500-year tradition of popular Catholicism – and was not the Southern European popular religion which the friars transplanted to the Americas itself the product of pagan and Catholic syncretisms? Today Catholicism in the Americas – but not apparently in Africa – is encumbered by a reflexive, more complicated and guilt-ridden relationship to popular culture than it was in the sixteenth century, and despite its post-modern resonance, this appreciation seems to have hobbled the Church's attempts to adapt to modernity in those countries. Maybe it is this lack of reflexivity on the part of the Pentecostals which gives them the edge.

Fundamentalism, then, is not a reaction against modernity.[8] But in the eyes of lay observers, its obsession with sexual control and obsessive hostility to the 'permissive society' in the West, and to the broadening of

---

[7] Though, in an even more extraordinary departure they came to describe their leader, who died in 1993, as the Messiah himself.

[8] In their judiciously worded Introductions to the various volumes of the Chicago Fundamentalism Project, Marty and Appleby describe it as a 'set of strategies by which beleaguered believers attempt to preserve their distinctive identity' (1993:3). At first reading this looks like a reaction against modernity, but closer inspection of the word 'beleaguered' shows that it leaves that issue out altogether. Later on they are careful to point out that fundamentalist movements select elements of tradition and modernity (ibid.) so clearly they do not see them straightforwardly as movements of opposition to modernity.

women's opportunities worldwide, is sufficient to tar it with the brush of backward-looking anti-modernism. There is, however, more to modernity than sex. If the term encapsulates Weberian rationalization in thought, in decision-making, in political and judicial life, then this account has shown that Pentecostalism at least, much as its growth may be a consequence of modernity (what is not?), is itself a catalyst of modernity, at least in Latin America. The notion that fundamentalism is merely a reaction against modernity, an attempt to reach back to a lost collective identity, is absurd. Even the Habad Hassidim, with their outlandish dress and hair-splitting prohibitions, are not trying to recreate the *shtetl*.

The effort to control female sexuality expresses a desire both to re-establish male authority and also to re-establish, or perhaps simply establish, the nuclear family as a stable unit. This has a distinctive significance in Brazil or the Caribbean, even in comparison with other Latin American countries, because of the prominence in the lower income groups of a matrifocal family structure headed by single women. My field work revealed a Pentecostalism in which not only were women a clear majority, but in which also the symbols and the metaphors deployed seemed to address their plight with particular poignancy: metaphors often related to sickness and extended to the family and the community in which women find themselves responsible for the welfare of their children in particular and indeed of the children of an extended network of female kin. For these women the churches provide a place in society, a source of respect from others, and thus possibly the self-confidence to assert themselves in the face of their men and indeed their children. In this context, the discourse on men, women, obedience and marriage, has multiple resonances. By preaching female obedience, the pastors are also heralding the context of that obedience, namely family stability and respectability in a nuclear household. They preach not obedience to men, but to husbands. Like the architecture of the churches and the mode of dress of the congregations, they are expressing an aspiration to an idealized *petit bourgeois* lifestyle, in which parents live together with their children in an isolated nuclear family, in a house 'of their own', with a car 'of their own', and in which husbands will both be obeyed and behave 'responsibly'. Indeed, if the establishment of male authority goes with the enforcement of male responsibility, it can be seen that an apparently male chauvinist appeal may have as its obverse, be it only in fantasy, the empowerment of women to force their men to shoulder responsibilities. It is therefore not surprising that side by side with a discourse of marital obedience, we hear a parallel discourse of empowerment, in which women speak of how after their conversion they have been able to bring their men to heel.

The projected image of the people

The term fundamentalism has given rise to many doubts and objections, derived from its pejorative connotations and the vast range of phenomena to which it is commonly applied. But in the final analysis the editors of the Fundamentalism Project are surely right when, in the Introduction to *Accounting for Fundamentalisms* (Marty and Appleby 1994) they defend their use of the term. In the politest possible way, yet not entirely concealing their impatience after no doubt many hours, days and weeks of agonizing, they say that the reservations of their authors with regard to its use have not led to the proposal of a catchy alternative, and above all have led to the proposal of other terms which, being too narrow, fail to capture the undoubted common elements among all these processes. And finally they ask, in effect: what can academicians do when a word has found its way into common parlance? In addition, we have found three features common to movements and organizations usually labelled as fundamentalist: anti-intellectualism; globalism and a strong emphasis, even an obsession with, control of women's sexuality.

There is little mileage in the view that fundamentalisms constitute an effort by disoriented or 'beleaguered' people, especially urban migrants, caught up in a maelstrom of change which is beyond their understanding, and yearning to go back to their roots, their origins, so as to recreate their identities. This view is naive,[9] yet we have seen that even while unashamedly borrowing an array of ritual and symbolic practices from the possession cults and many elements – such as belief in the Devil – from popular Catholicism, Brazilian Pentecostalism attempts to bring people to turn their backs on the past and on their roots – ironically during the same period as the highly rationalistic *basistas*, once so hostile to

---

[9] There is a related view (cogently criticized by Levine, 1995) which refers to the problem of anomie, and which is widely espoused by the Catholic Church, according to which many converts to Pentecostalism are migrants from the countryside who are wrenched from stable communities and are drawn to a secure community offering a stable set of values. Those communities are not as stable or secure as is assumed, and we have seen that even Jewish *hassidim* are more forward-looking and open to the modern world than would at first appear. There is much in all these fundamentalisms which involves tearing people away from their few remaining roots in family or community and creating new bonds – a technique which at the extreme leads to the formation of messianic and totalitarian sects and religious cults, but is present to a varying degree in all fundamentalisms.

superstition, are bringing samba drums into church, and with such apparently disappointing results.

The irony embodied in these radically different 'uses of popular religion' (Rostas and Droogers, 1993) reflects the deeper cultural dissidence represented in particular by Latin American Pentecostalism. For the rivalry between these profoundly different religious movements is cast in a struggle for legitimate control over the utterance 'the people' in societies where that word is not just a descriptive term, but an invocation, of a history, of a vocation, of solidarity and of collective loyalties. We are thus in the presence of more than a competition for numbers in Churches, or even for political power. Rather we are in the presence of a profound process of cultural change, and that change is located in the relationship of the intelligentsia to the people, of popular and erudite culture. It is also a process which differentiates the impact of Latin American Pentecostalism from other fundamentalisms.

Latin American Pentecostalism challenges this unique relationship, whose content is the construction by the intelligentsia of the concept and even the reality of the people, which has grown up in Latin America. Here 'popular culture' is the creation of a dialectical process of interaction between the intelligentsia and the people; it is neither pure fabrication of an idealized dissident culture − as Bourdieu would have it − nor the untainted product of the popular. It owes much to the region's Catholic heritage, most visible in the Mexican cult of the Virgin of Guadalupe, invented by the clergy in the colonial period and later elevated into a banner of nationalism;[10] but it is also evident in Peronism in Argentina; in Brazilian populism; in liberation theology and contemporary post-conciliar *basismo*, and also in secular *basista* enthusiasm for social movements and NGOs (Lehmann, 1990). In Brazil, it is the element of projection within that dialectic which has conditioned the evolution of music, of literature, of carnival, and of Catholicism, as the intelligentsia seek to construct the popular, to approximate to it, to struggle with the idealizations to which so often they themselves know they are irredeemably prone, and as the people, or the articulate members of that inchoate category, appropriate the projections, tacitly accept − or on occasion very self-consciously reject − the projections they see, and mould them to their own needs and interests, or deal with them in other ways.

---

[10] The cult of the Virgin of Guadalupe was encouraged by a clergy which saw in it 'a great national myth, all the more powerful because behind it lay the natural devotion of the Indian masses and the theological exaltation of the creole clergy' (Brading, 1985). In 1794 Fray Servando de Mier glorified the Mexican people as 'the chosen people' the privileged nation and the tender children of Mary' (Brading, 1984). The Brazilian attempt to do likewise with the Virgin of Aparecida has been less successful (Fernandes, 1988).

The Pentecostals bring about a radical cultural change because they break not with either popular or erudite culture, but because they break with this dialectic — that is, with the mirrored exchanges and projections constantly going on between the popular and the erudite in this culture, of which of course *basismo* is yet another manifestation. It was not planned like that — indeed the Pentecostals' 'plan' is to scandalize the establishment and confront the daily, weekly and annual rhythms of the popular — but the force of the change brought about by the Pentecostals lies in their disdain and turning away from this interplay which lies at the heart of Brazilian culture. Pentecostals glory in bad taste: whether 'good taste' is the artistic representation of popular traditions, or the erudite conformation of the avant-garde, they conduct an onslaught against both, looking to 'the United States' for a model, to the Holy Spirit for an inspiration, turning away from history and origins, and reconstructing every aspect of their daily lives. They reject the image of the people as projected by the intelligentsia, but they also reject the intelligentsia with great force. They do not care if they scandalize the establishment — be it that of the media moguls or of the political left. By attacking the culture of the people, even while speaking the language of the people, they constitute a force as potent as it is disconcerting.

Bibliography

Abbruzzese, Salvatore, 1989: *Comunione e Liberazione: identité catholique et disqualification du monde*. Paris, Cerf.

ACO (Açao Católica Operaria), n.d.: *A História do Povo de Deus: Introdução para uma Leitura da Bíblia, hoje*. vol. 2: *Do Exílio até o Fim da Dominação Grega*. Rio de Janeiro, ACO, Comissão Nacional de Pastoral Operária.

ACO (*Ação Católica Operaria*), c. 1985: *Revisão de Vida: Conhecer para Transformar – Ver-Julgar-Agor pelos 4 Lados*. Rio de Janeiro, ACO.

Agier, Michel, 1994: 'Une ville entre magie et industrie: nouvelles espaces d'identité à Bahia'. *Problèmes d'Amérique Latine*, Special issue on 'La ville et l'Amérique Latine', 14, July–September.

Anderson, Robert Mapes, 1979: *Vision of the Disinherited: the Making of American Pentecostalism*. New York, Oxford University Press.

Angell, Allan, 1972: *Politics and the Labour Movement in Chile*. London, Oxford University Press.

Antoniazzi, Alberto et al., 1994: *Nem anjos nem demonios: interpretações sociológicas do Pentecostalismo*. Petropolis, Vozes.

Arantes, Antonio Augusto, 1977: *Sociological Aspects of folhetos Literature in North-East Brazil*. Ph.D. thesis, Cambridge University.

Baer, Hans A. and Singer, Merrill, 1992: *African-American Religion in the Twentieth Century*. Knoxville, University of Tennessee Press.

Banck, Geert, 1990: 'Cultural dilemmas behind strategy: Brazilian neighbourhood movements and Catholic discourse'. *European Journal of Development Research*, 2,1.

Barthes, Roland, 1954: *Michelet par lui-même*. Paris, Seuil.

Bastian, Jean-Pierre, 1994: *Le protestantisme en Amérique Latine: une approche socio-historique*. Geneva, Labor et Fides.

Bayart, J.-F., 1989: *L'état en Afrique: la politique du ventre*. Paris, Fayard.

Bebbington, Anthony and Thiele, Graham, with Davies, Penelope, Prager, Martin and Riveros, Hernando, 1993: *Non-governmental Organizations and the*

State in Latin America: Rethinking Roles in Sustainable Agricultural Development. London, Routledge.

Berryman, Phillip, 1980: 'What happened at Puebla'. In Levine, (ed.) *Churches and Politics in Latin America.*

Boff, Leonardo, 1971: *Jesus Cristo Libertador.* Petropolis, Vozes. (Translation: *Jesus Christ Liberator*, Maryknoll, N.Y., Orbis Books, 1979).

Boff, Leonardo, 1977, *Eclesiogênese.* Petropolis, Vozes

Boff, Leonardo, 1985: *Church, charisma and power.* London, SPCK. (First published by Petropolis, Vozes, 1981).

Boff, Leonardo and Clodovis Boff, 1979: *Da Libertação: o teológico das libertaçoes sócio-históricas.* Petropolis, Vozes.

Bourdieu, Pierre, 1979: *La Distinction: critique sociale du jugement.* Paris, Ed. du Minuit.

Bourdieu, Pierre, 1994a: *Raisons pratiques: sur la théorie de l'action*, Paris, Seuil.

Bourdieu, Pierre, 1994b: 'Pieté religieuse et dévotion artistique: fidèles et amateurs d'art à Santa Maria Novella', *Actes de la recherche en sciences sociales.* 105, December.

Boyer-Araujo, Véronique, 1993a: *Femmes et cultes de possession au Brésil: les compagnons invisibles.* Paris, L'Harmattan.

Boyer-Araujo, Véronique, 1993b: ' "Les traditions risquent-elles d'être contaminées?" – paradigmes scientifiques et orthodoxie religieuse dans les cultes de possession au Brésil'. *Journal de la Société des Américanistes*, 79, 67–90.

Boyer-Araujo, Véronique, 1996a: 'Le don et l'initiation: de l'impact de la littérature sur les cultes de possession au Brésil'. *L'Homme*, 138, 7–24.

Boyer-Araujo, Véronique, 1996b, 'Possession et exorcisme dans une église pentecôtiste au Brésil', *Cahiers des Sciences Humaines* – ORSTOM.

Brading, David, 1984: *Prophecy and Myth in Mexican History.* Cambridge, Centre of Latin American Studies, University of Cambridge.

Brading, David, 1985: *The Origins of Mexican Nationalism.* Cambridge, Centre of Latin American Studies, University of Cambridge.

Brading, David, 1991: *The First America: The Spanish Monarchy, Creole Patriots and the Liberal State, 1492–1867.* Cambridge, Cambridge University Press.

Brandão, Carlos Rodriguez, 1980: *Os Deuses do Povo.* São Paulo, Brasiliense.

Brown, Diana DeG., 1986: *Umbanda: Religion and Politics in Urban Brazil.* Ann Arbor, Michigan, UMI Press. (2nd edition, New York, Columbia University Press, 1994).

Brown, Peter, 1981: *The Cult of the Saints.* London, SCM Press.

Bruneau, Thomas C., 1964: *The Political Transformation of the Brazilian Catholic Church.* Cambridge, Cambridge University Press.

Brusco, Elisabeth, 1986: 'The household basis of evangelical religion and the reformation of machismo in Colombia'. Ph.D. thesis, City University of New York.

Burdick, John, 1990: 'Looking for God in Brazil: the progressive Catholic Church in urban Brazil's religious arena'. Ph.D. thesis, City University of New York.

Burdick, John, 1991: 'Observaçoes sobre a Campanha da Fraternidade de 1988 na Baixada Fluminense'. *Comunicações do ISER*, ano 10, no. 40.

Burdick, John, 1993: *Looking for God in Brazil: The Progressive Catholic Church in Urban Brazil's Religious Arena*. Berkeley, University of California Press.

Burke, Peter, 1978: *Popular Culture in Early Modern Europe*. London, Temple Smith.

Burns, Gene, 1992: *The Frontiers of Catholicism: The Politics of Ideology in a Liberal World*. Berkeley, University of California Press.

Campbell, John, 1964: *Honour, Family and Patronage*. Oxford, Oxford University Press.

Campos, Renato Carneiro, 1959 (2nd. edn., 1977): *Ideologia dos poetas populares*. Recife, Ministerio da Educação e da Cultura (MEC), FUNARTE, Instituto Joaquim Nabuco de Pesquisas Sociais, Serie Estudos e Pesquisas, no.5.

Cardoso, Ruth, 1983: 'Movimentos sociais urbanos: um balanço crítico'. In Bernardo Sorj et al. (eds), *Sociedade e política no Brasil pós-64*, São Paulo, Brasiliense.

Carroll, Thomas, 1992: *Intermediary NGOs: The Supporting Link in Grassroots Development*. West Hartford, Connecticut, Kumarian Press.

Castañeda, Jorge 1993: *Utopia Unarmed: The Latin American Left after the Cold War*. New York, Vintage Books.

Castells, Manuel, 1983: *The City and the Grass Roots: A Cross Cultural Theory of Urban Social Movements*. London, Edward Arnold.

Castro, Ruy, 1993: *Chega de saudade: a historia e as historias da Bossa Nova*. São Paulo, Companhia das Letras.

CELAM (Latin American Episcopal Council) 1992a: *Elementos para uma reflexão pastoral em preparação à IV Conferencia Geral do Episcopado Latino-Americano*. São Paulo, Edições Loyola.

CELAM (Latin American Episcopal Council) 1992b: *Santo Domingo: nueva evangelización, promoción humana, cultura cristiana*, (Document of the Fourth General Conference of Latin American Bishops, Santo Domingo, 1992). Madrid, Ediciones Paulinas.

Clark, John, 1991: *Democratizing Development: The Role of Voluntary Organizations*. London, Earthscan.

Clarke, Peter, 1993: 'The dilemmas of a popular religion: the case of candomblé'. In Rostas and Droogers (eds.), *The Popular Uses of Popular Religion*.

Clendinnen, Inga, 1991, *Aztecs: An Interpretation*. Cambridge, Cambridge University Press.

Clifford, James and Marcus, George, 1986: *Writing Culture: The Poetics and Politics of Ethnography*. Berkeley, University of California Press.

Coleman, Kenneth M., Aguilar, Edwin Eloy, Sandoval, José Miguel and Steigenga, Timothy J., 1993: 'Protestantism in El Salvador: conventional wisdom versus the survey evidence'. In Stoll and Garrard-Burnett (eds), *Rethinking Protestantism in Latin America*.

Comblin, José, 1990: 'Algumas questões a partir da prática das Comunidades Eclesiais de Base no Nordeste. *Revista Eclesiástica Brasileira*, 50, 335–81.

Corten, André, 1995: *Le pentecôtisme au Brésil: emotion du pauvre et romantisme theologique*. Paris, Karthala.

DaMatta, Roberto, 1979: *Carnaval, malandros e herois: para uma sociologia do dilema brasileiro*, Rio, Zahar. (Translation: *Carnival, Rogues and Heroes: Interpretation of the Brazilian Dilemma*, Notre Dame, Indiana, Notre Dame University Press, 1992).

DaMatta, Roberto, 1986: *O qué faz o brasil, Brasil?*. Rio de Janeiro, Rocco.

Dantas, Beatriz Góis, 1988: *Vovó Nagô e Papai Branco: usos e abusos da Africa no Brasil*. Rio de Janeiro, Graal.

Davis, Natalie Zenon, 1974: 'Some tasks and themes in the study of popular religion'. In Charles Trinkaus and Heiko Oberman (eds.), *The Pursuit of Holiness in Late Medieval and Renaissance Religion*. Leiden, E.J. Brill.

Degler, Carl, 1971: *Neither Black nor White: Slavery and Race Relations in Brazil and the United States*. New York, Macmillan.

Deiros, Pablo, 1991: 'Protestant fundamentalism in Latin America'. In Marty and Appleby (eds.), *Fundamentalisms Observed*.

Délano, Priscilla and Lehmann, David, 1993: 'Women workers in labour-intensive factories: the case of Chile's fish industry'. *European Journal of Development Research*, V,2.

della Cava, Ralph, 1970: *Miracle at Juazeiro*. New York, Columbia University Press.

De Kadt, Emanuel, 1970: *Catholic Radicals in Brazil*. London, Oxford University Press.

Descola, Philippe, 1993: *La lance des crépuscules: relations Jivaros-Haute Amazonie*. Paris, Plon.

De Theije, Marjo, 1990: ' "Brotherhoods throw more weight around than the Pope": Catholic traditionalism and lay brotherhoods in Brazil'. *Sociological Analysis*, 51, 2.

Don-Yehiya, Eliezer, 1994: 'The Book and the Sword: the nationalist *yeshivoth* and political radicalism in Israel'. In Marty and Appleby (eds.), *Accounting for Fundamentalisms*.

Dumont, Louis, 1960: 'Caste, racisme et stratification'. *Cahiers Internationaux de Sociologie*, 29, 91–112. (Reprinted in *Homo hierarchicus*, London, Paladin, 1972).

Elbein dos Santos, Juana, 1986: *Os Nago e a Morte: Pade, Asese e o Culto Egun na Bahia*. Petropolis, Vozes.

Enayat, Hamid, 1982: *Modern Islamic Political Thought: The Response of the Shi'i and Sunni Muslims to the Twentieth Century*. London, Macmillan.

Escobar, Arturo and Alvarez, Sonia (eds.) 1992: *The Making of Social Movements in Latin America: Identity, Strategy and Democracy*. Boulder, Colorado, Westview Press.

Fernandes, Rubem César, 1988: '*Aparecida, nossa rainha, senhora e mãe, saravá!*'. In Viola Sachs et al. (eds) *Brasil & EUA: religião e identidade nacional.*

Fernandes, Rubem Cesar, 1994: 'Governo das almas: as denominações evangélicas no Grande Rio'. In Antoniazzi et al. (eds), *Nem anjos nem demonios.*

Foucault, Michel, 1971: *L'ordre du discours.* Paris, Gallimard.

Freston, Paul 1993a: 'Protestantes e Política no Brasil: da constituinte ão impeachment'. Doctoral thesis, State University of Campinas.

Freston, Paul 1993b: 'Brother votes for brother: the new politics of Pentecostalism in Brazil'. In Stoll and Garrard Burnett (eds.), *Rethinking Protestantism in Latin America.*

Freston, Paul 1994: 'Breve historia do Pentecostalismo brasileiro'. In Antoniazzi et al. (eds), *Nem anjos nem demonios.*

Freyre, Gilberto, 1933: *Casa-grande e senzala.* Rio de Janeiro, Maia e Schmidt Ltda. (1st. edn.) (Translation: *The Masters and the Slaves.* New York, Borzoi Books, 1970).

Friedman, Menachem, 1994: 'Habad as messianic fundamentalism: from local particularism to universal Jewish mission'. In Marty and Appleby (eds.), *Accounting for Fundamentalisms.*

Friedmann, John, 1992: *Empowerment: The Politics of Alternative Development.* Oxford, Basil Blackwell.

Furtado, Celso, 1959: *A Formação econômica do Brasil.* Rio de Janeiro, Fundo Universal da Cultura, (Translation by R.W. de Aguiar and E.C. Drysdale: *The Economic Growth of Brazil*, University of California Press, 1963).

Galvão, Walnicy Nogueira, 1974: *No calor da hora: a Guerra de Canudos nos Jornais – 4a. expedição.* São Paulo, Atica.

Geertz, Clifford, 1988: *Works and Lives: The Anthropologist as Author*, Cambridge, Polity.

Gifford, Paul, 1993: *Christianity and the State in Doe's Liberia.* Cambridge, Cambridge University Press.

Gomes, Wilson da Silva 1991: 'Relatorio de pesquisa sobre a Igreja Universal do Reino de Deus no contexto das seitas'. Unpublished manuscript, Salvador.

Gomes, Wilson da Silva, 1994: 'Nem anjos nem demonios'. In Antoniazzi et al. (eds), *New anjos nem demonioss.*

Goody, Jack, 1983: *The Development of the Family and Marriage in Europe.* Cambridge, Cambridge University Press.

Gorriti Ellenbogen, Gustavo, 1990: *Sendero: historia de la guerra milenaria en el Perú.* Lima, Apoyo.

Guillermoprieto, Alma, 1990: *Samba.* New York, Alfred A. Knopf.

Gutierrez, Gustavo, 1972: *Teología de la liberación: perspectivas.* Salamanca, Sígueme. (Translation: *A Theology of Liberation: History, Politics and Salvation.* Maryknoll, New York, Orbis Books, 1973).

Gutierrez, Gustavo, 1984: *We Drink From our Own Wells.* London, SCM Press.

Gutierrez, Gustavo, 1990: *La verdad os hará libres.* Salamanca, Sígueme.

Gutierrez, Gustavo, 1993: *En busca de los pobres de Jesucristo: el pensamiento de Bartolomé de las Casas*, Salamanca, Sígueme.

Hewitt, W.E. 1987: 'The influence of social class on activity preferences of CEBs in the Archdiocese of São Paulo'. *Journal of Latin American Studies*, 19, 1.

Hewitt, W.E., 1991: *Base Christian Communities and Social Change in Brazil*, Lincoln and London, University of Nebraska Press.

Hill, Michael, 1965: *The Religious Order: A Study of Virtuoso Religion and its Legitimation in the Nineteenth Century Church of England*. London, Heinemann.

Hirst, Paul 1994: 'The evolution of consciousness: identity and personality in historical perspective'. *Economy and Society*, 23, 1.

Hoffnagel, Judith, 1978: 'The believers: Pentecostalism in a Brazilian city'. Ph.D. thesis, Indiana University.

Hunter, James Davidson 1987: *Evangelicalism: The Coming Generation*. Chicago, University of Chicago Press.

Hymes, Dell, 1969: *Reinventing Anthropology*. New York, Pantheon Books.

Ireland, Rowan, 1992: *Kingdoms Come: Religion and Politics in Brazil*. Pittsburgh, Pittsburgh University Press.

Jelín, Elizabeth (ed.), 1985: *Los Nuevos movimientos sociales*. Buenos Aires, Centro Editor de América Latina.

Kamsteeg, Frans, 1993: 'The message and the people: different meanings of a Pentecostal evangelistic campaign. A case from Southern Peru'. In Rostas and Droogers (eds.)

Keck, Margaret, 1992: *The Workers' Party and Democratization in Brazil*. London and New Haven, Yale University Press.

Kepel, Gilles 1991: *La revanche de Dieu: chrétiens, juifs et musulmans à la reconquête du monde*. Paris, Seuil. (Translation: *The Revenge of God*, Cambridge, Polity, 1994).

Kepel, Gilles, 1994: *A l'ouest d'Allah*. Paris, Seuil. (Translation: *West of Allah*, Cambridge, Polity, 1996, forthcoming).

Kinzo, Maria D'Alva, 1993: 'The 1989 Presidential election: electoral behaviour in a Brazilian city'. *Journal of Latin American Studies*, 23,2.

Küng, Hans, 1964: *Structures of the Church*. London, Burns and Oates.

Laclau, Ernesto, 1977: *Politics and Ideology in Marxist Theory*. London, New Left Books.

Lancaster, Roger, 1989: *In the Name of God and the Revolution*. Berkeley, University of California Press.

Landim, Leila (ed.), 1990: *Sinais dos tempos: diversidade religiosa no Brasil*. Cadernos do ISER no. 23, Rio de Janeiro.

Lanternari, 1960: *Movimenti religiosi di libertà e di salvezza dei populi oppressi*. Milan, Feltrinelli.

Le Bot, Yvon, 1993: *La guerre en terre maya*. Paris, Karthala.

Lehmann, David, 1990: *Democracy and Development in Latin America: Economics, Politics and Religion in the Postwar Period*. Cambridge, Polity.

Levine, Daniel (ed.), 1980: *Churches and Politics in Latin America*. Beverly Hills, Sage Publications.

Levine, Daniel, 1992: *Popular Voices in Latin American Catholicism*. Princeton, Princeton University Press

Levine, Daniel, 1995: 'Protestants and Catholics in Latin America: a family portrait'. In Marty and Appleby (eds), *Fundamentalisms Compared*.

Levine, Robert M., 1992: *Vale of Tears*. Berkeley, University of California Press.

Lévi-Strauss, Claude, 1971: *L'Homme Nu*. Paris, Plon.

Lewis, Lowell, 1992: *Ring of Liberation: Deceptive Discourse in Brazilian Capóeira*. Chicago,University of Chicago Press.

McDonnell, Kilian (ed.), 1980: *Presence, Power and Praise: Documents on the Charismatic Renewal*. 3 vols., Collegeville, Minnesota, The Liturgical Press.

Bispo (Bishop) Edir Macedo, 1988: *Orixas, caboclos e guias: deuses ou demonios?* Universal Edições, Rio de Janeiro (11th edition, 100,000 copies) (first edition: 1982)

Mackenzie, John L., 1969: *The Roman Catholic Church*. London, Weidenfeld and Nicolson.

Mainwaring, Scott, 1986: *The Catholic Church and Politics in Brazil*. Stanford, Stanford University Press.

Mainwaring, Scott and Wilde, Alexander (eds.), 1989, *The Progressive Church in Latin America*, Notre Dame, Indiana, University of Notre Dame Press.

Marin, Richard, 1995: *Dom Helder Camara: les puissants et les pauvres. Pour une histoire de l'Eglise des pauvres dans le nordeste brésilien*. (1955–1985). Paris, Les Editions de l'Atelier/Editions Ouvrières.

Mariz, Cecilia Loreto, 1989: 'Religion and coping with poverty in Brazil'. Ph.D. Thesis, Boston University.

Mariz, Cecilia Loreto, 1993: *Coping with Poverty: Pentecostals and Christian Base Communities in Brazil*. Philadelphia, Temple University Press.

Marshall, Ruth, 1991: 'Power in the name of Jesus'. *Review of African Political Economy*, 52, November.

Martin, David, 1990: *Tongues of Fire: The Explosion of Protestantism in Latin America*. Oxford, Basil Blackwell.

Martin, David, 1995: 'Evangelical religion and capitalist society in Chile'. In Richard H. Roberts (ed.), *Religion and the Tranformations of Capitalism: Comparative Approaches*. London and New York, Routledge.

Martinez, Tomás Eloy, 1986: La novela de Perón. Buenos Aires, Legasa.

Martins, Heloisa T. de Souza, 1994: *Igreja e movimento operario no ABC, 1954–1975*, São Paulo-São Caetano do Sul, HUCITEC-Prefeitura de São Caetano do Sul.

Martins, José de Souza, 1994: *O poder do atraso: ensaios de sociologia da historia lenta*. São Paulo, HUCITEC.

Marty, Martin A. and Appleby, R. Scott (eds.), 1991: *Fundamentalisms Observed*. Chicago, University of Chicago Press.

Marty, Martin A. and Appleby, R. Scott (eds.), 1993a: *Fundamentalisms and Society*. Chicago, University of Chicago Press.

Marty, Martin and Appleby, R. Scott, (eds.), 1993b: *Fundamentalisms and the State*. Chicago, University of Chicago Press.

Marty, Martin A. and Appleby, R. Scott (eds.), 1994: *Accounting for Fundamentalisms*. Chicago, University of Chicago Press.

Marty, Martin A. and Appleby, R. Scott (eds.), 1995: *Fundamentalisms Compared*. Chicago, University of Chicago Press.

Mattoso, Katia M.de Queirós, 1992: *Bahia, século XIX: uma provincia no Imperio*. Rio de Janeiro, Nova Fronteira.

Mattoso, Katia M. de Queirós, 1994: 'Au Bresil: cent ans de mémoire de l'esclavage'. *Cahiers des Amériques Latines*. 17.

Melucci, Alberto, 1989: *Nomads of the Present: Social Movements and the Individual Needs in Contemporary Society*. London, Hutchinson Radius.

Mignone, Emilio, 1986: *Iglesia y dictadura: el papel de la Iglesia a la luz de sus relaciones con el régimen militar*. Buenos Aires, Ediciones del Pensamiento Nacional.

Moises, Alvaro and Verena Martinez-Alier, 1977: 'A revolta dos suburbanos, ou "patrão o tren atrasou" '. In Jose Alvaro Moises et al.: *Contradições urbanas e movimentos sociais*. Sao Paulo, CEDEC/Paz e Terra.

Monteiro, Douglas Teixeira, 1974: *Os errantes do novo século: um estudo sobre o surto milenarista do Contestado*. São Paulo, Duas Cidades.

Moynihan, Daniel, 1969: *Maximum Feasible Misunderstanding*. New York.

Muratorio, Blanca, 1980: 'Protestantism and capitalism revisited in the Highlands of Ecuador'. *Journal of Peasant Studies*. 8,1.

Napolitano, Valentina, 1995: 'Self and identity in a "colonia popular" of Guadalajara'. Ph.D. thesis, London University.

Oliveira, Pedro A. Ribeiro de, 1986: 'Comunidade, Igreja e poder: em busca de um conceito sociológico de "igreja" '. *Religiao e Sociedade*. 13,3.

Ortiz, Renato, 1978: *A morte branca do feiticeiro negro: umbanda e sociedade brasileira*. São Paulo, Brasiliense.

Olmi, Massimo, 1987: 'Opus Dei: its development and structure'. *The Month*. July.

Page, John Joseph, 1984: 'Brasil para Cristo: the cultural construction of Pentecostal networks in Brazil'. Ph.D. thesis, New York University.

Paiva, Vainilda, 1980: *Paulo Freire e o nacionalismo desenvolvimentista*. Rio de Janeiro, Civilização Brasileira.

Paiva, Vainilda, 1985: 'A Igreja moderna no Brasil'. In Vainilda Paiva (ed.) *Igreja e questão agraria*, São Paulo, Loyola.

Peel, John D.Y., 1968: *Aladura: A Religious Movement among the Yoruba*. London, Oxford University Press for the International African Institute.

Pepper, Joanne, 1991: 'The historical development of Pentecostalism in Northeastern Brazil, with specific reference to working class women in Recife'. Ph.D. thesis, University of Warwick.

Pereira, Cláudio Luz, 1993: ' "Linguas de fogo, rios de água viva . . .": etnografia da experiencia religiosa pentecostal em Salvador, Ba.' Masters' thesis, Federal University of Bahia.

Pereira de Queiroz, Maria Isaura, 1977: *O messianismo no Brasil e no mundo*. São Paulo, Alfa-Omega.

Pereira de Queiroz, Maria Isaura, 1986: 'Identité nationale, religion, expressions culturelles: la création religieuse au Brésil'. *Information sur les Sciences Sociales*. 25, 1.

Pereira de Queiroz, Maria Isaura, 1988: 'Identidade nacional, religiao e expressões culturais: a criação religiosa no Brasil'. In Sachs et al. (ed.), *Brasil & EUA*.

Pereira de Queiroz, Maria Isaura, 1992: *Carnaval brésilien: le vécu et le mythe*. Paris, Gallimard.

Peristiany, J.G., 1974: *Honour and Shame: The Values of Mediterranean Society*. Chicago, Chicago University Press.

Pitt-Rivers, Julian 1954: *The People of the Sierra*, Chicago, University of Chicago Press.

Prévot-Schapera, 1995: 'De l'utopie au pragmatisme: l'héritage du basisme dans les gestions municipales du Grand Buenos Aires'. unpublished manuscript.

Raboteau, Albert J. 1978: *Slave Religion: The 'Invisible Institution' in the Antebellum South*. New York, Oxford University Press.

Rappoport, Joanne, 1984: 'Las misiones Protestantes y la resistencia indígena en el sur de Colombia'. *América Indígena*, 44(1), 111–26.

Review of African Political Economy, 1991: Special Issue on Fundamentalism in Africa, November.

Rostas, Susanna, 1993: 'The Mexica's reformulation of the concheros' dance: the popular use of autochthonous religion in Mexico City'. In Rostas and Drooghers (eds.), *The Popular Uses of Popular Religion*.

Rostas, Susanna and André Droogers (eds.), 1993: *The Popular Uses of Popular Religion in Latin America*. Amsterdam, CEDLA, CEDLA Latin American Studies, no. 70.

Rose, Susan, 1993: 'Christian fundamentalism and education in the United States'. In Marty and Appleby (eds.), *Fundamentalism and Society*.

Rowe, William and Schelling, Vivian, 1991: *Memory and Modernity: Popular Culture in Latin America*. London, Verso.

Sachs, Viola (ed.), et al. (1988): *Brasil & EUA: religiao e identidade nacional*. Rio de Janeiro, Graal.

Sansone, Livio, 1994: 'Couleur, classe et modernité à travers deux lieux bahianais'. *Cahiers des Amériques Latines*. 17.

Schelling, Vivian, 1991: *A presença do povo na cultura brasileira: ensaio sobre o pensamento de Mario de Andrade e Paulo Freire*. Campinas, Editora Unicamp.

Shorter, Aylward, 1988: *Towards a Theology of Inculturation*. London, Geoffrey Chapman.

Skinner, Quentin 1978: *The Foundations of Modern Political Thought*. 2 vols. Cambridge, Cambridge University Press.

Slater, Candice, 1982: *Stories on a String: The Brazilian Literatura de Cordel*. Berkeley, University of California Press.

Smith, Christian, 1991: *The Emergence of Liberation Theology: Radical Religion and Social Movement Theory*. Chicago, Chicago University Press.

Soares, Marisa de Carvalho, 1990: 'Guerra Santa no país do sincretismo'. In Landim (ed.), *Sinais dos tempos*.

Sobrino, Jon, 1993: *Jesus the Liberator: A Historical-Theological Reading of Jesus of Nazareth*. Tunbridge Wells, Burnes and Oates (originally published as: *Jesucristo liberador. Una lectura histórico-teológica de la vida de Jesús de Nazareth*, Madrid, Editorial Trotta, 1991.)

Spier, Fred 1993: 'Rural protestantism in Southern Andean Peru: a case study'. In Rostas and Droogers (eds.), *The Popular Uses of Popular Religion*.

Stoll, David, 1990: *Is Latin America turning Protestant?*. Berkeley, University of California Press.

Stoll, David, 1993: *Between Two Armies in the Ixil Towns of Guatemala*. New York, Columbia University Press.

Stoll, David and Virginia Garrard Burnett, 1993: *Rethinking Protestantism in Latin America*. Philadelphia, Temple University Press.

Sundkler, Berngt, 1961: *Bantu Prophets in South Africa*. London, Oxford University Press for the International African Institute.

Swope, John W., 1992: 'The production, recontextualization and popular transmission of religious discourse: a case of Liberation Theology and Basic Christian Communities in Santiago, Chile'. Ph.D. thesis, Institute of Education, University of London.

Taylor, Anne Christine, 1991: 'Equateur: les indiens de l'Amazonie et la question ethnique'. *Problèmes d'Amérique Latine*. 3.

Telles, Edward, 1993: 'Racial distance and region in Brazil: intermarriage in Brazilian urban areas', *Latin American Research Review*. 28, 2.

Tendler, Judith and S. Freedheim, 1994: 'Trust in a rent-seeking world: health and government transformed in Northeast Brazil'. *World Development*. 22, 12.

Thomas, Keith, 1973: *Religion and the Decline of Magic*. London, Weidenfeld and Nicolson.

Touraine, Alain, 1965: *Sociologie de l'Action*. Paris, Seuil.

Touraine, Alain, 1973: *Production de la société*, Paris, Seuil.

Touraine, Alain, 1988: *La parole et le sang: politique et société en Amérique Latine*. Paris, Odile Jacob.

Turner, Victor, 1967: 'Betwixt and between: the liminal period in *rites de passage*'. In Turner, V. *The Forest of Symbols*, Ithaca, Cornell University Press.

Vasconcelos, Itamar de Abreu, 1986: 'Pentecostalismo e neopentecostalismo no Recife', *Symposium* (Revista da Universidade Católica de Pernambuco), 28, 1.

Verger, Pierre Fatumbi, 1982: *Orisha: les dieux Yoruba en Afrique et au Nouveau Monde*. Paris, Editions A.M. Metailié.

Vinhas de Queiroz, Mauricio, 1977: *Messianismo e conflito social (A guerra sertaneja do Contestado, 1912–1916)*. São Paulo, Atica.

Walsh, Michael, 1989: *The Secret World of Opus Dei*. London, Grafton Books.

Warner, Lloyd, 1959: *The Living and the Dead*. New Haven, Yale University Press.

Washington, Joseph R. Jr., 1972: *Black Sects and Cults*. Garden City, New York, Doubleday.

Weyland, K., 1995: 'Social movements and the state: the politics of health reform in Brazil', *World Development*, 23, 10.

Wilson, Bryan, 1961: *Sects and Society*. London, Heinemann.

Wilson, Bryan R. 1973: *Magic and the Millenium: A Sociological Study of Religious Movements of Protest among Tribal and Third-World Peoples*. London, Heinemann.

Wood, C. and J.A. Magno de Carvalho, 1988: *The Demography of Inequality in Brazil*. Cambridge, Cambridge University Press.

Worsley, Peter, 1957: *The Trumpet Shall Sound: A Study of 'Cargo' Cults in Melanesia*. London, MacGibbon and Kee.

Young, Kate, 1993: *Planning Development with Women: Making a World of Difference*. London, Macmillan.

Zadra, Dario, 1994: 'Comunione e liberazione: a fundamentalist idea of power'. In Marty and Appleby (eds.), *Accounting for Fundamentalisms*.

Zamosc, Leo, 1994: 'Agrarian protest and the Indian movement in the Ecuadorian highlands'. *Latin American Research Review*. 29, 3.

Index

ACO (Catholic Workers' Action) 26,
58–9, 82–5; in Argentina and Chile,
61–2, 82; JOC's (Catholic Workers'
Youth) shift to the left, 60; pamphlet
literature, 82–5; seminar, 97–100
Afro-Brazilian religion, *see candomblé*;
possession cults
anomie, as explanation of Pentecostal
growth, 226 n. 9
architecture: Pentecostal and Catholic
Churches, 182–8; reflecting social
mobility, 187–8
Argentina, 'Third World Priests'
movement, 51
Assemblies of God, 118, 119–22;
architecture, 184; and money, 204; in
Recife, 125, 128, 130, 131, 190–1;
respectability in, 175; training in,
131–2; use of Bible, 174–6, 180–1; *see
also* neo-Pentecostalism; Pentecostalism

assistencialismo, 60 n. 11, 81, 102
authenticity, idea of in international
basismo, 33

baptism, in Pentecostal Churches, 121
basismo: aversion to authority, 81;
compared to Pentecostalism, 6, 54,
218–19, 221–5; compared with
Communion and Liberation, 40; and
co-optation, 34; defined, 13; definition
as progressive Catholicism rejected,
5–6; its denial of leadership, 103;
divergent interpretations of religion,
78–9; influence on institutional
Catholic Church in Brazil, 63–4;
influence in policy-making and at the
grassroots, 113; influence in society,
34; institutions at the grassroots,

90–1; a minority tendency within the
Catholic Church, 112; its network
culture, 31; and *obreirismo*, 59; partial
incorporation into official Church
doctrine, 76; as a political culture, 5;
and popular culture, 18; and a popular
intelligentsia, 14; the problem of
elitism in, 95; shift in emphasis from
political power to communion with the
people, 69; shop-floor activism by
intellectuals, 60–1; its social base, 34;
and the state, 34–5; and theory of
social movements, 28–30; unstated
complicities in, 96; the unstructured
character of its organization, 81; *see
also basista* Catholicism; biblical
interpretation; boundaries; education;
intelligentsia; pamphlet literature;
populism; poverty; projection; projects;
ritual; theology of liberation;
workerism
basista Catholicism, 36; contrasted with
Pentecostalism, 6, 54, 218–19,
221–5; disproportion between 'voice'
and 'mass', 76; its long-term view, 80;
as a minority tendency within the
Catholic Church, 76; priority of
method over content, 80; usage
defended, 5–6; *see also basismo*; Bible;
Exodus story; *folheto* literature;
Kingdom of God; leadership; popular
intelligentsia; ritual defined
Bible: in *basista* commentary, 109–10; as
represented in pamphlet literature,
82–5; sacred character of text defined,
85; as source of identity in *basismo*,
84–5; in Universal Church 176; use of
in Pentecostalism, 85, 141, 178–81;
see also popular religion

biblical interpretation: and anti-intellectualism, 177–8; in *basismo*, 82–5; esotericism in, 176–7; inerrancy, 173; in Islamism, 178; Pentecostal interpretation, 174–5; pressure towards professionalization of, 176; use of quotation, 173–4

Boff, Leonardo, 55, 64, 110

Bolivia, 51

boundaries between sacred and profane in *basismo* and Pentecostalism, 83

Bourdieu, Pierre, 18–19, 163–8, 182, 184

Brandão, Carlos Rodriguez, 14–19

breaking away, in Pentecostal Churches, 123, 127, 128

Câmara, Dom Helder, 46, 51, 57, 60; *see also* CELAM

candomblé, its accoutrements brought into Catholic services, 156; *see also* possession cults

capóeira; its attributed meaning in popular culture, 105

carnival, 169–70; and class relationships and exchanges, 158; Pentecostal view of, 193

Catholic Church in Brazil: conversion to *basismo*, 63; support for grassroots movements, 63–4; *see also* architecture; *candomblé*; cosmopolitanism; France; Universal Church of the Kingdom of God

CEBs (Base Christian Communities): in Central America, 53; compared to Pentecostal meetings, 54; consciousness-raising *versus* care and counselling and devotional activity, 54–5; dependence on episcopal support, 54, 56–7; their ethos, 53; and the imposition (or not) of political views, 55; their institutionalization, 112; their many forms, 52–3; as modern version of parish structure, 55–7; in Northeast Brazil, 57; their politics tamed, 57; their reification, 58; social status of participants, 54; variations in political involvement, 55; *see also* clergy; race

CELAM (Latin American Bishops Conference): and Charismatic Renewal, 44, 51; and Dom Helder Câmara, 49; Medellín meeting and its effects, 50,

52; Puebla and Santo Domingo meetings, 75–7; *see also* inculturation

Central America: CEBs in, 53; as inspiration for eschatological vision of the Kingdom, 53; and theology of liberation, 73–5

Charismatic Renewal, 40–6; and CNBB (National Conference of Brazilian Bishops), 43; compared with Pentecostals, 41, 46; and hierarchical authority 42, 45; political opinions in 44; social composition, 43–4; and theology of liberation, 44; tongues in, 46

charity, its low priority in Universal Church, 208

Chile, Christian Democracy post-Medellín, 51

Church attendance, Pentecostal Churches, 191

Church finances in Pentecostal Churches: contributions by faithful, 203–7; *dizimistas* as community of the 'elect', 207; tithing, 206–7

clergy: change of role in approach to popular Catholicism, 88; number and resignations, 48; role in CEBs and grassroots organizations, 54, 93

Colombia, 200, 218; and Camilo Torres, 51

Communione e Liberazione (CL), 39–40; relations with politics and the Vatican, 40

confession, in community, 108

conversion, in Pentecostalism, 194–5; and cures, 197; and material wellbeing, 197; and women, 198–9

cordel (*literatura de*), *see folheto* literature

cosmopolitanism: in Catholicism, 8; and globalism, 8, 222

counselling, in Universal Church, 192

cult of the saints, 110; post-Vatican II, 106–7

Damatta, Roberto, 161–2, 169–70

Deus é Amor Church, 118, 125, 153; architecture, 184, 191–2; and Biblical quotation, 174–6; *see also* neo-Pentecostalism; Pentecostalism

Devil, 150–4; doctrinal, practical and ritual significance in Pentecostalism, 139–41; exorcism, 140–1; and family disorganization, 197–8; and sex, 196

discourse, defined, 113
dress: as marker, 201–2; rules of in
    Pentecostal Churches, 192, 200–1

education: desirability of its 'critical'
    quality, 103–4; its importance in
    basismo, 103–4
entrepreneurship in Pentecostal churches,
    see Pentecostalism
Exodus story in *basista* imaginary, 10
exorcism, 117, 124

family: as channel of missionary activity,
    200; in Pentecostal discourse, 196–9;
    as vehicle of church participation,
    190–1
field work, 19–22; methodological issues
    in, 10–11
fiestas in Pentecostal calendar, 193, 200
folheto literature: as adapted and
    politicized in *basista* pamphlets, 86–7;
    and modernism, and the culture
    industry, 89
Four-Square Gospel Church, 118, 125,
    130; *see also* neo-Pentecostalism;
    Pentecostalism
France, influence on Brazilian
    Catholicism, 83
Freire, Paulo, 63, 104–5
fundamentalism, 220–8; biblical
    inerrancy in, 220; definition and
    explanation of, 226; origins of the
    term, 173; *see also* Islam; Judaism

globalism: and fundamentalism, 222–4;
    in Islamic fundamentalism, 224; its
    methodological implications, 8; in
    Pentecostalism, 8
Globo TV Network, 217–18
GSOs (Grassroot Support Organizations),
    31; financial dependence of, 31, 91–2;
    see also clergy; NGOs; projects
Guatemala, 53, 215, 218
Gutierrez, Gustavo, 67–72, 79

healing, in Pentecostalism and possession
    cults, 145, 197
hierarchy, in Pentecostal Churches,
    119–20, 123–4
high culture, disdained by Pentecostals,
    167–8

inculturation, official definition of, 8,

n. 7; and CELAM, 71, 79; and later
    Gutierrez, 70
Indians: in las Casas, 70; as 'new Israel'
    in 16th century, 71; in theology of
    liberation, 69
intelligentsia, 220–2; in international
    basismo, 32; *see also* popular
    intelligentsia
Islam, 66; fundamentalism in, 219, 220,
    224; *see also* biblical interpretation, in
    Islamism

Jesuits (Society of Jesus), 38–9
John Paul II, Pope, in Nicaragua, 2
Judaism, 60; fundamentalism in, 220,
    224–5

Kingdom of God, in *basista* discussions,
    100

las Casas, Bartolomé de: as icon, 70; as
    precursor of theology of liberation,
    69–70
leadership: role of grassroots groups in
    forming it, 94; valuations of within
    basista Catholicism, 94–5

marxism: Catholic converts to, 62; and
    theology of liberation, 68
media, Universal Church and, 185, 217
Messiah, in pamphlet literature, 83
Mexico, 35, 53
miracles, their counter-intuitive message,
    73
modernism in Brazil, 7, 157–8
modernity and fundamentalism, 224ff.
money: as incentive in Pentecostal
    Church organization, 125; secrecy
    concerning in many churches, 125
music in Catholic and Pentecostal
    churches, 188

Nation of Islam, 159–60
neo-Pentecostalism, 15; 118; in Africa,
    208; Leninist organization in, 13,
    125, 128–9; in relation to
    Pentecostalism as a whole, 154
NGOs (Non-governmental organizations),
    30; multinationalism, in, 32; national
    and international, 31
Nicaragua, 1, 65 n. 19; *see also* John
    Paul II, Pope
Nigeria, 124; Aladura Churches, 146–8
Northeast Brazil, 21, 198; *see also* CEBs

'option for the poor', 35; addition of 'preferential', 75; effects on Church politics, 50–1

Opus Dei, 38

ordination in Pentecostal Churches, 122–3

organization in Pentecostal churches: autonomy of local congregations, 128; hierarchies, 123–4; patterns of affiliation to federal or 'superior' bodies, 126; role of material incentives, 125; training of personnel, 129–31

pamphlet literature: in *basismo*, 82–90; techniques of story-telling, 82–6

Partido dos Trabalhados (PT), 34; mentioned at ACO meeting, 99

Paul VI, Pope, 106

Pentecostalism: age of followers, 211; architecture in, 182–8; church splits, 123, 127, 128; compared with Charismatic Renewal, 41, 46; contrasted with *basista* Catholicism, 6, 54, 218–19, 221–5; entrepreneurship in, 122–3; ritual in, 136, 192–3; sacred and profane in, 83; social class/ status and, 212; social mobility as propounded in, 214; *see also* anomie; baptism; Bible, use of in; biblical interpretation; breaking away, in Pentecostal Churches; carnival; Church finances; conversion; counselling; Devil; dress; family; globalism; healing; media; money; music; neo-Pentecostalism; ordination; organization; possession cults; preaching styles; race; rationalization; respectability; sex and guilt; taste; United States; women; worship

People of God, 111

People's Church: in Central America, 53; and the Pope, 65 n. 19; as Slogan, 54

personal life: conflicts with socio-political commitment, 99; as distinct from faith, or not, 98–9

politics: and Pentecostalism, 35, 215–18; and Universal Church, 185; *see also* Communione e Liberazione

popular culture: and 'authenticity', 18–19; authenticity in, 155; in Bourdieu, 165–6; conceived as culture of resistance, 17, 79; and the dialectic

of the erudite and the popular, 17; in dialectic with the erudite, 169–73; and innovations in Catholic worship, 79; interaction with the erudite, 2; its peculiar construction in Latin America, 227; search for resistance in, 105; as target of fundamentalisms, 219–20; the 'two-tier' model, 168

popular intelligentsia, 104–5; inspired by Bible, 85; creation in *basista* Catholicism, 89

popular religion; concept of in Brandão, 14ff.; as dialectic with the erudite, 14–19, 83; use of the Bible in changing the content of, 88

populism, in contrast to *basismo*, 5

possession cults: main features, 141; their names, 154–5; and Pentecostalism, 143–55, 168–71; *see also* healing

poverty: concept of in theology of liberation, 68–9; as cultural impoverishment, 71–2; and the faith of the innocent, 69; grasping the point of view of the poor, 72; the poor distinguished by a way of thought, 69; in Sobrino, 74

poverty: *basista* desperation to touch its depths, 98; idealization of poor replaced by idealization of the people, 101; identity of the poor in theology of liberation, 74; its innocence, 98

progressive, as term applied to Catholicism, 5–6

projection: 111, 226–8; further levels of, 95; as manifested in erudite treatment of *folheto* literature, 89; and the Northeast in Brazilian culture, 21; of the popular, 89–90, 227–8; of the popular in church architecture and music, 188; of popular classes in pamphlet literature, 82–4; in the relations between anthropologists and cult practitioners, 171; in the relations between erudite and popular culture, 169–70; its role in the invocation of the people, 7

projects: characteristic of grassroots movements, 93; their job-creating function, 93–4

race: Brazil and the USA compared, 158–61; in CEBs and Pentecostal Churches compared, 162;

race *continued*
discrimination and its significance in
Brazil; 156; in erudite culture, 157–8;
in Pentecostalism, 155; and
Protestantism in US and Latin
America, 12; and religion in the USA,
158–60; and youth culture, 162
rationalization: and Church contributions,
205; in Nigerian Aladura Churches,
146–7
ritual: in conversion, 194; defined, 135;
as liminarity, 138; in Pentecostal
Churches, 136, 192–3; its relation to
belief in *basista* practice, 109

sacred and profane, boundaries between,
in *basismo* and Pentecostalism, 83
Salvador da Bahia, 19–22
samba, 169; schools, 171
São Paulo Archdiocese, 54–6
sect, concept of, 118
'see-judge-act' method of spiritual
exercise, 82–3
self-examination and self-realization, in
ACO seminar, 98–9
seminarians, dissatisfaction with option
for the poor, 64
sex and guilt: conversion, 196; repression
of in Pentecostalism, 225
Sobrino, John, 73–5
social class and religious affiliation,
210–14
social movements: *basismo* as an
international social movement, 30;
grassroots movements defined, 29;
theory of, 27–8

taste, good and bad, 166–7, 173, 228;
in Bourdieu, 182; Pentecostal, 183–5
theology: as a profession, 66, 177; its
role in Church, 66
theology of liberation (TL), 25; in
Central America, 73–5; change in G.
Gutierrez's writings, 67; conception of
Kingdom of God, 68, 74; its
diffusion, 49; freedom, concept of in,
72; G. Gutierrez and marxism and

socialism, 68; Gutierrez and Sobrino
contrasted, 65–75; maturation,
sanitization, differentiation, 67; origins
in 16th century, 69; not a political
theology, 66; shifting emphasis in
Brazil, 64; and theology as discipline,
65; *see also* poverty
tithing, *see* Church finances
Touraine, Alain, 26–9, 33

United States: effect on Pentecostalism in
Latin America, 12; in history of
Pentecostal imagination, 11; as 'land
of plenty' in Pentecostal imaginary,
11; in modern ultra-Orthodox
Judaism, 223; Pentecostalism in,
11–12; *see also* race
Universal Church of the Kingdom of
God, 118, 120, 122–5, 129, 191–2,
193, 201; architecture, 185, 187; in
Bahia, 136–8; Catholic borrowings,
209; Devil in, 140–1; international
expansion, 202; money in, 202,
205–7; and possession cults, 151–5;
ritual peculiarities, 136–7; 139–42; *see
also* Bible; charity; counselling in;
media; neo-Pentecostalism;
Pentecostalism

Vatican II, 25, 47, 48–9; Dom Helder
Câmara at, 49; effect on relationship
between priests and laity, 107; its
effects, 49; its place in history, 111;
popular response to, 106–8;
significance for experience of religious
life, 106

women, 211; and fundamentalism, 225;
in Pentecostal church organization,
131–3; their plight emphasized in a
Pentecostal service, 141; their
uniforms as *obreiras*, 131–2; *see also*
basismo and *obreirismo*
workerism, in Catholic movements,
59–62
worship, its intensity in Pentecostal
Churches, 135